POLICE AND PUBLIC SECURITY IN MEXICO

Edited by Robert A. Donnelly
and David A. Shirk

University Readers™
San Diego, CA

First published in the United States of America in 2010 by University Readers, Inc.

14 13 12 11 10 1 2 3 4 5

Printed in the United States of America

ISBN: 978-1-935551-50-8

University Readers™

800.200.3908 | www.universityreaders.com

Preface

THIS MONOGRAPH IS a product of research conducted through the Justice in Mexico Project, a multiyear collaborative initiative focused on the rule of law and administration of justice in Mexico. In this publication we bring together the works of seven exceptional scholars to examine and explain recent trends in Mexican public security, with special emphasis on the role of police in the administration of justice. Like an earlier project publication, *Accountability and Transparency in Mexico: Comparative, National, and Local Perspectives*, co-edited by Alejandra Ríos Cázares and David Shirk, this monograph examines key aspects of Mexico's criminal justice sector and the tremendous challenges related to improving the rule of law in Mexico. Also significantly shaping the contours and direction of this monograph was an earlier edited volume, *Reforming the Administration of Justice in Mexico*, co-edited by Wayne A. Cornelius and David Shirk, which provided a broad overview of Mexico's public security situation and criminal justice system.

The deliberations of the authors and other experts on the topics addressed in this monograph were the subject of a July 2007 binational workshop titled "Public Security and Criminal Justice Reform in Mexico," which was organized by the project at the University of Guadalajara. That meeting gathered two dozen experts from Mexico and the United States to discuss the militarization of Mexican public security at a time of intense nationwide debate on the legality and net effectiveness of a cornerstone of President Felipe Calderón's primary counternarcotics strategy: large-scale troop deployments to drug-trafficking hotspots. More than a purely academic discussion, the meeting also diagnosed Mexico's principal public security challenges, proposed policy solutions, and included the input of key state and local public security officials as well as legislators.

While this monograph is not a memorial of the meeting, the findings reached at the Guadalajara workshop were essential to assembling its theoretical armature and for identifying the most important issues for ongoing discussion. At its inception, this monograph was intended to focus exclusively on the question of the rapidly increasing militarization of public security in Mexico. In particular, Sigrid Arzt's succinct analysis of the challenges presented by the militarization of Mexico's Office of the Federal Attorney General (Procuraduría General de la República, PGR) strongly informed our outlook. According to Arzt, "The militarization of the PGR suggests that the armed forces have been able to expand their influence without serious civilian scrutiny, and they have been able to convince political elites that the military is the only entity capable of preventing the disintegration of the civilian security apparatus. In a nascent democracy, where the military has a culture lacking transparency and a history of human rights abuses, this continued (even expanded) role for the military in public security presents serious concerns."

Through our deliberations, it became evident that the increased involvement of Mexico's military in domestic law enforcement matters was a symptom of much larger problems related to police and policing. Moreover, while there is a general sense that police forces in Mexico are inadequate to the tasks with which they are charged—and are often a menace to society—relatively little is known about police and police organizations. Hence, as this project took shape, it became clear that there was a need for a holistic discussion of the larger public security situation in Mexico. Accordingly, we asked our authors to probe more deeply into these questions.

This monograph is therefore organized around the following set of broad themes that we consider essential to a comprehensive treatment of the military's role in civilian policing duties: (1) Mexico's current public security crisis, (2) the relationship between the state and organized crime, (3) Mexican police structures and cultures, (4) the contemporary role and organization of the Mexican military, and (5) human rights issues and the social construction of crime. Though these are not the only subject headings available in an analysis of such complicated subjects, they are essential to understanding the frameworks that have guided this project.

At the same time, it is important to note that this monograph evolved in response to dramatic and rapidly moving developments, given that much occurred in the process of compiling our research. Over the course of the first three years of the administration of President Calderón (2006–2012), Mexico has deployed tens of thousands of troops to combat violent organized crime groups. In 2008 the Mexican Congress passed sweeping legislation and constitutional amendments that will result in a massive overhaul of Mexico's judicial system, with major implications for law enforcement and overall security over the next decade. Following on these reforms, Mexico's Congress also approved sweeping changes to the federal law enforcement apparatus, merging the police functions of the Federal Agency for Investigation (Agencia Federal de Investigación, AFI) with the Public Security Ministry's Federal Preventative Police (Policía Federal Preventiva, PFP) to create a new, consolidated Federal Police agency in 2009.

In addition, over the last few years Mexican and U.S. officials have initiated unprecedented measures to promote cross-border collaboration in law enforcement and security, including the multi-billion-dollar Mérida Initiative counternarcotics program and other efforts to share responsibilities in fighting the war on drugs. Unfortunately, despite these new reforms and security measures, Mexico's public security situation had not improved dramatically as this monograph went to print; by midyear 2009, levels of cartel violence remained on par with those seen in the last six months of 2008, the bloodiest year on record. Indeed, all things remaining constant, the number of cartel-related deaths in 2009 appears likely to match or exceed those seen in 2008. Hence we feel the publication of this monograph is particularly timely, and we hope that the analysis contained herein will engage and inform policy makers from both countries on the weighty rule-of-law challenges facing Mexico today.

There are, of course, many we must thank for their contributions to this publication. The Justice in Mexico Project is generously supported by the William and Flora Hewlett Foundation and the Tinker Foundation. We must also thank the academics and public officials who participated in the July 2007 workshop that inspired this monograph: Luis Astorga, Bruce Bagley, Nauhcatzin T. Bravo Aguilar, Jorge Chabat, Carlos Flores, Javier Galván Guerrero, Aurelio Hernández Márquez, Omar Williams López Ovalle, Francisco Macías Medina, Carlos Mercado Casillas, Leonardo Mier, Luis Carlos Nájera Gutiérrez de Velasco, Jorge Rocha Quintero, Octavio Rodríguez, Celso Rodríguez González, Erubiel Tirado, and Randy Willoughby. Thanks are also due to personnel at the U.S. Consulate in Guadalajara, particularly Lynn Roche, for providing kind assistance and support for this workshop.

The institutional support of the University of Guadalajara, and particularly that of Marco Antonio Cortés Guardado, made possible not only our initial meeting but also ongoing collaboration that will continue to advance the larger goals of this project. The Trans-Border Institute and all of its initiatives also benefit from the institutional support of the Joan B. Kroc School of Peace and Justice at the University of San Diego. We are very appreciative of the efforts and assistance of the Institute's staff and students, especially those of Charles Pope, Claudia Ornelas, Theresa Firestine, Judith Dávila, Ruth Gómez, Stephanie Borrowdale, and Rommel Rico. In a very special way, we would like to acknowledge Cory Molzahn and Anna Cearley, whose contributions to our monthly news reports are incorporated liberally in certain sections of the introduction and conclusion to the monograph. Carlos J. Díaz de León and his team from Ogma Translating and Interpreting Services ably assisted us with the careful translation of all chapters originally authored in Spanish, and Sandra del Castillo provided her excellent editing services for the entire monograph. Seidy Cruz, Jessica Knott, Monica Hui, Ross Rinehart, and the publications team at University Readers were exceedingly patient and helpful in their production of the monograph. Naturally, as the editors of this monograph, we are deeply indebted to our talented authors, who shared with us their tremendous depth of knowledge across a wide range of topics. While we are very proud of the enormous contribution that they have made to the study of the rule of law in Mexico, as editors we bear primary responsibility for all errors and omissions in this work.

Above all, on behalf of all the authors in this volume, we express our collective hope that this monograph will serve as a useful resource for those who seek to understand and improve policing and public security in Mexico.

Robert A. Donnelly, Washington, DC
David A. Shirk, San Diego, CA

Contents

Introduction

Robert A. Donnelly and David A. Shirk

One of the most pressing public concerns in Mexico in recent years has been the proliferation of crime and violence that has seriously undermined the rule of law. With some important exceptions, notably homicide, other violent crime rates in Mexico appeared to grow in tandem with a series of economic crises starting in the mid-1970s. Meanwhile, high-profile violence related to organized crime, primarily drug trafficking, has also grown significantly over the last two decades. In the face of these trends, Mexican law enforcement and judicial institutions have demonstrated significant limitations—and in some cases, troubling dysfunctions—that have undermined public confidence in Mexico's justice sector. Indeed, frustrated by the ineffectiveness, corruption, and even criminal activities of law enforcement officials, the public has issued repeated calls for public authorities to address these concerns, prompting tougher criminal penalties and even increased reliance on the Mexican military.

This monograph explores Mexico's public security challenges, particularly its embattled law enforcement agencies, the growing role of the military, the problem of drug violence and corruption, and the possible strategies for moving forward. Drawing on the insights of some of the foremost scholars in this area, we examine some of the serious and persistent public security challenges that have plagued Mexico in recent years. Studying these issues is especially timely due to Mexicans' heightened concerns about crime and violence, but also in light of growing U.S.-Mexican collaboration in this area in the context of the Mérida Initiative approved in June 2008. The goal of this monograph is to provide a careful analysis of Mexico's public security apparatus, examine the institutional problems and practices that undermine effective law enforcement, and identify practical recommendations for addressing these challenges. We begin by providing an overview of Mexico's current public security situation, and particularly recent trends in "common" and high-profile violence related to organized crime. We then move to an exploration of Mexican law enforcement organizations and a discussion of the increasing role that the Mexican military has played in domestic policing.

CRIME AND INSECURITY IN MEXICO

The recent wave of crime in Mexico consists of steep increases in reported crime and people's concerns about public security in Mexico, as well as violence related to organized crime activities, most notably drug trafficking. While there are still significant limitations to the available data about crime, there are some identifiable and disturbing trends on a number of indicators, which suggest much higher levels of criminal activity over the past decade and point to the limited effectiveness of Mexico's law enforcement apparatus. Meanwhile, this trend has been accompanied by greater violence related to organized crime, particularly with the breakdown of Mexico's major cartels over the last decade. Below we outline these major trends to provide a backdrop for our discussion of Mexico's public security apparatus.

Common Crime in Mexico

For more than a decade, Mexico has experienced elevated levels of crime and violence, problems that have been consistently ranked among the top concerns of its citizens. Yet due to the public's lack of confidence in the justice sector, an estimated 75 percent of crimes go unreported because the public perceives that reporting crimes is a futile exercise. Estimates produced by the Citizens' Institute for the Study of Insecurity (Instituto Ciudadano de Estudios Sobre la Inseguridad, ICESI) suggest that as few as a quarter of all crimes are actually reported in Mexico. This further exacerbates Mexico's severe problems of criminal impunity and makes it virtually impossible to accurately measure actual levels of crime. Large numbers of cases are not investigated, and many cases that are investigated do not yield a suspect. Hence, in the absence of reliable crime reporting and successful investigations, other proxy measures—like the number of criminals arrested for specific crimes—are very inadequate. Data on arrests tend to seriously undercount crime, even though multiple persons may be arrested and convicted for the same crime. Arrest rates may also reflect socioeconomic factors (such as class bias), law enforcement resource constraints, bureaucratic inefficiencies, or other circumstances that would affect crime reporting, criminal investigations, and apprehensions.

Still, judicial sector data are available for most of the twentieth century in Mexico. Though they have serious limitations, such data (particularly arrests) can be suggestive of the overall caseload handled by law enforcement, which presumably fluctuates in response to actual levels of crime. Taking this into consideration, they offer some useful clues about larger trends in common crime in Mexico over the last few decades.[1] For this reason, the Justice in Mexico Project compiled a historical dataset of arrests reported by the National Institute for Statistics, Geography, and Informatics (Instituto Nacional de Estadística y Geografía, INEGI) from 1926 to 2005 in four major categories of violent crime: homicide, robbery, assault, and rape.[2] Figure 1.1 below expands data originally presented in the introduction to the edited volume titled *Reforming the Administration of Justice in Mexico* (Cornelius and Shirk 2007).

These data suggest a number of trends over the last eight decades. First, there was a general decline in homicide, assault, and robbery for most of the period from the 1920s through the 1960s. For example, the peak in homicides came between 1936 and 1940, when the average rate reached 38 homicide suspects per 100,000 people. Then, over the course of the next three decades, the number of homicide arrests declined nearly 75 percent, to an average of 10 or fewer per 100,000 people from 1976 to 2000. By 2005, however, the number of homicide arrests tipped up to 12.3 per 100,000 people.

It is also noteworthy that in two other categories—robbery and assault—we see an important point of departure from homicide beginning in the mid-1970s. Controlling for population, the rate of suspects accused of assault increased by more than 25 percent over the course of the 1980s (from roughly 31 per 100,000 in 1980 to 39 per 100,000 in 1990). While the rate of criminals arrested for assault dropped to 31 per 100,000 by 1997, it rose and fluctuated after 2000 (between 34 and 37 per 100,000). More significantly, arrest rates for robbery nearly doubled from 1976 to 1986 (growing from 22 per 100,000 to 40 per 100,000) and increased nearly 50

1 The rate of accused criminals is a problematic proxy because it only measures the number of suspects identified in cases investigated by authorities, not actual rates of crime. The INEGI database used by the Justice in Mexico Project dates back to 1926 and is available on line at www.justiceinmexico.org.

2 The rate of arrests is a problematic proxy because it only measures the number of suspects identified in cases investigated by authorities, not actual rates of crime. Large numbers of cases are not investigated, and many cases investigated do not yield a suspect. Nonetheless, this variable is somewhat useful because data are suggestive of the overall caseload handled by police, which presumably fluctuates in response to actual levels of crime. Accused suspect data are also available over a relatively long period; the INEGI database used by the Justice in Mexico Project dates back to 1926 and is available on line at www.justiceinmexico.org.

Figure 1.1 Accused Criminals per 100,000 Persons, for Common and Federal Crimes from 1926 to 2005 (homicide, assault, robbery, and rape)

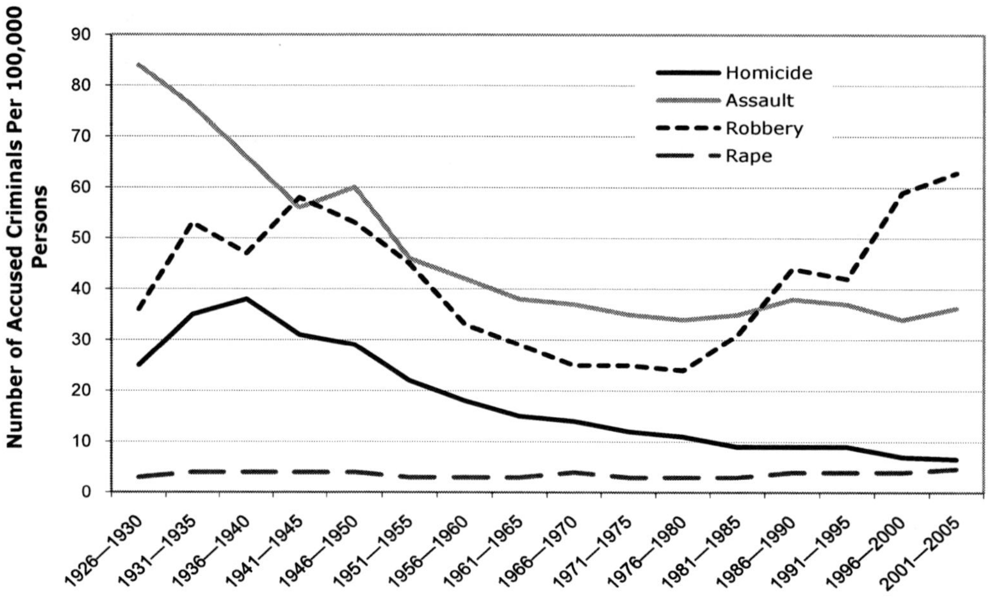

Source: Data on crime suspects *(presuntos delincuentes)* compiled from INEGI by Pablo Piccato for 1926–2001 and by David Shirk and Rommel Rico for 2001–2005.

percent over the next decade (reaching 59 per 100,000 in 1996).[3] By 2005, robbery arrests climbed another 13 percent, to 67 per 100,000.

Another, less visible trend relates to arrests for rape. Rape arrests tend to be drowned out in figure 1.1 due to the much higher rates in other categories of violent crime. Of course, it must be noted that rape data are notoriously problematic. Both male and female victims are extremely reluctant to report rape crimes. Moreover, historically crimes against women have been taken less seriously by police in Mexico (and elsewhere). This said, data on arrests demonstrate a remarkable trend over the last

3 These figures reflect only local jurisdiction *(fuero común)* and exclude federal-level crimes *(fuero federal)*.

eighty years. When broken out as a single category of crime, we see a very significant general increase in arrests for rape, with rates doubling in the 1950s and increasing dramatically in each subsequent decade (figure 1.2). Indeed, after an unusually stable lull from 1975 to 1985, the rate of arrests on rape charges (per 100,000 people) fluctuated and generally increased—by more than 50 percent—in the 1990s and the early 2000s.

These trends offer several useful points for reflection. First, it is worth noting that late-twentieth-century increases in arrests for violent crime—especially robbery—appeared to follow in the aftermath of the severe economic crises that occurred in 1976, 1982, and 1994. These brought significant slowdowns in the Mexican economy, severe devaluations of the peso, rampant inflation, and other problems. It is likely that conditions associated with these trends—unemployment, eroding wages, inequality, and so on—contributed to measurable increases in criminal activity. Second, the increase in arrests for rape is open to a number of plausible explanations, both positive and negative. It may be that the rate of rape has actually increased over time. It also may be that victims have become less reluctant to report crimes and police have become more inclined and better able to arrest suspects for rape. Third, the general downward trend in homicide may be partly explained by the consolidation of the Mexican political system, as postrevolutionary, antistate violence declined significantly after the 1930s and especially after the 1960s. At the same time, there were important improvements in medical technology over the twentieth century that helped to treat potentially fatal injuries and therefore may have reduced the number of homicides (while contributing to a general increase in assault charges). Whatever the case, the recent increase in the number of homicide arrests represents a disturbing reversal of a six-decade trend and appears to correspond to the intensification of drug-related violence that began in 2005.

Lastly, what is especially important to note about the general trends identified here is that—whether or not arrests represent an actual increase in violent crime—there has been an enormous increase in activity by Mexico's public security apparatus over the last two decades. This in itself represents a significant challenge for police agencies and the overall justice system. Moreover, the fact that increased arrest rates probably reflect actual crime trends at least partially suggests that Mexico is in the midst of a serious public security challenge, for which it may not have adequate institutional response mechanisms. While this may be true for "everyday" forms of crime such as

Figure 1.2 Arrests for Rape per 100,000 Persons, 1927–2005

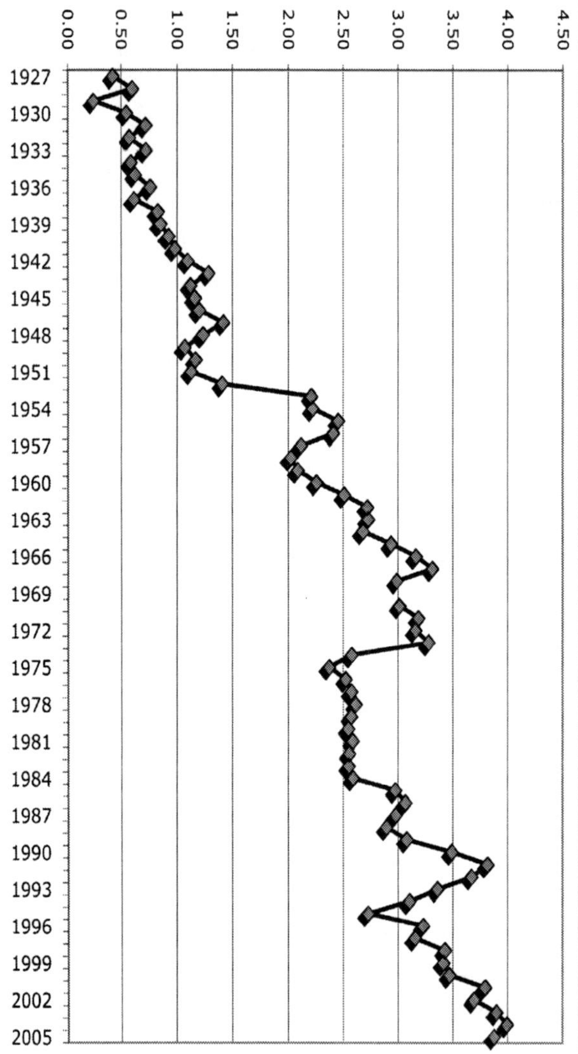

Source: Data on crime suspects *(presuntos delincuentes)* compiled from INEGI by Pablo Piccato for 1926–2001 and by David Shirk and Rommel Rico for 2001–2005.

those discussed above, it may be even more so for violent organized crime. We turn to these challenges below.

Organized Crime in Mexico: Drug Trafficking, Arms Trafficking, and Kidnapping

The growth of "common" crime over the last two decades has been accompanied by increased activity by organized crime groups. Amid the apparent inability of public officials to address even minor forms of crime, the impunity of organized crime syndicates in Mexico has provoked a severe degree of public frustration and concern. Because organized crime is technically defined in Mexico as any criminal activity involving three or more persons, there is arguably some overlap between what registers as "common" and "organized" crime. Low-level organized crime might therefore include a mugging, a burglary, or a small-time prostitution ring. Higher-level crime syndicates, however, operate sophisticated domestic and international operations that include a diverse array of activities, including kidnapping and the smuggling of drugs, weapons, cash, and people. Here we concentrate our analysis on three interrelated forms of organized crime—drug trafficking, arms trafficking, and kidnapping—which have been especially prominent in recent years.

DRUG TRAFFICKING

Arguably, the most serious challenge facing Mexico's law enforcement authorities is the growth of violence related to drug-trafficking organizations. In the early twentieth century, Mexico had been an important but low-level supplier of drugs to the United States, notably products like marijuana and opium that were homegrown in places like the "Golden Triangle," where the northern states of Durango, Chihuahua, and Sinaloa meet. However, as Carlos Antonio Flores notes in his chapter in this monograph, drug trafficking in Mexico began to increase in the 1960s and 1970s, thanks in part to increased U.S. drug consumption. During this period, the popularity of countercultural lifestyles among U.S. middle-class youth and soldiers returning from Vietnam led to heightened drug trafficking and drug cultivation in Mexico. Also, with the growth of cocaine use, Mexico and the Caribbean became important transshipment points for Colombian cartels, as most Andean product was moved into the United States via the Miami connection through the Gulf of Mexico.

Subsequently, these changing patterns of drug consumption and U.S. anti-drug efforts were accompanied by a major shift. Successful interdiction efforts in the Gulf of Mexico and the disruption of Colombia's cartels appeared to empower the Mexican drug-trafficking organizations, which proliferated and became increasingly involved in the direct control of the drug trade. Yet, according to Flores, changing patterns in Mexican drug trafficking are not solely attributable to exogenous shifts in U.S. counter-drug strategy, patterns of drug consumption, or the weakening of Colombian organized crime. Rather, Flores asserts that political democratization in Mexico has led to a proliferation of atomized and diffuse power relationships between drug-trafficking organizations and mid-level state actors beginning in the 1990s. Indeed, Flores divides Mexico's drug history into two main eras: 1960–1994 and 1994–present.

First, according to Flores, the drug-trafficking regime that developed in Mexico in the 1960s was one in which the model of organized crime was highly centralized, and hierarchical regional organizations operated with a disturbing degree of influence at the highest levels of government. In Mexico, this rise in drug activity led to the expanded use of the military in destruction-and-interdiction operations targeting marijuana and opium poppy growers and traffickers in rural states in the North and Northwest in particular. Ultimately this "permanent campaign" led to a spoils system in which military commanders colluded with and extorted traffickers within their districts for personal enrichment. In sharp contrast to the government's blanket campaign against political insurgents at the time, anti-drug operations by the military were neutered by a complex web of bureaucratic Catch-22s, Flores notes. He describes a Mexican national security apparatus that, threatened by antigovernment forces, engaged in a "dirty war" against political dissidents but largely turned a blind eye to traffickers. It is only when errant traffickers ran afoul of a high-level military figure that they risked "being disappeared" like political subversives. The apogee of state-directed centralization and control over trafficking networks came in the 1974–1985 period. It was then that a powerful domestic intelligence agency, the Federal Security Directorate (DSF), essentially operated above the law and exerted deep control over organized crime activity. With the introduction of large-scale cocaine trafficking and the neutralization of the leftist revolutionary threat in the 1980s, the Directorate turned its attention fully to drug trafficking, becoming in the process a breeding ground for corruption. Ultimately the Directorate's rising power sparked a sharp rivalry with the Office of the Federal Attorney General (PGR). However, the Directorate was abruptly dismantled in 1985 after the controversial torture and murder of undercover U.S. Drug Enforcement Administration (DEA) Agent Enrique Camarena provoked U.S. allegations of high-level corruption.

A second epoch of Mexican drug trafficking began in 1994 during the presidency of Ernesto Zedillo. By the 1990s the centralized, hierarchical model collapsed because of greater political plurality at the state level, the ascension of a president incapable or unwilling to exert total control over state governors, the undermining of established agreements and conspiracies between organized crime and government authorities, and the gradual unsettling of a political order that culminated in the Institutional Revolutionary Party's (PRI) presidential loss in 2000. As evidence, Flores cites the high-profile arrest of Mexican anti-drug czar General Jesús Gutiérrez Rebollo in 1997 on charges of protecting a prominent drug lord, and he points to the enactment of judicial proceedings on organized crime charges against two ex-governors around the same time: Jorge Carrillo Olea of Morelos, after leaving office in 1998, and Mario Villanueva of Quintana Roo, after leaving office in 1999. According to Flores, these were signs that the erstwhile centralized model was fragmenting and that a more atomized and diffuse system, involving new actors and interests, was emerging.

Indeed, over time Mexico's drug cartels had become divided into increasingly fractionalized and autonomous regional organizations, typically centered in a given city or state. During the 1980s, Mexico's most powerful drug trafficker, Miguel Ángel Félix Gallardo, was based in Guadalajara and was one of the first to develop ties with Colombian suppliers. The two most prominent organizations in the 1990s, the Tijuana and Juárez cartels, arose after Félix Gallardo's arrest in 1989. The Tijuana cartel, operated by Félix Gallardo's nephews and nieces in the Arellano-Félix family (comprising seven brothers, four sisters, and other relatives), is involved in the smuggling of marijuana, cocaine, methamphetamines, and heroin.[4] Meanwhile, the Juárez cartel was operated in the 1990s by Amado Carrillo Fuentes, known as

4 At its peak, the Arellano-Félix organization was believed to dole out over US$50 million a year in bribes. Some estimates suggest that bribes from the Arellano-Félix cartel ranged as high as $75 million per year (Padgett and Shannon 2001).

the "Lord of the Skies" because he pioneered airborne Mexican smuggling routes into the United States for the Colombians.[5]

By the late 1990s two additional cartels gained prominence, in the Gulf of Mexico and in Sinaloa. The Gulf cartel was brought to fruition by Juan García Abrego. After his arrest and extradition in 1996, an internal contest for power led to the rise of Osiel Cárdenas Guillén, a former *"madrina,"* or quasi-official police hit man.[6] After his arrest in 2003, Cárdenas continued to coordinate the cartel's operations directly from his jail cell. These operations included his direction of masked commando units known as "Zetas," apparently comprising corrupt former elite military forces employed by Cárdenas, and ended only when he was extradited to the United States in January 2007.[7] The Sinaloa cartel was started in the 1970s by Héctor "El Güero" Palma Salazar, who broke with Félix Gallardo to form his own organization. After Palma was arrested in 1995, Ismael Zambada, Joaquín Guzmán Loera (alias "Shorty" or El Chapo), and members of the Beltrán Leyva family took over the cartel's operations. The Sinaloa cartel subsequently developed several enforcer groups—Los Negros, Los Pelones, and La Gente Nueva—to counter the Gulf cartel's Zeta commandos, and this cartel is believed to work with transnational gangs (like the Mara Salvatrucha and the Mexican Mafia) operating in the United States.

Hence, Flores argues that Mexican organized crime has experienced a shift from its former centralized, hierarchical model to one that is more atomized, multifaceted, and unpredictable, as each of the above-noted cartels has suffered major blows in the last decade.[8] The result has been disequilibrium and competition among and within

---

5 After Carrillo Fuentes mysteriously died—or not, as some speculate—on the operating table of his plastic surgeon in 1997, it is believed that Vicente Carrillo Fuentes, the brother of Amado, continued to coordinate the remnants of the Juárez cartel.

6 Abrego solidified the Gulf cartel organization's ties with Colombia's Cali cartel. The Gulf cartel was originally founded in Matamoros, Tamaulipas, in the 1970s by Abrego's uncle, Juan Nepomuceno Guerra, who got his start in cross-border smuggling as a bootlegger in the 1930s. Nepomuceno Guerra, who was never successfully charged with drug-related offenses, died on July 12, 2001 (Castillo García and Torres Barbosa 2003).

7 Thereafter, the cartel's operations continued under his brother Antonio "Tony" Esquiel Cárdenas Guillén and top lieutenant, Jorge "El Coss" Eduardo Costilla.

8 In 2002, Ramón Arellano Félix was killed in a shootout with police in Sinaloa (possibly in a clash with Zambada), and Benjamín Arellano Félix was arrested by Mexican authorities in a hideout in the

the cartels, which has produced a cascade of violence. In recent years the remnants of the Tijuana and Gulf cartels have been locked in a battle with the Juárez and Sinaloa cartels, whose evidently allied forces have become known as "The Federation" or the "Golden Triangle" alliance (Trahan, Londoño, and Corchado 2005). These organizations no longer operate in the structured, orderly, quasi-official framework that previously characterized Mexican drug trafficking. Hence there has been a newfound willingness by cartels to attack official targets. According to Flores, the willingness of Mexico's cartels to strike back against the state was evidenced by the prison escape of Sinaloa cartel leader Joaquín Guzmán in 2001 and an attempted jailbreak in 2005 at the maximum-security Almoloya prison in the State of Mexico (intended to free Gulf cartel leader Osiel Cárdenas and the Tijuana cartel's Benjamín Arellano). Flores suggests that this scornful disregard for state authority was uncharacteristic of organized crime in the 1980s and early 1990s, when it would have been unacceptable to overstep the boundaries of a centralized criminal hierarchy intimately interlinked with the state.

The result has been a wave of high-profile drug violence that began to intensify in 2005. That year, Mexico experienced the retaliatory murder of half a dozen Matamoros prison guards, the brazen assassination of Nuevo Laredo police chief Alejandro Domínguez only hours after being sworn in, thousands of drug-related homicides, and a series of kidnappings and assaults throughout the country (Grayson 2008). Over the next few years, drug violence in Mexico reached unprecedented proportions, with brutal violence that included killings, kidnappings, assaults, gun battles in the public square, and a series of gruesome beheaded and dismembered bodies appearing in states like Baja California, Chihuahua, Guerrero, and Michoacán.[9] Brazen attacks against military, police, and government targets continued through 2008 and represent a serious challenge to the Mexican state.

Because the Mexican government did not release official data on the number of drug-related killings until 2008 (and still releases such data only sporadically),

---

state of Puebla. That same year, the arrest of drug kingpin Osiel Cárdenas and top lieutenant Adán Medrano Rodríguez severely weakened the Gulf cartel. In 2004 and 2005, respectively, Juan José "El Azul" Esparragoza Moreno and Ricardo García Urquiza, major leaders of the Juárez cartel's operations, were arrested.

9 It is worth noting that the escalation of violence in Mexico to include video-recorded and Internet broadcasts of killings and beheadings appeared to follow the example of (or at least coincide with) similarly gruesome violence in the Middle East.

Figure 1.3 Distribution of Drug Killings in Mexico by State, 2006, 2007, and 2008

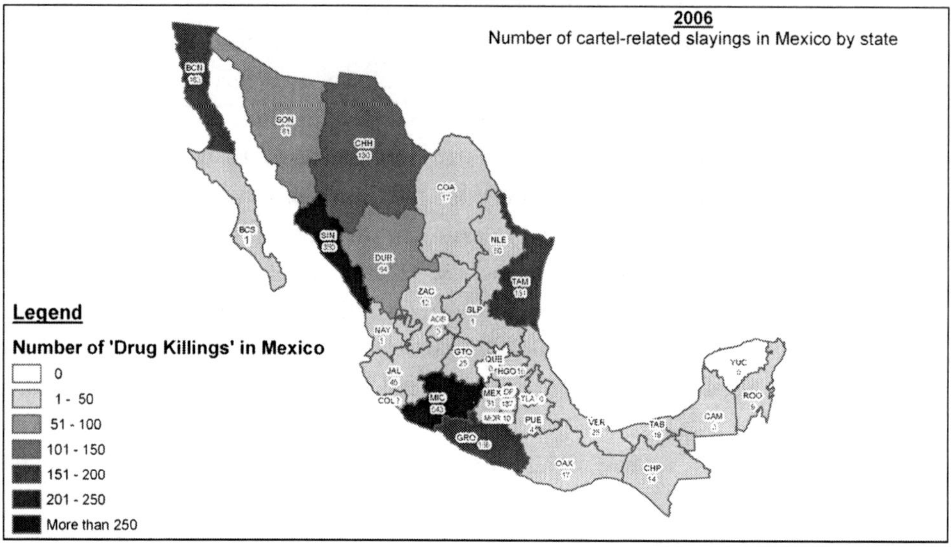

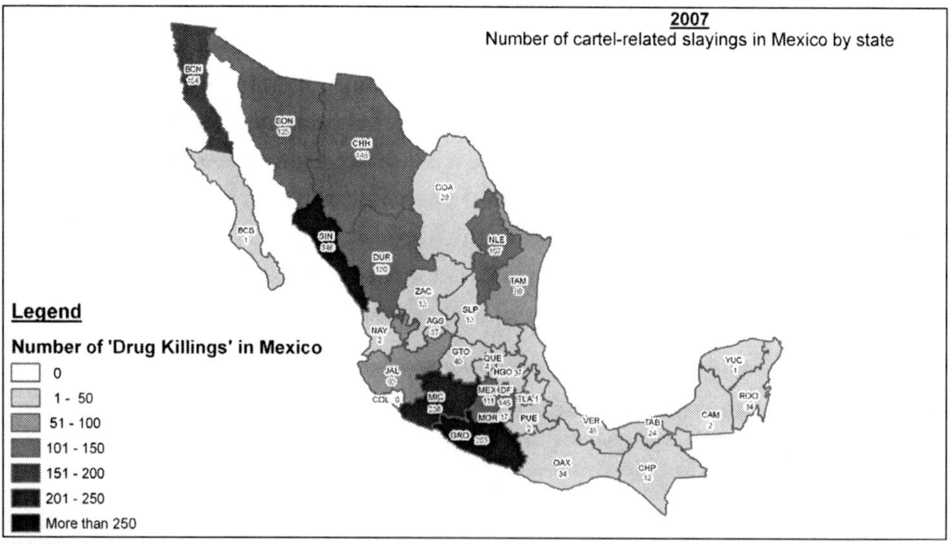

Figure 1.3 Distribution of Drug Killings in Mexico by State, 2006, 2007, and 2008 (*Continued*)

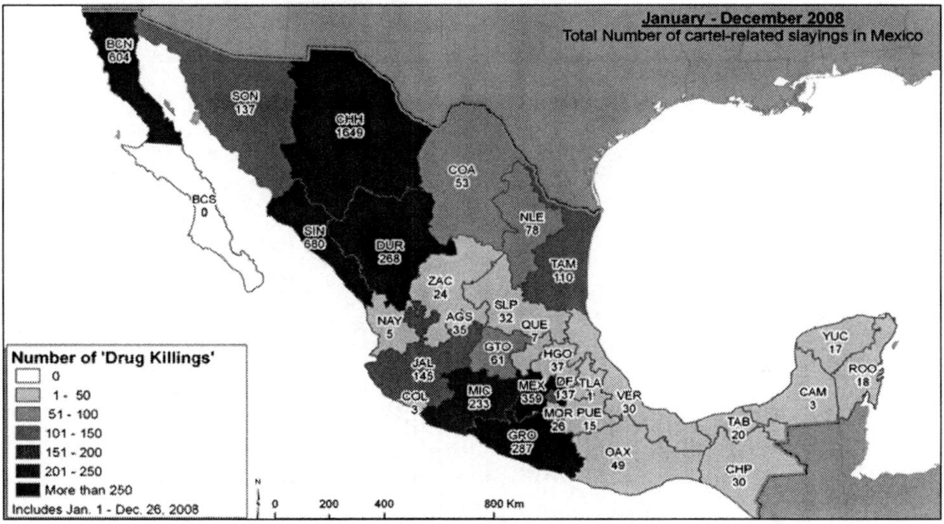

Sources: Trans-Border Institute. http://www.sandiego.edu/tbi/projects/maps.php. Maps reflect the state and national totals of cartel-related slayings in Mexico ("*ejecuciones*" and "*narcoejecuciones*") obtained from data provided by *Reforma* newspaper. Maximum values are: 543 (Michoacán) for 2006; 346 (Sinaloa) for 2007; and 1,649 (Chihuahua) through December 26, 2008. Maps developed by Theresa Firestine. Data gathering and analysis by Judith Dávila, Robert Donnelly, Ruth Gómez, Cory Molzahn, Charles Pope, and David Shirk.

Figure 1.4 Monthly Drug-Related Killings in Mexico, January 1, 2008–July 3, 2009

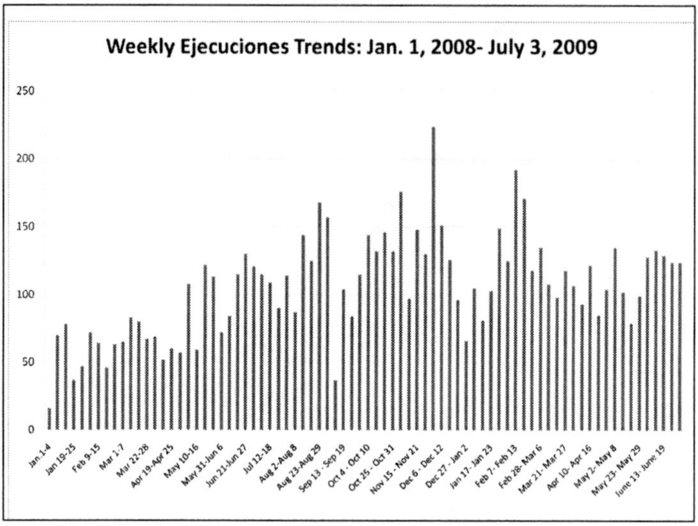

Note: Since early 2007, the Trans-Border Institute's Justice in Mexico Project has monitored Mexican media reports on the number of drug-related killings to generate a series of GIS maps tracking the violence. Thanks to support from research assistants Theresa Firestine, Cory Molzahn, Ruth Gómez, and Judith Dávila, these maps are available on the Justice in Mexico Project Web site: www.justiceinmexico.org.

the best available estimates for drug violence in recent years have come from news sources that track the figures informally. According to data compiled by the Mexican newspaper *Reforma*, the number of drug-related killings in Mexico totaled around 1,500 in 2005, over 2,100 in 2006, and 2,300 in 2007 (figure 1.3). A systematic analysis of drug-related murders reveals that central Mexican states like Michoacán and Guerrero experienced the largest number of killings in 2006.[10] Later, however,

10 In 2006 and 2007, Central Pacific Mexican states experienced the most killings, with 346 drug killings in Sinaloa (13.27 per 100,000), 238 in Michoacán (5.96 per 100,000), and 256 in Guerrero

the greatest number of drug killings shifted to northern and border states, with the most violence in 2007 concentrated in Baja California (154 drug killings, or 5.14 per 100,000), Sonora (125, or 5.07 per 100,000), and Chihuahua (148, or 4.45 per 100,000). In 2006 and 2007, the national rate of cartel-related killings stood at 2.1 and 2.3 per 100,000, respectively.

In 2008, Mexico experienced a dramatic escalation of cartel-related violence, with *Reforma* tracking a total of more than 5,000 cartel-related killings (the government reported more than 6,000). By 2008, cartel-related killings became overwhelmingly concentrated along the border and especially in the state of Chihuahua, with over 1,600 killings that year. Chihuahua's rate of killings increased fivefold to 49.3 per 100,000 people—nearly double the rate in Sinaloa (now more than 25.7 per 100,000) and more than fifteen times the national rate (5 per 100,000). By early July 2009, despite the massive deployment of troops earlier in the year, the number of cartel-related killings nationwide stood at 3,054 (see figure 1.4). This was only a slight decline—about 5 percent— compared to the previous six-month period, and was on track to exceed the total for 2008.[11] Still, despite the large volume of cartel-related killings, Mexican officials insist that homicide rates in Mexico have remained at around 10 murders per 100,000 in recent years (significantly lower than the rate of more than 90 killings per 100,000 that accompanied drug-related and paramilitary conflict in Colombia during the late 1980s and early 1990s).

Drawing from Flores's analysis, the recent increase in drug violence—from the Central Pacific Coast to northern border states—appears to be a "positive" outcome. No longer as complicit with organized crime as in the past, the Mexican federal government has adopted a more aggressive strategy in recent years. During the early 2000s, important gains made against drug traffickers—the arrest and prosecution of numerous high-ranking cartel members, tougher interdiction measures, and the extradition of major cartel leaders—seriously destabilized Mexico's organized crime syndicates and intensified the competition for lucrative smuggling routes into the

(8.03 per 100,000). In relative terms, Durango ranked among the top three states with the most drug killings, since its 130 killings in 2007 constituted a rate of 8.45 per 100,000.

11 The Federal Attorney General's Office released official figures in August which noted the deaths of more than 450 police officers between December 2006 and June 2008. At the time this paper was written, more than 50 police and military personnel had been murdered after June 2008, according to the newspaper *Reforma.*

United States. The ensuing struggles between—and within—the cartels have resulted in higher levels of violence.

ARMS TRAFFICKING

In recent years, Mexican organized crime groups have utilized a wide array of firearms, including 9mm pistols, .38 caliber "super" pistols (also known as cop killers), .45-caliber pistols, and AR-15 and AK-47-type assault rifles. From 2007 to 2008, the Mexican federal government saw significant increases in the number and array of weapons seized, with a significant increase in the proportion of high-powered weapons (including machine guns, grenades, and bazookas) (Calderón 2008, 24). From January to June 2008, 7,645 weapons were seized, compared to only 3,801 during the same period for the previous year. Particularly disturbing was the increase in the proportion of "long-arm" weapons (*armas largas*), which went from 1,877, or 49.3 percent of weapons seized in the first half of 2007, to 4,465, or 58.4 percent of weapons seized in the first half of 2008. The dramatic increase in the use of high-powered weapons means that Mexican law enforcement confronts a more lethal threat from organized crime.

Despite the large number of weapons confiscated in recent years, firearms are heavily restricted in Mexico. In 2007, there were an estimated 4,300 registered firearms in Mexico (Grillo 2007). Restrictions on the sale and personal possession of firearms in Mexico make arms trafficking the primary source of weapons for Mexican drug cartels and other organized crime syndicates (Lumpe 1997). The legal availability of firearms in the United States—including advanced high-caliber, semi-automatic weapons that are especially sought after by organized crime—creates a readily accessible market in which to purchase weapons that are illegally trafficked into Mexico.[12] Thus, in addition to crime related to the northbound flows of drugs, Mexico has faced significant challenges due to the southbound flow of weapons in recent years. Indeed, authorities estimate that 90 percent of weapons confiscated in Mexico come

12 According to the 2004 national firearms survey conducted by Hepburn et al. (2007), there are an estimated 218 million privately owned firearms in the United States. However, only one in four U.S. citizens (26 percent) and two in five households (38 percent) actually owned a firearm. This means that the vast majority of firearms are owned by a small percentage of the population, with nearly half of all individual gun owners (48 percent) possessing four or more weapons and only 20 percent of owners holding 65 percent of all guns.

Figure 1.5 Reported Rates of Kidnapping in Mexico, 1997–2007

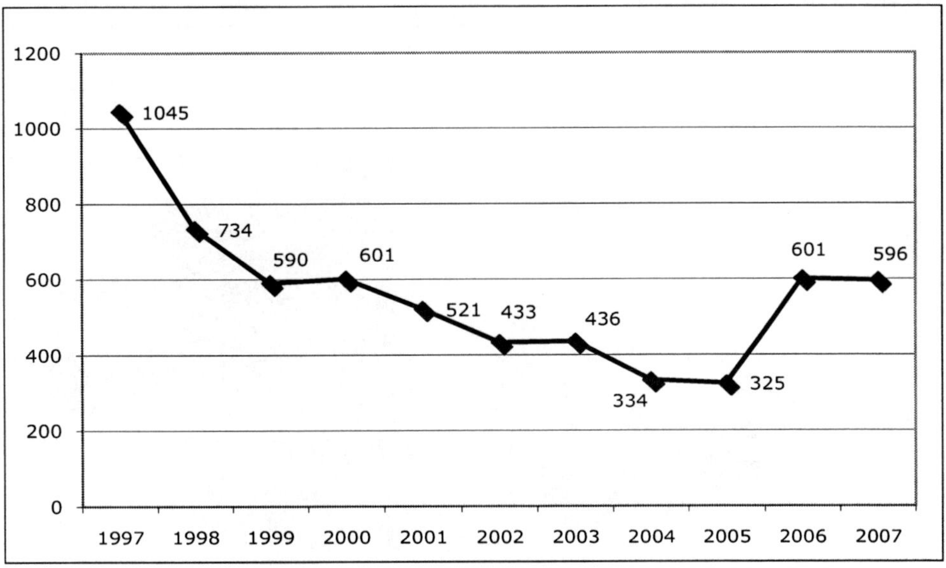

Source: Instituto Ciudadano de Estudios Sobre la Inseguridad.

from the United States, which effectively serves as a "gray market" for arms traffickers (Serrano 2008).

Within the United States there are several alternate legal sources of weapons, including the formal, regulated system of registered gun dealers, as well as an informal, unregulated (but legal) system of person-to-person sales (as, for example, through newspaper advertisements). In addition, there are numerous unlicensed hobby dealers and gun shows throughout the country. Many gun shops—an estimated 6,700

Figure 1.6 Preliminary Inquiries Initiated for Illegal Deprivation of Liberty, Registered with State Attorneys General, 2007

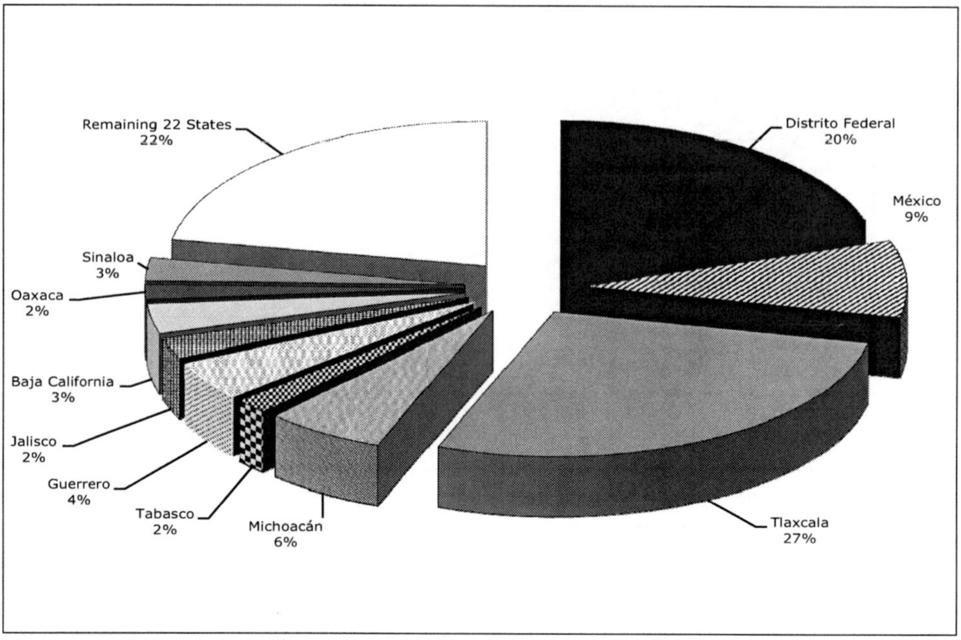

Source: Instituto Ciudadano de Estudios Sobre la Inseguridad.

dealers[13] out of some 54,000 nationwide[14]—are located along the U.S.-Mexico border. In 2007, an ATF (U.S. Bureau of Alcohol, Tobacco, and Firearms) trace of

13 Estimates for the number of drug shops along the border vary. In September 2007, George Grayson estimated the number at 1,200. In January 2008, Mexican Ambassador Arturo Sarukhán criticized the availability of weapons along the border: "Between Texas and Arizona alone, you've got 12,000 gun shops along that border with Mexico. And a lot of these gun shops provide weapons that feed into organized crime in Mexico, so we really need the support of the United States" (Corchado and Connolly 2008). More recently, the figure of 6,700—three dealers for every mile along the border—has been used in reports about the number of gun shops along the border (Serrano 2008).

14 Estimates for the total number of gun dealers in the United States vary, but by all accounts they have declined dramatically over the last decade—from 245,000 to 54,000—thanks to tougher enforcement by ATF and tighter gun regulations, such as the Brady Handgun Violence Protection Act of 1993 (Marks 2006; see also Vernick et al. 2006).

weapons confiscated in Mexico found that 1,805 of 2,455 weapons (73.5 percent) came from three border states: Arizona, California, and Texas. Moreover, gun shops are weakly regulated, with only 5 percent of all gun dealers in the country inspected annually (Marks 2006). Along the border there are an estimated 100 U.S. firearms agents and 35 inspectors.

Organized crime is involved in the purchasing—often through "straw" or substitute buyers—and trafficking of weapons into Mexico. Straw purchasers are often unfamiliar with the weapons they use, buy bulk quantities of like-model weapons, make their purchases in cash, and structure purchases in ways that avoid ATF reporting requirements.[15]

KIDNAPPING

As noted above, the increase in high-profile violence has coincided with a serious problem of kidnappings in Mexico since the mid-1990s. Although kidnapping can involve cases of intra-family abduction or other instances of individual or small-scale criminal activity, kidnapping in Mexico frequently involves organized crime. "Organized" kidnappings range from small-scale heists where an individual is carjacked or abducted in a taxicab to sophisticated operations involving corrupt law enforcement personnel. In the 1990s, so-called express kidnapping (*secuestro express*) became a major phenomenon, with two or more assailants abducting an individual for the purpose of extracting the maximum daily withdrawal from a bank card (and possibly holding the person until the next 24-hour cycle for a second withdrawal) before releasing him or her.[16] At the same time, more sophisticated operations included a clandestine group known as "La Hermandad"(The Brotherhood), which operated a crime syndicate that engaged in kidnapping and other forms of racketeering within the ranks of the Mexico City police.[17] However, not all kidnappings necessarily con-

15 Alcohol, Firearms, and Tobacco Factsheet. http://www.atf.gov/pub/fire-explo_pub/p3317_6.pdf.

16 The organization México Denuncia reports that an average of eight people are kidnapped per day and temporarily housed in various hotels and motels throughout Mexico City. http://www.mexicodenuncia.org. Accessed October 28, 2008.

17 México Denuncia reports that activities of La Hermandad include such criminal rackets as extortion, auto theft, pirated goods, and prostitution. http://www.mexicodenuncia.org. Accessed October 28, 2008. See also Osorio 2008.

stitute profit-making activity; in recent years, there have been a significant number of "pickups" or *"levantones,"* in which a victim is forcibly abducted to be tortured and killed.

As with other crime data in Mexico, existing statistics on kidnappings are quite unreliable because they reflect officially reported and acknowledged kidnappings. In Mexico, people are reluctant to report kidnappings, in part because of the perceived ineffectiveness or suspected involvement of police. Another problem is that different states seem to record and report kidnappings differently, depending on the nature of the abduction. Likewise, reporting rates also probably vary dramatically by state, due to differential rates of confidence among citizens in reporting crimes. However, as with other crime statistics, official data suggest some interesting trends that hint toward some general tendencies and tentative conclusions. One noticeable trend is that reported kidnappings appeared to decline dramatically from 1997 to 2005, then picking up slightly from 2005 to 2007 (figure 1.5). It is noteworthy that this post-2005 increase in kidnappings parallels trends observed in homicide, robbery, and assault after 2005.

In 2007, the absolute number of reported kidnappings was heavily concentrated in the greater Mexico City metropolitan area, particularly the Federal District, Mexico State, and Tlaxcala (figure 1.6). Meanwhile, collectively, other high drug-trafficking states (Michoacán, Guerrero, Baja California, Jalisco, and Sinaloa) also ranked in the "top ten" in terms of the absolute number of officially reported kidnappings.[18] These data may reflect a few different trends: (1) many people who are kidnapped may be involved in the drug trade; (2) law enforcement personnel also rank high among the victims of kidnapping (possibly in part because they may also fit into the first category); and/or (3) the breaking up of drug cartels has led to diversified criminal activities. In other words, there is some reason to believe that kidnapping in Mexico is strongly related to drug trafficking, law enforcement corruption, and the proliferation of more fractionalized criminal enterprises.

The increase in kidnappings has provoked a sharp response from Mexican citizens. In August 2008, the abduction and brutal murder of Fernando Martí, the fourteen-year-old son of prominent Mexico City businessman Alejandro Martí, triggered a nationwide series of anticrime demonstrations involving over 150,000 people. The

---

18 Aguascalientes is not known as a major drug-trafficking state, but it ranked eighth (above both Sinaloa and Jalisco) in total number of reported cases of kidnapping.

Mexican public was particularly outraged upon discovery of the involvement of law enforcement—including federal police officers—in the kidnapping ring. The Martí family had paid an estimated US$2 million to the kidnappers to secure their son's return, but the boy was brutally murdered. His body was discovered weeks later in the trunk of a car. In the wake of the Martí murder, new security measures were initiated by President Calderón and Mexico City Mayor Marcelo Ebrard, including tougher sentences and special police units to prevent and investigate cases of kidnapping. Also, representatives from all three federal branches of government and state authorities met in a televised session to discuss a new 74-point security plan to be implemented over the next hundred days. Although significant numbers of Mexicans supported these efforts, critics expressed skepticism given that harsher sentences are not a significant deterrent without a criminal justice system that can effectively address the problem of impunity.

MEXICAN PUBLIC SECURITY AND THE ADMINISTRATION OF JUSTICE

In the face of the public security crisis described above, Mexican law enforcement has exhibited significant limitations. In response to the failure of civilian police forces to provide basic public security, authorities have increasingly turned to the armed forces. The militarization of domestic security has included not only the deployment of more than twenty-five hundred federal police and military troops in troubled states, but also the appointment of military personnel to head civilian law enforcement agencies and the wholesale recruitment of soldiers to the ranks of law enforcement agencies. In contrast to Mexican police, who are viewed as ineffective and severely corrupted, the military enjoys a high degree of public confidence (higher than any other government institution) and is widely believed to be the best hope for restoring order. To provide a background for understanding this trend, below we examine Mexico's domestic law enforcement and security apparatus in more detail.

The recent escalation of the military's involvement in the provision of public security in Mexico is partly a symptom of deep and pervasive problems in domestic law enforcement. Mexican police, in particular, are viewed as highly ineffective and severely corrupted. Government authorities have insisted that the militarization of Mexican public security is therefore a necessary, limited, and temporary phenomenon that the country must endure until it makes greater gains in professionalizing domestic police forces. Yet civil libertarians, human rights advocates, and legislators have protested this trend toward militarization on the grounds that the use of combat tactics to ensure domestic security dramatically increases the risk of human rights abuses and military corruption.

Thus, even if the military can provide a "temporary fix" in restoring order, longer-term solutions to Mexico's public security crisis will require penetrating reforms to overhaul domestic law enforcement. As the authors in this volume make clear, at least three sets of problems are of particular concern: (1) problems with the recruitment, training, organization, and culture of Mexico's law enforcement corps; (2) larger problems of institutional design that undermine effective public policy and civil service in Mexico; and (3) the growing role of the Mexican armed forces. We discuss each of these in turn below.

Problems with Mexico's Law Enforcement Apparatus

Mexican law enforcement is much reviled and frequently disparaged. Mexican citizens view their law enforcement authorities as woefully ineffective, thoroughly corrupt, and frequently prone to abusive and criminal behavior. Yet, as the authors of this volume point out, the problem with Mexican law enforcement is rooted in institutional factors which practically guarantee that police will not only fail to adequately serve the public, but will become a menace to society. From the outset, police are poorly trained and equipped, underpaid, and subject to an incentive system that leads naturally down a twisted path of extortion and corruption. The criminal justice system is also organized in a way that creates a disconnect between critical police functions and simultaneously undermines effective police investigations, contributes to criminal impunity, and threatens the rights of criminals. This system is ultimately to blame for the problems of Mexican law enforcement, and it requires broad and penetrating reforms, some of which are already under way.

Perhaps no other Mexican academic has conducted such thorough research on the daily lives of Mexican police officers as Elena Azaola, a social anthropologist. In her chapter in this volume, Azaola issues a strong indictment of the systemic challenges that prevent police professionalism. Through exhaustive research, which includes detailed ethnographic analysis and interviews based largely in Mexico City, Azaola portrays a highly discretionary system absent of clearly delineated rules, expectations, or rewards—a "good ole boy" system where tacit understandings thrive and accountability is unknown. Yet Azaola finds police themselves a surprisingly sympathetic subject. She notes that Mexican police officers face deplorable working conditions, have terrible work schedules, must deal with a patronage-fueled promotions structure, and are poorly salaried. Police are routinely charged by superiors for items that are necessary for patrol work: ammunition, bulletproof jackets, and even vehicles. According to Azaola, such conditions harm morale and contribute to the susceptibility of police to corrupt practices. Forced to navigate an informal system that eclipses the paltry academic training they receive, entry-level officers who hope to advance invariably end up being corrupted themselves. Azaola closes her piece by noting that, for an integral reform to the corps, greater research is needed from the perspective of the rank-and-file police officer and his self-image.

María Eugenia Suárez, also an anthropologist, provides a similarly pessimistic assessment of public security forces in Mexico. Basing her observations on ethnographic research and interviews with police officers, she concludes that the state has proven largely incapable of meeting the public security demands of citizens. Moreover, this inability to provide for public security has foisted an ever-greater burden on citizens for ensuring personal safety, signaling a paradigmatic shift from the collectivization to the individualization of such responsibilities. Suárez's assessment is instructive to determining the efficacy of anticrime efforts that are focused on increasing the raw number of officers on the streets. If the state is viewed as incapable of reversing rising crime rates, then how effective are policies that boost manpower and firepower but do little else? More portentously, a state unable to ensure public security engenders a society ever more willing to accept coercion and force to fight crime. Suárez hints that a natural outcome of the failure to maintain public security includes vigilantism, mob violence, and other threats to the consolidation of democracy in Mexico. Perhaps tellingly, 71 percent of respondents in a 2007 AP-Ipsos poll said they favored the death penalty for murderers, possibly indicating a preference for an "ironfisted" approach to law enforcement.[19]

Unlike fellow anthropologist and contributor Elena Azaola, whose work attempts to derive conclusions about police systems at the macroscopic and structural levels, Suárez's ethnographic research focuses on the microscopic and individual relationships that dictate the expression of police power in everyday exchanges and settings. After all, the authority of the state is ultimately materialized in the person and

19 http://hosted.ap.org/specials/interactives/wdc/int_deathpenalty/index.html. Accessed June 15, 2009.

behavior of its most visible representative: the police officer is the face of the state. Suárez asserts that individual officers internalize exaggerated conceptions of masculinity and are transformed into almost psychopathic "men with guns," becoming "trapped, cornered, and paranoid" in the sadistic and repressive institution that is the stationhouse. An overriding and negative ethos pervades the police corps, she asserts, one that emphasizes discretion, aggression, hierarchy, and a stereotypical masculinity. It is a culture, she says, that exalts fearsome talismans of masculine power: militaristic uniforms, badges, and guns. And for average citizens its very real and natural consequences are the routine instances of brutality, abuse of authority, and due process violations that are committed by the very agents expected to uphold the rule of law.

Suárez furnishes a glimpse of common, everyday police dirty work: the use of men known as *madrinas*—literally "godmothers"—who are hired to do dirty enforcement jobs such as shaking down petty drug dealers, torturing suspects, and extracting confessions. She tells of cops who have been retaliated against for violating unspoken codes and who are "trapped" in a debasing, opaque, and abusive world. To the public these officers face a harsh stigmatization, attributable to the popular belief that they are impotent in the face of rampant crime (or at least impotent in the face of media-stoked perceptions of rampant crime) and are themselves the beneficiaries of illicit activity. Like Azaola's, Suárez's data also indicate low morale and low self-esteem among officers, given the abysmal public approval ratings they consistently obtain. But Suárez also produces examples of officers who derive satisfaction from the meager power to be gotten from owning a badge or, even more, because of its appeal to some women, a gun.

Though Suárez's research is primarily concerned with the processes guiding the identity formation of individual officers, she is mindful of the role that structures play in the self-perpetuation of the present broken system. She views the stationhouse as a microcosm of the clientelism that was elemental to the PRI party's domination of Mexican political life for most of the twentieth century, where, even after the end of its authoritarian rule, entrenched patronage enables only unethical officers to rise in the ranks and discourages promising candidates from ever applying. She also acknowledges the incompetence of the civilian leadership structure, which in the face of massive public protests against violent crime in past years has done little more than engage in empty posturing.

Table 1.1 Attributes of Accusatorial and Inquisitorial Legal Systems

Accusatorial System	Inquisitorial System
• Direct confrontation between the state (prosecutor) and the accused (defendant), with both prosecutors and defendants presenting arguments and evidence.	• Investigative process and presentation of evidence undertaken by the court or its investigative and prosecutorial representatives (e.g., *policía judicial, ministerio público*).
• Access to prosecutorial evidence (i.e., "discovery") provided to defendant in advance of proceedings.	• Consideration of evidence and testimony by a judge, who serves as impartial evaluator.
• Public forum where the judge serves as an impartial arbitrator in the presentation of arguments and evidence.	• Written proceedings, documentation of evidence, and testimony.
• Oral proceedings that permit contradiction between the parties in the review of arguments and evidence.	• Legal defense of the accused advocates for due process and proper adherence to criminal law procedure.
• Public proceedings are subject to public scrutiny, including the possibility of jury trials in certain cases.	• Proceedings are not subject to public scrutiny and rarely involve juries (Mexico's Constitution allows jury trials, but they have not been used for several decades).
• Commonly allows debate on cautionary measures to be applied to the accused during trial, such as the restraint of liberty.	• Commonly restrains liberty of the accused during pre-sentencing phase of trial procedure, upon presentation of compelling indications of guilt.

Table 1.2 Justice Sector Reforms in Selected States

State	Date of Implementation
Baja California	January 2009
Chihuahua	December 2006
Federal District	October 2008
Mexico State	August 2006
Morelos	January 2010
Nuevo León	January 2004
Oaxaca	September 2007
Veracruz	January 2010
Zacatecas	January 2009

Problems of Institutional Design

Many of the above-noted problems of police culture and organization relate to problems of institutional design. As Guillermo Zepeda and Daniel Sabet make clear in their respective chapters, these include the procedures Mexico has long used for criminal investigation, trial, and sentencing, as well as a lack of administrative continuity that contributes inadequate oversight, reduced job security, and limited opportunities for career development.

First, Guillermo Zepeda, a professor at the Instituto Tecnológico de Estudios Superiores del Oriente or ITESO, and a researcher at the Centro de Investigación para el Desarrollo, A.C., or CIDAC, observes that many of the problems with police in Mexico relate to the lack of checks and balances in Mexican criminal procedure. Mexico's legal system is rooted in a "civil law" tradition descended from Roman law, reinvigorated by Napoleonic law, and proliferated throughout Latin America by Spain.[20] Like other civil law systems, Mexico has traditionally relied on an inquisitorial model of criminal procedure, which places the judiciary in the position of gathering evidence and making determinations of guilt or innocence on behalf of the state.

In such systems, the judge or other actors effectively operating on behalf of the court—the public prosecutor (*ministerio público*) and the judicial police (*policía judicial*) in Mexico—have oversight of criminal investigations and an active role in the levying of charges against the accused. Hence, in a civil law system, the court may have compelling indications of guilt in advance of trial and sentencing, and the accused is often held in detention prior to sentencing. Pretrial release of the accused is therefore very rare, in part because of the preponderance of evidence indicating guilt and concerns that defendants may represent a flight risk. Thus, while Mexico theoretically maintains a "presumption of innocence" prior to the verdict of the court, defendants are commonly viewed as "guilty until proven innocent" and spend years in jail prior to receiving a formal sentence. Moreover, because court procedures rely much more on written than oral presentation of information, criminal procedure has tended to lack the degree of public scrutiny found elsewhere.

This contrasts with the accusatorial model used in the United States, which is more typically associated with common law systems. The accusatorial system derives from a historical and cultural tradition that challenges the legal position of the state and seeks to establish checks and balances in criminal procedure. That is, the accusatorial model allows for a more balanced treatment of the prosecution and the defense, viewing these as equally opposing forces in a criminal case. For this reason, the accusatorial system is sometimes also described as an "adversarial" system. In an accusatorial model, both parties—the prosecution and the defense—are granted the opportunity to present evidence and testimony in support of their positions. Moreover, the accusatorial model customarily allows each party to question and contradict the other's case before a judge in a public, oral proceeding. By comparison, the role of the defense in an inquisitorial system is typically limited to ensuring adherence to proper legal procedure, without the presentation of counterarguments or supporting evidence.

20 The defining characteristic of the civil law tradition is the strict application of legal codes or statutes (as written by the legislature) in judicial decisions, with the goal of ensuring that judges interpret the law consistently across all cases. Mexico's civil law system differs from the "common law" tradition that the United States inherited from Great Britain.

Both the inquisitorial and accusatorial systems have attributes with potential advantages and disadvantages (see table 1.1). In the United States, for example, prosecutors and the public often lament the reliance on highly paid defense attorneys who are skilled at subverting the state's evidence in criminal trials through legal technicalities. Also, the use of citizen juries to issue a verdict in accusatorial systems sometimes generates public criticism because of "jury rigging" and prejudicial juries.[21] Meanwhile, proponents of the accusatorial system claim that it provides for a more transparent and balanced presentation of arguments and evidence—as well as greater speed and efficiency—than the inquisitorial model.[22]

Despite the potential advantages of the inquisitorial model, its flaws are very visible in the Mexican experience. In Mexico, there is a strong role for the public prosecutor, there is very limited use of oral proceedings, and cases are presented primarily in written form. The problems that result include a lack of fluidity of the proceedings, enormous case backlogs and unsound prosecutorial investigations, inadequate disclosure of evidence to defense attorneys, insufficient involvement of the presiding judge, and a lack of alternative remedies for resolving criminal matters outside of court. The United Nations Commissioner for Human Rights in Mexico and numerous domestic and international nongovernmental organizations (NGOs) have criticized such problems as detrimental to the rights of the accused. Many also suggest that Mexico's inquisitorial model contributes, directly or indirectly, to botched criminal investigations, excessive criminal impunity, systemic problems of corruption, a lack of adherence to due process, and severe human rights abuses. In terms of the problems of Mexican police, the limited role of the defense in Mexican criminal procedure means that the checks and balances for law enforcement are exceedingly weak.

---

21 The accusatorial model need not rely on citizen juries, however. An accusatorial system could conceivably abandon the use of citizen juries in favor of rulings by an impartial judge or even by professional juries. Indeed, certain crimes in the United States are tried by "grand juries" comprising members of the judiciary.

22 It should be noted that elements of both systems can be combined. Indeed, prior to the 2008 justice-sector reforms, Article 20, Fraction VI of the Mexican Constitution included the possibility of jury trials, for instance (though these have been used only rarely in Mexican history). Also, Mexico has long employed "oral hearings" in the preliminary and adjudication phases. However, these are quite different from the oral, public proceedings found in most accusatorial systems. As we discuss in greater detail in the conclusion, recent reforms go much further in moving Mexico toward the accusatorial model.

TABLE 1.3 Major Federal Police and Military Deployments During the Calderón Administration

State	Month	Troops
Michoacán	Dec. 2006	6,700
Baja California	Jan. 2007	3,300
Guerrero	Jan. 2007	7,000
Golden Triangle (Chihuahua, Durango, Sinaloa)	Jan. 2007	4,000
Nuevo León and Tamaulipas	Feb. 2007	3,600
Veracruz	May 2007	1,200
Nuevo León	June 2007	1,600
Tamaulipas	Feb. 2008	n.a.
Chihuahua	Mar. 2008	2,500
Baja California	Oct. 2008	150
Chihuahua	Feb. 2009	1,800
Chihuahua	Mar. 2009	5,000
Chihuahua	Mar. 2009	1,500
Michoacan	July 2009	5,500

Source: *Justice in Mexico Monthly News Report* (www.justiceinmexico.org/news). Numbers reflect large-scale deployments of both soldiers and federal police, but does not include troop replacements.

As we discuss in further detail in the conclusion, Mexico responded to these concerns by passing sweeping legislation and major constitutional reforms in 2008 that will move the criminal justice system toward the accusatorial model, introducing legal innovations like oral trials and alternative dispute resolution mechanisms. In fact, prior to the passage of these federal reforms, several Mexican states had already passed similar legislation and had already begun to implement their reforms. As

Zepeda points out, there was significant variation in the extent of reform in these early reform states. Among the most progressive states were Chihuahua, Oaxaca, and Zacatecas, while others—like Mexico State—opted for half measures that in many ways made systematic "criminal injustice" more efficient. Thanks to the new federal reform package, all states will now have up to eight years to implement reforms, though some may fail to incorporate changes that will adequately guarantee the rights of the accused.

As Zepeda argues, these changes to Mexican criminal procedure will have important implications for policing. They will introduce the principle of contradiction, rights for the defendant, and greater due process that will provide a much-needed check on law enforcement agencies. In the face of a stronger, more empowered legal defense for criminal defendants, standards for proper evidence gathering and presentation of criminal cases will necessarily increase. Police and prosecutors will need to work together to build the strongest possible case to prove culpability or risk that criminals will walk free. Hence the modifications to criminal procedure that will be implemented over the next decade will significantly raise the bar for Mexican law enforcement.

Meanwhile, a second major area for institutional reform relates to the problem of administrative continuity and the development of a career civil service in Mexico. In his contribution to this monograph, Daniel Sabet, of Georgetown University, describes how sustained policy continuity across mayoral administrations and compliance with international best-practices accreditation programs have led to improved public perceptions of the Chihuahua City police. His empirical case study provides a model—or at least a precedent—for municipal-level reform efforts that do not necessitate wholesale and possibly volatile overhauls of existing law enforcement structures. Rather, Sabet's study suggests that small-scale modifications, feasibly implemented within the reduced time windows of Mexican municipal administrations, may improve police professionalization levels more efficiently than grandiose reform projects, which may be more comprehensive but also more complicated and costly. Sabet's study of the Chihuahua City police force is highly compelling and an important contribution to the study of municipal-level police reform efforts in Mexico. Like Azaola, Suárez, and Zepeda, Sabet provides a detailed diagnosis of Mexican police operations and structures. Focusing on the challenges complicating professionalization, he acknowledges the persistence of patronage-based systems of promotion and addresses the difficulties of effective interagency policy coordination in a federal system. Likewise, he focuses on the consequences of co-optation and infiltration that result from shortsighted police recruitment efforts. He also discusses the problem of perennial budget and operational shortcomings, particularly at a time when formidable organized crime syndicates pose real threats to the rule of law.

Sabet's analysis of the Chihuahua case subtly puts forth a prescriptive model for addressing these and other challenges to police professionalization in Mexico. His analysis suggests that compliance with prestigious international accreditation programs, combined with sustained policy continuity across administrations, can anchor a successful professionalization model. Moreover, the successful pursuit of certification from a prestigious nongovernmental organization, such as the Chihuahua force's accreditation by the U.S.-based Commission on Law Enforcement Accreditation (CALEA), may defuse the politicized issue of police professionalization, transforming it into a less polemical technical or scientific objective. Sabet's study also suggests that police professionalization efforts can benefit from the application of best practices, standards, and techniques developed in the fields of business administration and the management sciences—illustrated in the Chihuahua force's successful ISO-9000 credentialing. His case study further suggests that the exploitation of existing systems of incentives, such as the desire for the prestige obtained from successful accreditation, may be essential to any successful reform strategy.

Moreover, Sabet identifies policy continuity as an essential ingredient for sustained police professionalization efforts at the municipal level. Acknowledging that high barriers exist for such continuity given inflexible term limits on mayors, Sabet's study shows how successive mayoral administrations in Chihuahua City advanced and sustained the work of previous administrations, even within the logics of partisanship that define Mexican politics. Additionally, Sabet's study indicates a strong case for federally directed and long-term investment into those municipal police departments that are implementing successful professionalization efforts. Amid the consistently negative drumbeat of "bad news" about the police in Mexico, this "success story" of professionalization in the Chihuahua City preventive police force is very encouraging.

The Militarization of Public Security and the Role of the Armed Forces

Given the limitations and problems facing law enforcement agencies in Mexico, public authorities have increasingly resorted to extreme measures to try to get a grip on crime. Higher criminal sentences and even growing support for the death penalty reflect the growing frustration of both politicians and the public. But perhaps the most notable and potentially dangerous trend that has developed is the tendency of public authorities to draw on the military for the provision of basic public security and the staffing of civilian law enforcement agencies. On the one hand, the Mexican government has deployed thousands of federal troops to man checkpoints, establish street patrols, and oversee other domestic law enforcement functions in high drug violence states (see table 1.3). Precise data on the number of federal troops deployed are lacking, primarily because the government refuses to release such statistics for security reasons. However, media reports of deployments—which typically blur federal police and military personnel—provide an approximation of the size of deployments in recent years.

While there is no way to determine the length of deployments or the extent to which government forces are gradually drawn down or redeployed elsewhere, the size and significance of the initial deployments is notable. The first major deployments began at the outset of the Calderón administration, with the introduction of 6,700 troops in the state of Michoacán in December 2006 (see table 1.3). At the time, Michoacán had the highest level of drug-related killings in Mexico. These deployments were followed one month later by further deployments in Baja California, Guerrero, and the Golden Triangle area in January 2007. Throughout 2007, the government made smaller deployments to Nuevo León, Tamaulipas, and Veracruz. The most recent deployments have targeted the violence-ridden state of Chihuahua, where the number of killings exceeded 1,000 people by September 2008 (more than twice the number recorded in any other state).

In his chapter in this volume, Marcos Pablo Moloeznik examines the changing mandate of the Mexican military as its mission adapts to confront the national security threat posed by organized crime. He explains that the military's security detail has broadened in increasing proportion to the growing challenge the state faces from drug-trafficking organizations. And he cites specific examples of the gradual militarization of public security duties in Mexico since 1994. Moloeznik considers that two principal developments have enhanced the military's role in normally civilian police functions, and that these developments have cemented the military's place within the national security apparatus.

The first major development was the inclusion in 1996 of the military in the federal security cabinet, the National Public Security Council (Consejo Nacional de

Seguridad Pública, CNSP), a promotion that enabled the high brass's direct involvement in the elaboration and implementation of public and national security policy. Moloeznik considers the military's elevation to this upper stratum of security decision making to be the most prominent example of the militarization of security duties in Mexico in recent years. A second exemplary development of the militarization trend occurred also in 1996 when the Mexican Supreme Court gave its constitutional imprimatur to the use of the military in civilian-led public security operations. This high court decision, related to constitutional Article 129, has been interpreted as a legal redefinition of the mission of the corps, expanding the scope of its sworn duty to protect the nation. Besides its traditional call to arms against foreign invaders, the corps' mandate now orders it "to fight drug trafficking and organized crime or against acts that threaten the security of the nation," Moloeznik writes.

Moloeznik points out that there is a long history and tradition of military involvement in Mexico's domestic public security. Thus Moloeznik suggests that the use of the military in public security tasks is not a short-term measure, but rather that its role in top-level security policy making is becoming institutionalized and that this role has successively deepened over the past three presidential administrations. He closes by stressing that the rule of law demands that a stable horizon be fixed for the withdrawal of troops currently deployed in counternarcotics operations. He emphasizes the need for a schedule, or timetable, to govern the military's role in domestic policing activities and in those other activities he considers "beyond its nature."

Indeed, there are serious questions about the effectiveness of the military strategy even in the short term. Measured in terms of the reduction in drug violence, Mexico's military deployments have brought only mixed success at best. Some states, like Michoacán and Tamaulipas, saw significant reductions in drug-related violence shortly after federal forces were deployed there. Other states, like Baja California, Chihuahua, Guerrero, and Nuevo León, suffered continued or increased violence. A number of plausible hypotheses might explain these outcomes. One, which links back to Flores's claims, is that drug-trafficking organizations have successfully cultivated relationships with mid-level state actors in some states but not in others. Another, also related to Flores's observations, is that the fractionalization and atomization of drug cartels means that they are simply too erratic and unpredictable in their responses to state actions. Both of these hypotheses are compatible and troubling. If the government's strategy of last resort—exercising the chief tool of government coercive capability—is incapable of overcoming cartel violence, what are the prospects for the longer term?

Human rights researcher and act-ivist Jorge Rocha expresses similar concerns and offers a critique of the trend toward the militarization of Mexican domestic public security, which has contributed to human rights abuses, exposed the military to greater corruption, and increased the militarization of organized crime. Moreover, echoing Zepeda's concerns, Rocha warns that a "false dichotomy" has wrongly made civil liberties and law and order mutually exclusive concepts in Mexico, perpetuating the received "either/or" knowledge that the suppression of human rights is necessary for the improvement of public security. "One can read and hear in the local and national press ... different social actors ... vouch(ing) for the restriction of certain rights for the maintenance of personal security and the social order," Rocha notes. The widespread belief that such abrogations are necessary for the rule of law has aggravated conflicts between the state and civil society, especially with civil society that employs collective action, mass mobilization, or other political strategies that rely on "freedom of association," Rocha says. In many cases, the state's default repression or criminalization of such activities has served to expose its lack of effective noncoercive conflict-resolution capacities (such as political negotiation, labor mediation, and so on).

In fact, enforcement-heavy reactions have frequently led to even greater intransigence and stalemate in some state–civil society conflicts, further hardening positions and thwarting negotiated solutions. As a case in point, Rocha discusses in detail the 2006 Oaxaca City uprising, a months-long rebellion fundamentally ignited by a disastrous government attempt to break a massive teachers' strike. The state's mismanagement of the teachers' protest sparked a lengthy and volatile standoff, the vigilante killings of civilians, the illegal and arbitrary detentions of hundreds of protesters, and a politically costly federal intervention. The Oaxaca case exemplifies the state's need for a more constructive engagement with civil society, Rocha says. Such a rapprochement is possible when the state adopts the premise that political protests fundamentally arise from deeply embedded social and economic conditions, and when it rejects the automatic belief that such demonstrations are criminal or disruptive to the social order.

The state must also work to reverse the de facto stereotyping of certain vulnerable and marginalized groups as criminal or deviant, since such labeling rationalizes abusive practices against minorities, Rocha notes. Branding as criminals such groups as the indigenous, homosexuals, sex workers, drug addicts, and youths encourages their further marginalization and second-class citizenship, Rocha says. Not unilaterally blaming the state, he acknowledges the role of a sensationalistic news media in manufacturing such social constructions of crime and deviance. "What we have, in the face of a legal and institutional vacuum, is a de facto public security policy that socioculturally constructs criminality and pursues persons and social groups, not for having committed crimes, but for having belonged to certain social groups or having realized certain social practices."

Rocha considers the expanded use of the military in police duties part of a security doctrine that leans toward the criminalization of state–civil society conflict, that favors coercion, and that encourages the abrogation of individual liberties in the name of national defense. Such a doctrine, Rocha suggests, represents a "maximalist" vision of the role that security should play in the enactment of the rule of law in Mexico. The Calderón administration's protracted and large-scale troop deployments, making use of security checks and warrantless search capabilities, to fight organized crime throughout the country are emblematic of this doctrine. Yet in sharp contradistinction, another equally important component to the rule of law—human rights—possesses a highly circumscribed and minimalist iteration. Rocha suggests that "human rights" in Mexico are frequently subordinated to collectivist rights, that a "nucleus" of core rights is continuously being whittled down, and that a "race to the bottom" mentality characterizes recent trends. More portentously, he warns that a minimalist understanding of human rights can indirectly serve to justify claims for the suppression of individual rights, particularly in the name of national defense. Under such scenarios, Rocha warns, human rights violations become permissible because they are seen as necessary for the preservation of more important national rights. Ideally, the predominant vision of human rights in Mexico should be a maximalist one, continuously expanding its scope and responsibility rather than accommodating to a continuously diminished set of minimum standards.

In his contribution to this monograph, Rocha stresses the important connections between two concepts commonly considered in polar opposition: law and order and civil liberties. He suggests that a professional police force that upholds civil liberties in the performance of its security task begins to be viewed by citizens as an effective partner in the enactment of the rule of law. However, genuine and enforceable citizen monitoring of the police, heretofore lacking in Mexico, is essential to catalyze this improvement. In short, Rocha's essay helps to advance a fundamental thesis of the Justice in Mexico Project that generated this monograph: that the democratic rule of law is dependent on the development and interplay of three essential elements—order (law and order and security); accountability (transparency and effective public accountability of government actions); and access to justice (due process, protection of human rights, and just application of the law).

CONCLUSION

In short, this monograph provides a comprehensive and timely overview of the significant public security challenges Mexico faces today. Together, the authors represent some of the leading academic experts on Mexican policing, and their observations and recommendations offer tremendous insights into the possible policy directions for improving Mexican law enforcement. Collectively, these authors provide support for the idea that improving the overall effectiveness of civilian police forces is a better alternative than long-term reliance on the military for public security. In the short term, Mexico's reliance on the military may be a "necessary evil," but emphasis must be placed not only on the necessity but on the evils: human rights violations, heightened violence, and other threats to democratic governance are very clear and present dangers in Mexico's military strategy.

Thus there is a critical and urgent need to improve the capability of Mexican police to deal with crime, and especially organized crime. As these authors point out, efforts to improve Mexican law enforcement will necessarily address the systemic problems found in the function and organization of its police agencies. Improving the daily work conditions of police officers—with better pay, better equipment, and better training—will greatly enhance the function and effectiveness of Mexican law enforcement. Indeed, as this volume went to print, significant changes were made at the federal level seeking to address some of these issues. In May 2009, the Federal Attorney General Law and the Federal Police Law passed both chambers of Mexico's Congress, giving more investigative powers to the Public Security Ministry (SSP) through the creation of a new Federal Police agency. Meanwhile, scattered police reform efforts at the state and local levels—as illustrated by Sabet's discussion of the case of Chihuahua—offer some promise that police reform can make real headway in Mexico under the right institutional conditions.

Yet, while strengthening the capability of law enforcement is essential for improving the rule of law in Mexico, promoting greater police effectiveness is not enough. Indeed, without proper checks and balances to ensure accountability and fairness in the Mexican criminal justice system, improving the effectiveness and efficiency of police may actually contribute to greater problems and injustices. Hence guaranteeing the success of Mexico's justice-sector reform initiatives over the next decade will be essential to the longer-term promotion of both order and justice. These reforms will introduce the necessary checks and balances to ensure that police become more effective and more accountable.

REFERENCES

Calderón, President Felipe. 2008. *Segundo Informe de Gobierno*, September 1.

Castillo García, Gustavo, and Armando Torres Barbosa. 2003. "La historia del *cártel* del Golfo," *La Jornada*, March 15.

Corchado, Alfredo, and Tim Connolly. 2008. "Analyst: U.S. Anti-drug Aid Proposal Could Heighten Violence in Mexico," *Dallas Morning News*, January 3.

Cornelius, Wayne A., and David Shirk, eds. 2007. *Reforming the Administration of Justice in Mexico*. Notre Dame, IN: University of Notre Dame Press.

Grayson, George. 2007. "Drug War Allies," *San Diego Union-Tribune*, September 2.

———. 2008. "Los Zetas: The Ruthless Army Spawned by a Mexican Drug Cartel." Foreign Policy Research Institute. May. http://www.fpri.org/enotes/200805.grayson.loszetas.html. Accessed July 19, 2008.

Grillo, Ioan. 2007. "'Cop-killer' Guns from U.S. Seen Crossing into Mexico," Associated Press, August 18.

Hepburn, L., M. Miller, D. Azreal, and D. Hemenway. 2007. "The U.S. Gun Stock: Results from the 2004 National Firearms Survey," *Injury Prevention* 13: 15–19.

Lumpe, L. 1997. "The US Arms Both Sides of Mexico's Drug War," *Covert Action Quarterly* 61: 39–46.

Marks, Alexandra. 2006. "Why Gun Dealers Have Dwindled," *Christian Science Monitor*, March 14.

Osorio, Ernesto. 2008. "Avala Ebrard a mandos de SSP," *Reforma*, October 28.

Padgett, Tim, and Elaine Shannon. 2001. "The Border Monsters," *Time* 157, no. 23 (June 11).

Serrano, Richard A. 2008. "U.S. Guns Arm Mexican Drug Cartels," *Los Angeles Times*, August 10.

Trahan, Jason, Ernesto Londoño, and Alfredo Corchado. 2005. "Drug Wars' Long Shadow," *Dallas Morning News*, December 13.

Vernick, Jon S., Daniel W. Webster, Maria T. Bulzacchelli, and Julie Samia Mair. 2006. "Regulation of Firearm Dealers in the United States: An Analysis of State Law and Opportunities for Improvement," *Journal of Law, Medicine, and Ethics* 34, no. 4: 765–75.

Mexican Police and the Criminal Justice System

GUILLERMO ZEPEDA LECUONA

THERE ARE NEW, pragmatic reasons for undertaking an intense search for alternatives to the use of the criminal justice system as a tool of police work. This also means that there is a new incentive to cultivate a positive relationship with the community. Police forces need to replace the amorphous authority previously obtained from the criminal justice system and upon which they so deeply depended in the past. What better way to do this than by taking unto themselves what Robert Peel characterized in 1829 as the most powerful form of authority, the "public approval of its existence, actions and behavior" (Goldstein 1998, 123).

POLICE, POLITICS, AND THE CRIMINAL JUSTICE SYSTEM IN MEXICO

The shape of government institutions is a reflection of the configuration and distribution of political power in society. This is particularly applicable to the criminal justice system and the police subsystem.[1] It is in the justice system as a whole that we find the most delicate points of contact between the state and the sphere of the fundamental rights of the people living in a given society.

The attributes of surveillance, investigation, and, when necessary, punishment of members of society imply weighing and restricting such rights as freedom of movement and even physical integrity. Therefore, in regulating what to watch, what to control, what to punish, and how to do it, society and its elected officials evidence the whys that justify, validate, and legitimize the actions of government entities and their officials in the exercise of their monopoly of legal coercion.

Within the framework of the criminal justice process, the accusatorial model tends to be associated with "liberal regimes, jealously guarding the principle of separation of public [government] power and the rights of citizens," whereas the

1 As James Goldschmidt has pointed out in reference to procedural institutions: "the principles of a nation's procedural policy are nothing more than segments of state policy in general" (in García Ramírez 2003, 546).

inquisitorial model "is proper to tyrannical, absolutist or authoritarian regimes … where the interests of society prevail over all others" (Alfredo Etcheberry, in García Ramírez 1989, 101).

Police forces are among the government bodies that are closest to the people, representing in many cases the first face of the state and, in the words of one author as regards the criminal justice system, have the "monopoly of contact with the community" (Rusconi 1998, 193). They also have at their disposal a level of discretionary power that can be regulated but not eliminated. Therefore, the police are a vital component for the legitimacy and efficiency of the system.[2]

For decades, the police and criminal justice institutions in Mexico had been a reflection of a hegemonic regime that had de facto deactivated the formally established system of checks and balances. The operation of the criminal justice system focused on social control and the selective and arbitrary application of the law. In addition, its operation was neither transparent nor accountable to society. Police functions of community service and crime prevention were marginalized and left to a broad discretionary scope. Police forces were principally focused on the administrative application of regulations and serving as auxiliaries of the criminal justice system.

In the past fifteen years or so, institutional reforms have strengthened the oversight and control of power by such entities as Mexico's Supreme Court; the right to learn how public power is exercised has been guaranteed and made more transparent; and a trustworthy electoral system has been built. Mexico has moved from a hegemonic-party political regime to a multiparty system with alternation in power, which has permitted the conformation of multiparty legislative bodies and a better operation of the mechanisms of separation of, and balance between, branches of government. This new reality goes hand in hand with a more active, informed, and demanding public.

The criminal justice system has not remained isolated from the transformation of the political and institutional context in Mexico. Mexicans are dissatisfied with their criminal justice system, with its serious qualitative problems (inquisitorial model, absence of judges at hearings, typewritten files, limited transparency, and systematic violations of human rights) as well as its quantitative or efficiency problems (court

---

2 "The criminal justice system is defined in great measure during the stage of police investigation of crimes" (Duce and González 1998, 52).

backlogs and jail overcrowding, impunity rates of 97 percent, and inefficient and irrational use of material and human resources).

A deep reform of the criminal justice system is needed to restore the accusatorial model foreseen in the Constitution, a reform that confers the right to contradict the prosecution's case and the right to a quality defense, and also strengthens due process provisions. To this end, the federal government passed a package of criminal justice reforms in 2008. As noted by Donnelley and Shirk in the introductory chapter to this volume, this reform was preceded by similar measures in a few states—including Chihuahua, Oaxaca, and Zacatecas—which introduced profound qualitative and quantitative transformations to criminal procedure and helped move these states toward a more just and efficient system. Other states, such as Coahuila and Nuevo León, were halfway down this road, with measures that introduced principles of restorative justice and greater transparency. In still others, criminal justice reform efforts met with resistance, falling into the paradox of adopting measures to "de-saturate" and "efficientize" (such as arbitration and alternative sentencing) without transforming the bias of the inquisitorial model or addressing systemic qualitative problems. In these states, such as Mexico State and Jalisco, criminal injustice was being made more efficient.[3]

Over the next eight years, the 2008 legal changes at the federal level will require all states to implement reforms to strengthen the procedural principle of contradiction, the rights to a competent defense, and due process. As these reforms are implemented, a new conception of the exercise of public power must guide the police forces in their work with the community. That is, the transformation of the justice system must also be reflected in the organizations that provide police services; otherwise, there is a risk of implementing the judicial reforms Chilean-style, but without the guns.

As Luigi Ferrajoli has pointed out: "It would matter little if the Constitution guarantees habeas corpus in principle, and the exclusive monopoly of legal authorities in matters of personal freedom, if in the end arrests by police are done illegally or if, indeed, the law itself confers upon the police broad discretionary powers to restrict said freedom" (1995, 763). Likewise, the police must no longer be considered the custodians of an order established by the state. They must transition from being an instrument of public power that protects the security of the state, to become

3 Law enforcement reform is also being promoted in states and municipalities across Mexico, including Chihuahua, Coahuila, Querétaro, and Mexico State.

protectors of the security of the people (moving through the intermediate concepts of public safety and residents' safety).

AN EXHAUSTED MODEL OF LAW ENFORCEMENT

What exists in Mexico is less a model of law enforcement than an inertial pattern of police practices developed over decades in an environment shaped by a hegemonic political system and an inquisitorial and arbitrary model of criminal procedure, with very little public participation. The police, as noted, were relegated to the selective application of administrative regulations and to auxiliary tasks in support of criminal justice authorities.

Generally speaking, both society as a whole and the authorities themselves mistrust the police, but instead of taking steps to improve the police, the police have seen their functions stripped away piece by piece. The police cannot take crime reports but must wait for information from prosecutors or attorneys before beginning their intelligence and crime-mapping activities. Nor can they act after a crime has been committed because, unless the perpetrator is caught red-handed, the investigation and arrest of suspects is also reserved to the prosecutors.

The deficiencies in the criminal justice system have become increasingly visible since 1994, when the levels of both organized crime and common crime began to climb. In response to this increase in criminal activity, police forces moved away from administrative functions and community service to make crime fighting their top priority, even though they lack the human and material resources to wage an effective battle.

Even though experts, noting the deficiencies in the nation's police forces, pointed to the need for their professionalization as fundamental to the country's safety and security policies, law enforcement decision makers have responded primarily with quantitative measures. Budgets have risen, along with the number of public servants assigned to public safety, procurement of justice, and the penal system (traditionally called "the state of national forces").[4]

---

4 This denomination, a military one, is used by government officials, law enforcement, justice personnel, penal system administrators, and prosecutors themselves. The term illustrates how all subsystems of the Mexican criminal justice system (including private security company personnel) are focused, independently of the roles established under law, on combating crime, adopting traces of what has been called "criminal law for enemies." A new usage appeared in a June 2007 report that replaced "state of

Figure 2.1 Total Number of Public Servants in Public Safety and Criminal Justice Institutions in Mexico and Number of Police

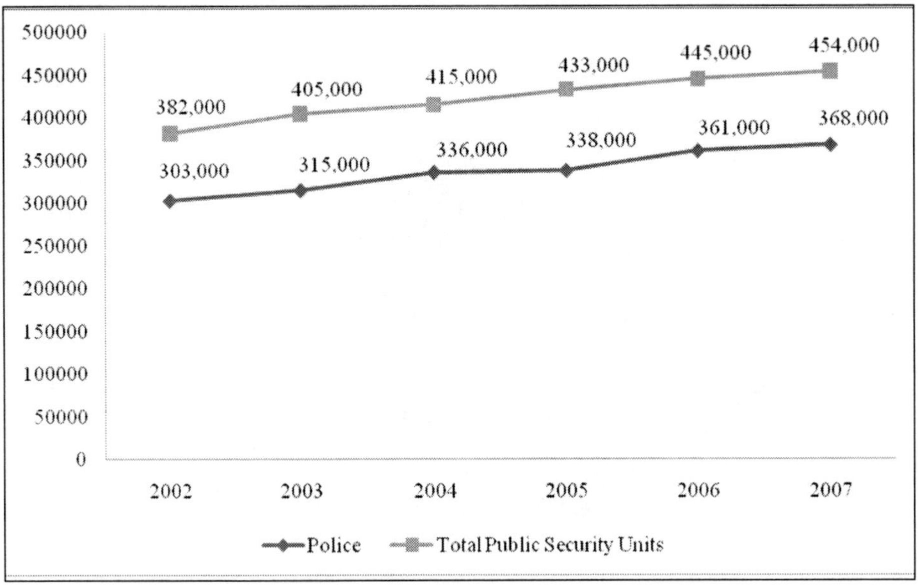

Sources: For 2002 and 2003, SNSP-CON 2004a; for 2004–June 2007, SNSP-CON 2007.

By June 2007, this number had reached 454,574, plus an additional 122,973 private security guards.[5]

The number of public servants dedicated to crime prevention, public safety, the administration of justice, and social rehabilitation has continued to rise in recent

---

national forces" with "active public and private security personnel" (although the focus on public safety continues to apply among public officials dedicated to reviewing expert opinion regulations). Another indicator of this closing of ranks against crime under the logic of "criminal law for enemies" can be found in the General Law which establishes the basis for coordination of the National Public Security System. In Article 3 it states that "the public safety function shall be carried out in the various areas of competence by preventive police authorities, prosecutors, and tribunals" (emphasis added). That is, the court system is included; courts must oversee the constitutionality and legality of the actions of police and prosecutors, as well as deal with the evidence they present, always presuming the innocence of the accused. In other words, the task of the courts cannot be to provide public safety and security, but under the logic of criminal law for enemies, there are only allies and enemies.

5 Moloeznik (this volume) suggests this number may be as high as 140,966.

Figure 2.2 Public Servants in Safety and Justice Institutions in Mexico, June 2007

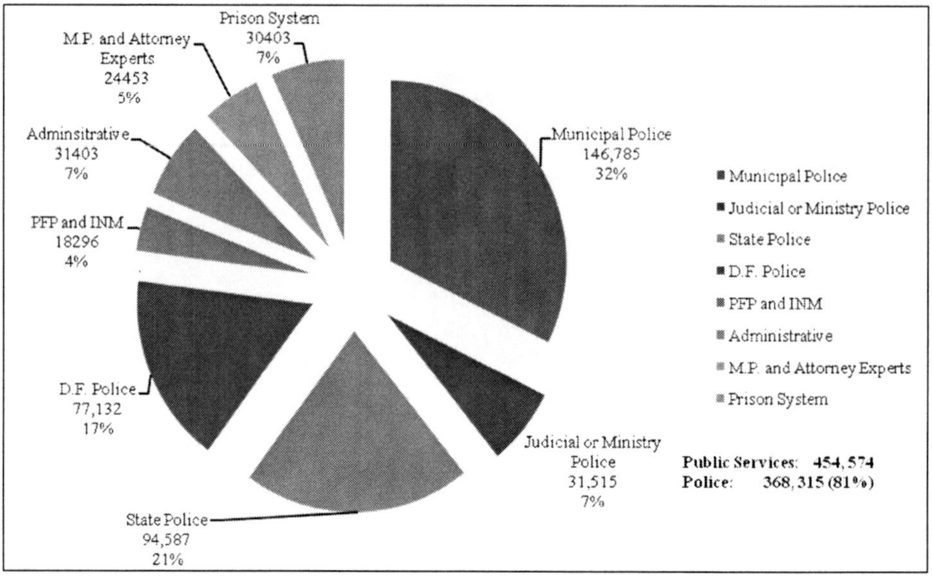

Source: SSP-CON 2007.

years, with a preponderance of these individuals dedicated to police tasks, as indicated in figure 2.1.

The police are the most geographically dispersed face of government in Mexico, with a municipal-level presence across the country. And though the citizenry directs its demands for safety and security to all levels of government, these tend to concentrate at the local level.[6] Of the 454,574 public servants working in the various subsystems of the justice sector in 2007,[7] 81 percent (368,315) were police. Of these, 8.6 percent

6 This contrasts with other components of the justice system, which are centralized at the state and federal levels and are, therefore, part of the structural conditions that promote police use of discretionary power and hinder efforts to control police actions (see Rusconi 1998).

7 Official sources differ on the number of people in law enforcement in Mexico. I am using the most trustworthy source, the National Public Security System (SNSP), which reported 368,315 police

Figure 2.3 International Comparison of Law Enforcement Personnel per 100,000 People

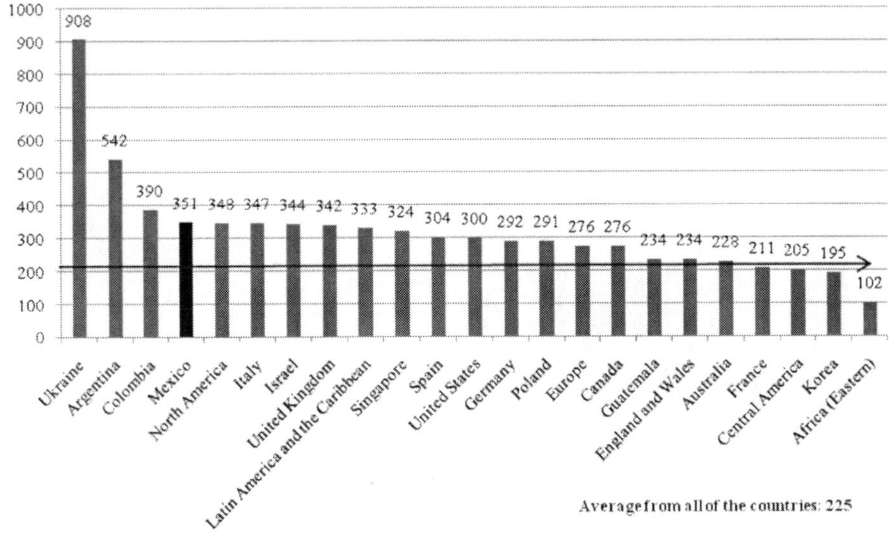

Sources: For regions, Shaw, Van Dijk, and Rhomberg 2003, 56. For Mexico, CIDAC calculation based on SSP information. For Colombia, speech by Colombian President Álvaro Uribe at the United Nations in 2006, available at the United Nations Web site. For the United States, U.S. Department of Justice. For all other countries, Seguridad Estratégica Regional (www.ser2000.org.ar).

officers in June 2007 (SNSP-CON 2007). Yet the Ministry of Public Security counts 426,528 police officers in the country in February 2007 (SSP 2007, 3), and in July 2007 the head of the SSP indicated there were 439,248 police officers (SSP-CON 2007). If these numbers were correct, the police would represent between 94.7 and 97.5 percent of all public servants across all subsystems. Our hypothesis is that at some point between January 2006 and February 2007, the SSP counted the police forces of Mexico City twice, since in November 2004 (SNSP-CON 2004b) there was a total of 151,124 state-level law enforcement officers (76,907 in Mexico City and 74,217 in the remainder of the country), and in December 2006 (SNSP-CON 2007) there were 170,235 (77,820 in Mexico City and 92,415 elsewhere). Yet by February 2007, there are 234,855 state-level law enforcement officers reported (77,862 in Mexico City and 156,993 in the rest of the states), which would imply that in one month, state law enforcement personnel would have experienced a 70 percent increase. This matches neither the SNSP information for June 2007 nor trends in states for which there are disaggregated data. In addition, this is not consistent with the total number of public servants in various subsystems reported by the SSP itself. As regards municipal-level preventive police, that number has remained between 133,625 and 146,785 (in June 2007).

Figure 2.4 Police Officers per 100,000 Residents, by State, June 2007

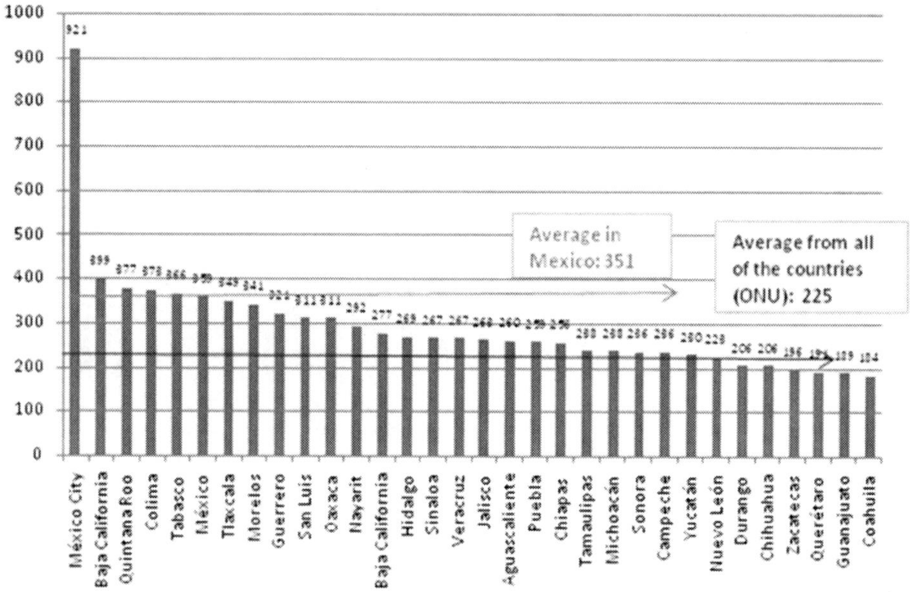

Sources: Calculations based on INEGI population projections and SSP-CON 2007.

were police investigators, and the remaining 91.4 percent were uniformed preventive police (see figure 2.2).

The United Nations recommendation on police personnel is that societies have 280 law enforcement officers per 100,000 people, though some experts argue for lower numbers, even suggesting that 150 police officers per 100,000 people is adequate in cases of political instability (Dobbins et al., in Jones et al. 2005, 19). In practice, most countries have about 200 officers per 100,000 people. An international survey conducted by the United Nations every four years yielded an average of 225 police officers per 100,000 people across all countries surveyed in 2002. Mexico's rate is far higher: 351 law enforcement personnel per 100,000 people (see figure 2.3).

However, it is important to note that Mexico's national-level indicator includes a high concentration of police in Mexico City. One of every five Mexican police

Table 2.1 National Budget for Public Safety, Criminal Justice System, and Social Rehabilitation, 2005 (millions of pesos)

	Municipal	State	Federal	Mexico City	Subtotals
Preventive police	15,561.8	8,656.0	5,146.5	11,804.0	41,168.8
Prosecutors		10,183.6	8,143.6	2,955.1	21,282.3
Criminal courts		2,514.0	5,575.0	848.5	8,937.5
Social rehabilitation	N. A.	10,470.0	1,839.0	1,075.5	13,384.6
Totals	15,561.8	31,823.6	20,704.1	16,682.1	84,773.2

Sources: Disaggregated data from the federal budget and the Mexico City budget. Disaggregated data was accessed in some states, as well as data from the National Public Security System for municipalities. Disaggregated data from twenty-three of the thirty-two states was used for state-level estimates.

Note: For the information on municipal preventive police, data were drawn from municipal funding for public safety, weighing the estimate according to the level of strength of the municipal preventive police in the states, as reported by the General Directorate of the National Public Security Information System. In the majority of states, information was not available for expenditures in municipal prisons, which in many cases are funded mainly or exclusively from local treasuries. Although human rights commissions consider municipal jails unconstitutional, 15 percent of the country's jail population is held in these facilities.

officers works in the nation's capital; elsewhere the number of police drops to 299 per 100,000 inhabitants. Yet despite Mexico's strong ratio of police to population, responses to public safety concerns continue to focus on quantitative solutions. During his campaign and into his administration, Mexico City Mayor Marcelo Ebrard reiterated the city's need for twenty thousand more officers and vowed to make increasing the police force a priority.[8]

8 When asked what would be needed to eradicate crime, Ebrard responded: "Three things are needed: 20,000 new officers in the neighborhood cop model; merge crime prosecution tasks with the city's surveillance, and, third, modify the current prison system" (El Universal 2005). In another interview, Ebrard was asked what he would do to reestablish security for the people of Mexico City. His response

Figure 2.5 Nationwide Distribution of Budgetary Resources for Public Safety, Criminal Justice System, and Social Rehabilitation, 2005 (millions of pesos)

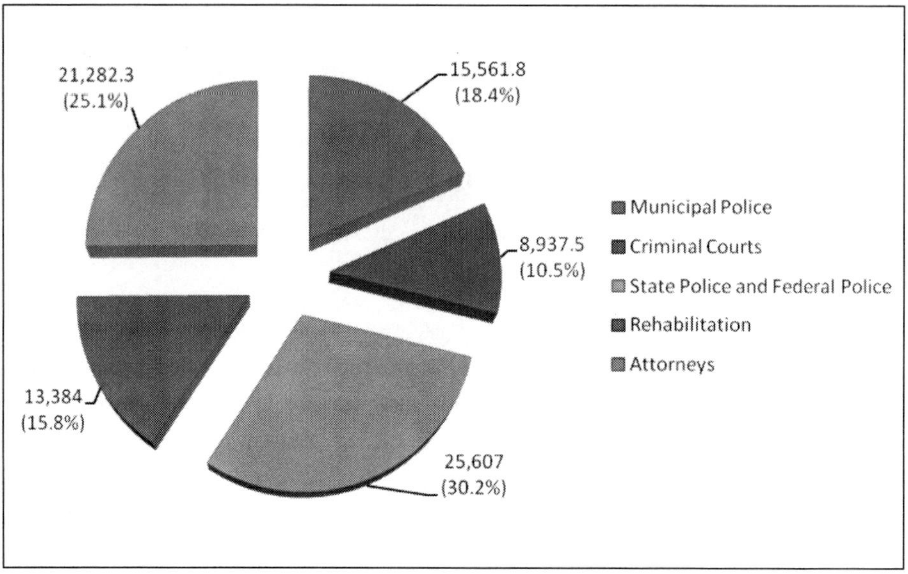

Sources: Calculations based on INEGI population projections and SSP-CON 2007.

Figure 2.4 presents the ratios of police to population in Mexico City and the states. Of note are the differences between the nation's capital and the states, and also the differences among the states, from a high of over 300 officers per 100,000 in ten states to a low of 184 per 100,000 in Coahuila. Curiously, the lowest numbers are found in the very same states—Saltillo, Chihuahua, and Querétaro—that are making significant efforts in law enforcement reform and pursuing certification by international organizations, reinforcing the argument that the most effective measures are not quantitative in nature.

was: "Well, we're going to hire 20,000 new police officers, high school graduates, well paid, well trained" (Vázquez Raña 2006).

There is also a lack of parity in the distribution of financial resources, with the uniformed preventive police, who account for 75 percent of personnel, receiving 48.6 percent of the monies budgeted for public safety, the criminal justice system, and social rehabilitation. In 2005 almost half of the resources for public security and the criminal justice system went to the preventive police (see table 2.1 and figure 2.5).

Notwithstanding the strong allocation of resources to policing and the authorities' continued focus on quantitative measures, there is no authentic law enforcement career in Mexico. To be a police officer in Mexico implies a low-paid, high-risk job that carries a strong social stigma. Policemen leave the job as soon as a better option arises, leading to a high turnover rate. Based on information from the National Public Security Program (through 2000) on police training and preparation over the preceding ten years, Miguel Sarre reports that for every active agent there are "3.5 [former agents] who no longer render their services to the state." Thus, if we currently have 368,000 active law enforcement agents, approximately 1.6 million police were trained in the previous decade, and more than a million of them could not be convinced to remain with the police.

Preliminary results from ongoing research on Guadalajara's metropolitan police indicate that the average tenure for police personnel is 2 years, 86 days. There are always vacancies in the municipal police, and the urgent need to fill these positions results in a relaxation of entrance requirements over time.[9]

Turnover also affects the higher ranks of the police, with police chiefs often changing posts every three or six years, along with the change in elected officials. Given the politicization of the public safety issue and the fact that there is no law enforcement civil service, newly elected mayors and governors appoint people they trust to head the police force in their respective municipality or state, independent of whether these individuals have any law enforcement experience. The group that currently controls the municipal police in Zapopan, Jalisco, provides an example of the rotation in police leadership. During the previous three-year administration, this group headed the force in León, Guanajuato; three years prior to that, several of its members were police commanders in Guadalajara; three years before that they were

9 For instance, at the July 2007 workshop that gave rise to this monograph, Marcos Pablo Moloeznik pointed out that recruitment shortfalls often compel Mexican police forces to accept applicants over thirty-five years of age.

in charge of the police in San Juan de los Lagos, Jalisco; and in the three years prior to that, they led the police force in Lagos de Moreno, Jalisco. Many police commanders spend a quarter of their time looking for their next job, in the knowledge that the next mayor or governor will oust them in order to appoint his or her own people.

Given the high turnover in law enforcement, including in community services and outreach programs, citizens must continuously deal with a new group of officials. Moreover, organizational learning is lost when experienced people leave. And finally, the local police forces that are supposed to combat organized crime must reinvent themselves every few years.

After more than a decade of efforts to improve police forces, officers still have an average of only 8.8 years of education (López Portillo 2004, 19). Because of poor training and inadequate equipment, more officers than criminals die in clashes between the two groups. Sixty percent of officers suffer from illnesses such as hypertension, obesity, diabetes, and gastritis; and approximately 40 percent of injuries suffered by uniformed police are self-inflicted or from "friendly fire" in weapons practice or during operations.

Police officers feel they are under attack from three sides: from criminals (especially organized crime groups), who generally have better training, information, and equipment; from their superiors, who impose harsh working conditions and unrealistic performance goals and also often expose them to corrupt practices; and from a society that despises them and is indifferent to their efforts and sacrifices.

Law enforcement officials tremble in hostage takings or riots because agents are not trained to intervene in crisis situations and prefer to negotiate rather than risk a bloodbath. Officers seen fleeing from machete-wielding demonstrators or providing nonsensical legalistic statements to the media are the sad images of an incapable and impotent police.

The reduced response capability of the police and the taint of corruption hanging over them have stigmatized the profession. In surveys, 80 percent of respondents state that they distrust the police. On a scale of 0 to 10 (where 0 is "no trust" and 10 is "high trust"), law enforcement receives a rating of 4.48 (just slightly above members of the federal legislature). Further, the majority of respondents view the police as incapable and corrupt (Concha et al. 2004, 62).

Yet the heroism and sacrifice demonstrated by many honest uniformed officers requires that we make an effort to retain all that is beneficial among the police and reform what is not. Undertaking a legal and administrative reform of law enforcement organizations, making law enforcement an attractive career, and improving training, wages, and working conditions are all indispensable to developing the full potential of the preventive police in the following areas, among others: advising the public; crime prevention and public information, especially for vulnerable groups and in problem areas; intervention, channeling, and resolution of minor conflicts; maintenance of order and intervention in crisis situations; crime mapping and design of high-impact prevention programs; intelligence; and the elite tasks of fighting organized crime. In a word, the goal is to build a new, leaner, capable, and solvent force, one that is closer to the public. Given good recruits and better training, the current level of personnel could likely be reduced by half.

A MINIMUM AGENDA FOR CHANGE

What is needed in Mexico is a paradigm shift from reactive and punitive policing to a model of police work focused on public service and managing social conflict. For decades a characteristic of the police has been its function as an auxiliary of the criminal justice system, which has meant marginalizing its functions of interacting with the public, preventing crime, and intervening in the early stages of social conflict.

The old orientation is reinforced by the nation's current climate of insecurity and the adoption of an official discourse of emergency. Lamentably, public and political criteria converge in demands for social control and even tolerance of repression. These criteria are translated into goals that emphasize "products" more than "results." Arrest quotas are set, which the police usually fill with "easy arrests," detaining people for disorderly conduct, public drinking, or loitering in residential areas. Thus, as Eugenio Raúl Zaffaroni points out, the crime most prosecuted by Latin American police is simply "having the wrong look" (in Maya 2004), to which we can add the increasingly significant crime of "being poor."

These policies have resulted in an irrational use of the material and human resources dedicated to public security and the criminal justice system. In Mexico, the prison population doubled between 2000 and 2008, and 70 percent of resources are focused on arrest, investigation (in that order, regrettably), prosecution, and punishment related to minor crimes.

Police officers and officials are aware that these measures do not help return safety and security to their communities, but they are trapped by short-term policies focused on meeting numerical goals and maximizing media coverage. To change course would imply a paradigm shift in political and technical evaluation criteria.

In democratic societies only about 15 percent of police activity corresponds to fighting crime.[10] To move toward more community-oriented public service, the bulk of police attention must be focused on communicating with the public, mapping crime, designing patrols, interacting with the citizenry, and conducting preventive measures, particularly among vulnerable groups.

Social Policy and the Prevention of Social Conflicts

A significant number of social conflicts—most of which are not legal offenses—are tied to the socioeconomic conditions of a community. García Ramírez has noted that we cannot ask the criminal justice system to do what the social justice system cannot (2000, 479).

An adequate mapping of social conflicts permits a much more efficient (and less costly) preventive effort than can be achieved through reactive and punitive measures after the violence escalates. For example, in opinion polls in urban areas, a major public concern involves the proliferation of groups of young people who take over public spaces and devolve into gangs waging violent turf wars. Such behavior often reflects the lack of educational and work opportunities, as well as the absence of recreational space for sports or cultural activities. Social programs have scored great success in rescuing public spaces and improving quality of life in marginalized urban areas. Policies to improve social and urban environments also play a very important role as regards law breaking. For instance, the absence of public lighting and similar services can generate unsafe conditions for people in marginalized areas.

Local authorities' involvement in preventive actions is invaluable for improving safety as a component of communities' quality of life. The police, as the face of the state that is closest to the people, can make a considerable contribution here. When the police win the trust of the public, they are able to take crime reports and make note of inadequacies in community infrastructure, services, and so on.

---

10 Duce and González (1998, 57), citing empirical studies, in particular Newman and Anderson 1998.

TABLE 2.2 Guidelines for Law Enforcement Tasks in Various Types of Social Conflict

Misdemeanors or Emerging Social Conflicts	High-frequency, Unintentional Misdemeanors	Organized Crime	Violent Crimes/ Felonies
• Police trained in proximity actions • Follow up on agreements • Community support actions • Community participation	• Police intelligence, crime mapping • Patrols, rounds, operations, prevention and investigation-based outreach • Community participation	• Police intelligence and anticipation • Capacity for immediate reaction/ response • Elite groups • Specialization	• Securing crime scene professionally • Preliminary questioning for investigation • Capacity for immediate reaction/response • Crisis intervention

The Principle of Police Service and Proportionality

The principle of proportionality of response is fundamental to ensure that police actions do not infringe on people's legal rights. Further, in the event that this does happen, it must be under circumstances that are so extraordinary that they justify the state's actions. Even then, police actions must comply with established rules and procedures.

This principle is absolutely crucial in law enforcement, given the potential for the legitimate use of force and the need for police to respond quickly in the face of sudden events. There must be exhaustive rules defining the conditions under which the police can use their discretionary powers in responding to specific situations, and police procedures and training must imprint the principle of proportionality on these public servants.

The principle of proportionality must guide the police not only in their usual service activities, but also in interventions in emerging social conflicts and in matters related to the criminal justice system (where the principles of proportionality and minimum penal intervention apply). This principle is the very foundation of law enforcement in a democratic society. A new paradigm for Mexico's police would follow an organizational model that privileges "a greater level of contact between police personnel and the community, in order to achieve a more individualized approach to the different categories of conflicts that require a solution, and in that way find a rational and adequate response to the different types of cases" (Duce and González 1998, 57).

The principle of proportionality has a fundamental application in terms of the rational use of force, with all options being considered before a suspect is arrested and turned over to the criminal justice system. In Mexico, improper arrests and detentions for minor infractions contravene the principle of proportionality, delegitimize the police, and overload the penal system.

Reorienting Mexican Policing

Some general guidelines for ways in which law enforcement efforts could address social conflicts, ranging all the way from a minor problem between neighbors or family members up to organized crime, are sketched out in table 2.2 and discussed in further detail below.

Early-Stage Social Conflicts and Police Services

Many minor social conflicts arise between neighbors, family members, or co-workers. The majority of these can be channeled through conciliation and restorative justice mechanisms, where the goal is to reestablish social harmony. Conciliation and mediation professionals can facilitate everything from the recognition that a conflict exists to proposals for its resolution and the adoption of a mutually acceptable and sustainable conciliatory or restorative agreement.[11]

In Mexico, the criminal justice system has been the place of recourse for many of these minor social conflicts. Their criminalization is neither a proportional nor an appropriate channel for their resolution. In placing a state-imposed punishment on the table, the criminal justice system polarizes the situation and radicalizes the

11 There is a strong tendency in Mexico for victims to tolerate violations of their rights rather than pursue formalized and poorly accessible mechanisms of conflict resolution.

parties' positions. In general, litigation in this area takes a conflict into a spiral of polarization and violence. The disproportionality of recurring to the criminal justice system for incipient social conflicts has been described as swatting flies with a hammer (Goldstein 1998, 124) or using a Cadillac maintenance manual to repair a bicycle (Biebesheimer and Cordovez 1999, 39).

In addition, the involvement of legal professionals increases costs and reduces the likelihood of reaching a mutually satisfactory resolution, transforming a minor conflict into an all-or-nothing criminal process that leads to a verdict of guilt or innocence but does not achieve society's goal of reestablishing harmony between the parties in conflict. This argues strongly for a review of the legal conflict resolution framework and the decriminalization of minor conflicts.

Local-level instruments, such as civil courts, legal aid agencies, and police outreach programs offer more adequate measures for resolving minor social conflicts. To this end, specialists should be trained in mediation, conciliation, and facilitation of restorative justice. For the police, this means training a significant fraction of personnel in outreach programs and public relations, as well as other activities that enhance the legitimacy of the police in the community. Police should also be trained in first contact with the public in order to direct conflicts toward resolution arenas and follow up to ensure that problems have been addressed (Goldstein 1998, 122). This approach runs directly counter to the tendency to train police in punitive logic within the "criminal law for enemies" context.

Unintentional and Low-Danger Misdemeanors and Police Services

Misdemeanors such as traffic accidents, fraud, and nonviolent theft account for over half of all police reports in Mexico. In these cases, the aim should be to simplify procedures, develop alternate solutions, and facilitate mechanisms for victim protection and assistance and for reparation for damages.

The police have a broad range of responsibilities related to these types of misdemeanors. They obtain information and enter the misdemeanors on the incidence map. They look for infrastructure problems, such as unclear signage which could cause traffic accidents, and take measures to correct them.[12] Incidence patterns of

12 This is especially important in a country where accidental deaths are the fourth leading cause of death (www.cidac.org and Zepeda 2007). Carelessness and accidents resulted in 13.5 deaths per

nonviolent theft provide information on highly vulnerable or high-incidence population groups or territorial jurisdictions, and police could use these to determine where outreach and prevention activities are most needed. However, prosecutors currently receive these reports, and sharing these data with the preventive police would require a high level of coordination and trust between institutions, a level of cooperation that is rarely seen.

The police must also receive basic training in criminology and investigation techniques. This will enable the police to secure crime scenes and perform preliminary inquiries (for instance, collecting contact information so witnesses can be reached later, or gathering information for later use in the investigation). Police assistance in these areas would facilitate the work of police experts and investigators in determining the facts of the case and, ultimately, assigning responsibility.[13]

Violent Misdemeanors and Organized Crime

If minor infractions are decriminalized and procedures for handling low-impact misdemeanors are simplified, the resources that become available as a result could be used to further police intelligence work to anticipate the actions of crime syndicates; to strengthen elite units to combat specific types of crime; to build capacity for immediate reaction and intervention in crisis situations (such as hostage taking); and to maximize efforts to deter the kinds of crime that most harm society and ensure that such acts, when committed, do not go unpunished because of omissions or deficiencies on the part of the authorities.

A preponderant share of high-impact crimes (kidnappings, car theft, executions) are committed by organized crime groups. When combating organized crime, the police must address its three main aspects: sophisticated and articulated operations (cybercrime, logistics, safe houses); financial engineering (money laundering, profit distribution, and bribes); and protection provided by the institutions charged with combating crime (mainly police and prosecutors).[14]

100,000 people in Mexico in 2006, compared to Spain, with accidental death rates of 3 per 100,000 people.

13 On this very interesting point, see Gómez Morán 2007.

14 Posited by Magistrate Giovanni Falcone, in Arzt 2003, 182.

Only elite police squads with proper training, specialization, and equipment can counter the sophisticated methods of the organized underworld. Only through police intelligence work can organized crime's operations be detected, their actions anticipated, and their gangs fractured and arrested. Specialization and monitoring by prosecutors' offices will also support the detection of financial operations that run parallel to criminal organizations. On the other hand, only when there is respect for the law enforcement profession and institutional support and protection for officers can a professional police force be shielded from criminal infiltration and its officers not feel vulnerable or abandoned when threatened by agents of organized crime.

The battle against organized crime requires a policy that concentrates efforts and resources toward that goal. It requires a professional police force and efficient criminal investigations conducted by highly professional, specialized, and not overburdened prosecutors to ensure that cases brought before the courts are solid, thereby eliminating the reigning impunity in this sector. Organized criminals may be responsible for less than 20 percent of crimes committed, but their actions are the root of Mexicans' perceptions of vulnerability and lack of security in an environment of escalating violence.

In addition to the acts perpetrated by organized crime syndicates, there is a set of violent crimes that exert a strong impact on public perception. One example is the violence in rural areas in southeastern Mexico, with its alarming toll of injuries and deaths.[15] Another example is the urban violence between youth groups, where gang members aim to inflict injury and, increasingly, to kill. Rapes and other acts of violence against women are also on the rise (though they are seldom reported). The police must counter these types of violent crime with intelligence work, efforts to anticipate and prevent them, immediate response, and effective preliminary criminal investigations.

INSTITUTIONAL DEVELOPMENT: BETWEEN DISCRETION AND

15 Oaxaca's homicide rate is 40 per 100,000, compared to a national rate of 11 per 100,000, and some states—such as Yucatán and Aguascalientes—have only 1.5 homicides per 100,000. One of every four intentional killings in Mexico takes place in Oaxaca, Tlaxcala, Guerrero, or Chiapas, and most of these are related to rural violence.

CONTROL

By the very nature of their functions, combined with their territorial decentralization and their monopoly over contact with the citizenry, the police will always have broad discretionary powers. However, this largely ignored fact has not been addressed from a regulatory standpoint, which is why discretion often devolves into arbitrariness and abuse. As Ferrajoli (1995) notes, the police represent the absence of law, holding, as they do, broad discretion in both preventive administrative law and in ante, post, or extra criminal law.

Rules, regulations, and procedural manuals must recognize and control police discretionary power in all its modalities, providing police with guidelines both for their day-to-day activities and for specific situations.

Regulation is fundamental. The first instrument for preventing abuse of police power is the principle of legality. Strong criteria for admission to the police and personality profiles are also vitally important, as are specific training and refresher programs. These steps will bring operation protocols in line with regulations and will support the development of skills to apply the criteria in the exercise of police duties, especially in crisis situations. Regulation should not paralyze the police but rather should establish the legal requirements for police actions, as well as outline factors to be taken into account in cases where police must employ their discretional authority.

As Goldstein points out: "Those worried about control, however, must recognize that the control methods upon which we currently depend are much less effective than first thought. Preparation to give more power to individual agents supposes changes in recruitment and training standards, the establishment of instructions for the exercise of discretion, and the inculcation of values that, in the absence of specific instructions, guide decision-making" (1998: 124–25). When limits are set on the conditions and criteria of action, the scope of discretion is reduced and becomes susceptible to control by both internal and external mechanisms.

The mechanisms to prevent, correct, and (if necessary) punish abuses of power can take the form of the aforementioned regulations and procedural manuals; guidelines from superiors that accord with the framework of formal behavior;[16] other internal

16 This marks an extended research agenda that analyzes the agent-principal problems, as well as organizational communications problems that can devolve into a proliferation of informal practices and criteria, in clear conflict with official regulations. In many cases these informal guidelines are imposed

mechanisms, such as the ex post procedures derived from complaints and observations, which should receive expeditious processing and follow-up by an autonomous and independent office to determine if further proceedings are warranted; and an internal affairs unit or similar watchdog groups of officials and members of the public to hear complaints and detect possible abuses.

If abuse is widespread, there should also be: (1) internal investigative and disciplinary commissions, in addition, of course, to the courts to deal with violations or crimes where police are allegedly involved; and (2) court oversight of police actions, such as evidence handling, so that in cases where legal requirements are not met or procedural criteria are not observed, the questionable evidence will not be used and those responsible for its mishandling may be sanctioned.[17]

An organized society and public opinion generally play a crucial role in exerting control over police forces. When public opinion is closed to arguments in support of human rights (as is typical in an environment of fear and insecurity), this promotes hard-line incentives, public tolerance of arbitrary police actions, and a police force focused on criminal justice issues.

CONCLUSION

The agenda for changing policing in Mexico must be reflected in a profound transformation of police organizations and procedures. The paradigm shift must involve a police force that is open to society, less militarized, and more oriented toward a broad range of community services that are often unrelated to crime.18 In short, the police must develop a more benevolent relationship toward the public it protects and serves.

Such a radical change must encompass the admissions profile, academy training programs, procedural manuals, and other training and skills upgrading for members

---

and maintained by mid-level officials, which is why they often supersede formal guidelines in the everyday performance of police duties.

17 Varenik 2005 is an excellent source on the various models of police control and accountability.

18 In some law enforcement organizations, other public servants—such as firefighters, paramedics, and roadside assistance—are housed within the police, underscoring a public service role over and above the orientation toward crime fighting. Merging these services also increases police forces' legitimacy in the public eye.

of the force. There must also be a revolution regarding police performance and evaluation criteria, giving greater weight to community service and discarding quantitative or "product" variables in favor of qualitative variables for evaluating performance.

Also key to police reform is the issue of professionalizing and institutionalizing law enforcement as a career, and then safeguarding those who enter the profession. This factor is crucial if there is to be a continuation of the reform process. Incentives must be put in place to promote the professionalization, specialization, and retention of police officers and to make police service an attractive career, with levels of pay and benefits that enable officers and their families to enjoy a decent standard of living. Reforming police organizations and strengthening a professional police service will dignify police work and improve the public's perception of their community police. Professionalization is a sine qua non for police reform, placing it first on the agenda of police transformations.

A police force oriented toward crime prevention must strengthen its links with agencies that serve the public through public works, infrastructure, and services that improve quality of life and reduce crime's impacts on society.

Police forces must be exposed to the broad spectrum of preventive measures, as well as sensitized to the socioeconomic factors that may underpin conflicts in the community. Police must also be trained to mediate conflicts and to direct individuals in early stages of conflict toward conciliation mechanisms, legal aid agencies, and restorative justice channels. They must also hold a clear vision of their overarching responsibility to aid and support these forms of conflict resolution, and to follow up on agreements reached to confirm that a conflict has been resolved and social harmony has been restored.

The police must have sufficient knowledge of criminology and investigative techniques to act in support of prosecution and the criminal justice system. In the case of preventive police, this must include knowing how to secure a crime scene, make initial inquiries, collect valuable information, and support special operations and enforce rulings by the appropriate authorities. The ministerial police, of course, will have a higher degree of specialization pertinent to this aspect of police action.

Police forces must establish and develop intelligence and information services, not only for crime mapping, patrol design, special operations, and outreach and prevention, but also for employing disaggregated data, making diagnoses, and planning elite operations to deal with violent and organized crime.

Likewise, procedures must be made transparent, limits to police discretion must be set and enforced, and internal and external control instruments must be improved.

A thoroughgoing reform of justice and police institutions requires political will and courage. It implies concerted and continuous efforts to design, plan, and implement a reform program. Much of the resistance to adopting a modern public safety system befitting a democratic society is rooted in two counterarguments: (1) that Mexico's police are not ready for this challenge, and (2) that it would require too much effort.

Indeed, it is easier to change the law—for example, increasing prison sentences or adding new infractions to the catalog of serious crimes—than to reform institutions from the bottom up. Reform implies political will and a social commitment to prepare the institutions to efficiently undertake their responsibilities to society, a society that is no longer convinced by the fallacious argument that they must go without quality community services in exchange for a promise of public safety. Police reform implies a political step and an ethical leap.

REFERENCES

Arzt, Sigrid. 2003. "El combate a la delincuencia organizada en México: ¿Una misión (im) posible?" In Crimen trasnacional y seguridad pública: Desafíos para México y Estados Unidos, ed. John Bailey and Jorge Chabat. Mexico: Plaza y Janés.

Biebesheimer, Christina, and Carlos Cordovez, eds. 1999. La justicia más allá de nuestras fronteras: Experiencias de reforma útiles para América Latina y el Caribe. Washington, DC: Inter-American Development Bank.

Concha, Hugo, Héctor Fix Fierro, Julia Flores, and Diego Valadés, eds. 2004. Cultura de la Constitución en México: Una encuesta nacional de actitudes, percepciones y valores, Mexico: Universidad Nacional Autónoma de México, Tribunal Electoral del Poder Judicial Federal, and Comisión Federal de Mejora Regulatoria.

Duce, Mauricio, and Felipe González. 1998. "Policía y estado de derecho: Problemas en torno a su función y organización," Policía y Sociedad Democrática, Pena y Estado, Revista Latinoamericana de Política Criminal [Instituto de Estudios Comparados en Ciencias Penales y Sociales, Buenos Aires] 3, no. 3: 51–62.

El Universal. 2005. "No soy salinista: Marcelo Ebrard," September 22.

Ferrajoli, Luigi. 1995. Derecho y razón: Teoría del garantismo penal. Madrid: Trotta.

García Ramírez, Sergio. 1989. Curso de derecho procesal penal. Mexico: Porrúa.

———. 2000. "El sistema penal," Estudios Jurídicos [Instituto de Investigaciones Jurídicas, Universidad Nacional Autónoma de México].

———. 2003. "Principios del proceso penal: Legalidad y oportunidad." In La influencia de la ciencia penal alemana en Iberoamérica: Libro homenaje a Claus Roxin. Vol. 1. Mexico: Instituto Nacional de Ciencias Penales.

Goldstein, Herman. 1998. "La nueva orientación policial: Confrontando la complejidad," Policía y Sociedad Democrática, Pena y Estado, Revista Latinoamericana de Política Criminal [Instituto de Estudios Comparados en Ciencias Penales y Sociales, Buenos Aires] 3, no. 3: 117–28.

Gómez Morán, Edgar Estuardo. 2007. "La formación de las habilidades de macro investigación en los oficiales preventivos del municipio de Guadalajara." Master's thesis, Universidad de Guadalajara.

Jones, Seth G., Jeremy M. Wilson, Andrew Rathmell, and Jack Riley. 2005. Establishing Law and Order after Conflict. Santa Monica, CA: Rand Corporation.

López Portillo, Ernesto. 2004. "La reforma a la seguridad y a la justicia," Nexos 323 (November): 17–24.

Maya, Rafael. 2004. "Misógino de origen, el sistema penal en el mundo," CIMAC Noticias, April 30. http://www.cimacnoticias.com/04abr/04043010.html.

Newman, Donald, and Patrick Anderson. 1998. Introduction to Criminal Justice. New York: McGraw-Hill.

Rusconi, Maximiliano. 1998. "Reformulación de los sistemas de justicia penal en América Latina y policía: Algunas reflexiones," Policía y Sociedad Democrática, Pena y Estado, Revista Latinoamericana de Política Criminal [Instituto de Estudios Comparados en Ciencias Penales y Sociales, Buenos Aires] 3, no. 3: 189–98.

Shaw, Mark, Jan Van Dijk, and Wolfgang Rhomberg. 2003. "Determining Trends in Global Crime and Justice: An Overview of Results," Forum on Crime and Society 3, nos. 1–2 (December): 35–63.

SNSP-CON (Sistema Nacional de Seguridad Pública, Unidad de Enlace de la Secretaría de Seguridad Pública). 2004a. Information request No. 0002200037804. Estado de fuerza de julio de 2002 a octubre de 2004. http://buscador.ifai.org.mx/buscador/bienvenido.do.

———. 2004b. The information request number was not retained nor was the document located on the Internet. The author has only a photocopy of the information on Estado de fuerza nacional al 1 de noviembre de 2004.

———. 2007. Information request No. 2210300001307. Estado de fuerza nacional al 31 de enero de 2007. http://buscador.ifai.org.mx/buscador/bienvenido.do.

SSP (Secretaría de Seguridad Pública). 2007. Reingeniería al modelo al combate al delito. Mexico: SSP. February.

SSP-CON. (Secretaría de Seguridad Pública del Gobierno Federal, Unidad de Enlace). 2007. Request No. 0002200077107, Estado de fuerza nacional al 29 de diciembre de 2005 y al 31 de diciembre de 2006, and Reporte de elementos activos del personal de seguridad pública y privada al 30 de junio de 2007. July. Not yet available on the Internet; obtained through SISI system of the Instituto Federal de Acceso a la Información Pública.

Vázquez Raña, Mario. 2006. "El DF no crece por culpa del gobierno federal: Ebrard," Organización Editorial Mexicana, June 24.

Varenik, Robert O. 2005. Accountability, sistema policial de rendición de cuentas: Estudio internacional comparado. Mexico: Instituto para la Seguridad y la Democracia A.C. (Insyde) and Centro de Investigación y Docencia Económicas (CIDE).

Zepeda Lecuona, Guillermo. 2007. "La violencia imprudencial en México," Salud Pública de México 49 (March): 247–53.

The Militarization of Public Security and the Role of the Military in Mexico

Marcos Pablo Moloeznik

President Felipe Calderón's decision early in his administration to use the military to fight drug trafficking, reestablish public order, and achieve social peace in Mexico did not introduce something unique or previously unknown in Mexico. Indeed, the militarization of public safety functions has a long history in Mexico (Barrón Cruz 2005, 302ff). The military has had a role in policing duties and missions at least since the 1910 Mexican Revolution.[1] This role continues today, requiring us to give attention to the high political costs associated with it, in particular the autonomy of the Mexican armed forces and the implications for Mexico's nascent democracy.

THE UNDERLYING CAUSES OF MILITARIZATION

The recent militarization of public safety in Mexico is rooted in the public's discontent with the performance of civilian police institutions, which are responsible for public safety under Article 21 of the Mexican Constitution. Mexico's police agencies are decentralized as per the federal government's protections for municipal autonomy. Different police agencies coexist at each government level, with two main types of police forces: (1). the preventive, uniformed, and administrative police, which operate at all three levels of government (federal, state, and municipal); and (2) the judicial, investigative, and ministerial police, which operate only at the federal and state levels. Preventive police focus on preventing and responding to crimes in flagrante, while investigative police agencies operate ex post to the commission of a crime, aiding the Attorney General's Office (prosecutor) in the investigation and prosecution of the crime.[2] Table 3.1 illustrates the basic structure of Mexico's police agencies and the number of their personnel.

---

1 See, for example, Lozoya 1984, 40–58. The decree creating the armed forces was passed by the Twenty-Second Legislature of the State of Coahuila on February 19, 1913, a month prior to the Plan de Guadalupe, launched by Venustiano Carranza, governor of the state.

2 For more detailed information on this topic, see Moloeznik 2005a.

Table 3.1 Mexican Police Forces and Number of Personnel, 2007

Level		
Federal	Ministry of Public Safety 19,597 [a]	Federal Investigative Agency 5,945
State	Preventive 190,730	Judicial/Ministerial 25,495
Municipal	Preventive 144,276	
Total	Preventive and Investigative 386,043 [b]	

Source: SSP 2007.

a Includes 15,464 federal preventive police (10,964 assigned to regional safety and intelligence for crime prevention, and 4,500 to federal support forces), 2,832 operations agents of the National Immigration Institute, and 1,301 federal prison police.

b Does not include agents, experts, or administrative personnel of district attorneys' offices. If these were included, the total of public security personnel in Mexico would rise to 450,846.

Available information indicates that Mexican police are woefully underprepared to accomplish their essential function of protecting society. Police academies give only four months of basic training, on average, and only seventeen of the fifty-eight training institutes in the country require applicants to have a minimum education level. Thus it is not surprising that a 2002 study found that 55.6 percent of police in the various public safety agencies either lacked formal education or had only completed grade school (López Portillo 2002, 119).

From a strictly quantitative point of view, Mexico does not suffer from a lack of police personnel. On the contrary, Mexico enjoys an enviable ratio of 386 police per 100,000 residents, one of the highest in the world. In 2006, Mexican states with the highest numbers of preventive police (both state and municipal) were the Federal District (Mexico City) (77,820), Mexico State (48,213), Veracruz (18,185), Jalisco (16,596), Puebla (12,587), Chiapas (11,862), Oaxaca (9,856), Nuevo León (8,957), and Michoacán (8,343). The states with the highest numbers of officers assigned to the judicial or ministerial police that assist in investigations and prosecutions were the Federal District (4,056), Mexico State (1,447), Guerrero (1,238), Michoacán

(1,216), Veracruz (1,089), Jalisco (1,040), Puebla (1,121), and Oaxaca (1019). The same study identified 140,966 employees of private security firms (SSP 2007).

It would seem that a shortage of personnel is not the problem. It may be more productive, then, to consider intangibles, such as the guiding principles set forth in constitutional Article 21: legality, efficiency, professionalism, and honesty. However, one can hardly expect Mexico's public servants (particularly police officers) to uphold the law and punish violators, given that—according to Latinobarómetro—Mexico's police are the most amenable to bribery among all the police forces in Latin America (see table 3.2). Indeed, the probability of being able to bribe a public official, judge, or police officer in Mexico is three times higher than in Chile or El Salvador. Hence, paradoxically, government employees in Mexico—responsible for upholding and enforcing the law—are, in fact, its worst violators.

The violation of basic human rights is another constant in police behavior. According to a 2005 Amnesty International report: "Human rights violations persisted, particularly at a state level, where arbitrary arrests, torture, and mistreatment, and abuses of the judicial system were commonplace." Police officers' failure to adhere to a code of conduct is reflected in the public's low levels of trust in the police. Mexico's citizens gave the police as an institution a rating of 5.55 on a scale of 1 to 10, where 1 indicated "no trust" and 10 indicated "complete trust." This compares poorly with the public's trust in the National Human Rights Commission (6.91) and Mexico's armed forces (7.72) (Secretaría de Gobernación 2005).

It is not surprising, then, that over half of the Mexican population (54 percent) feel unsafe, a fact that President Calderón acknowledged when he announced his crime-fighting strategy at the outset of his administration. In the second of four proposals, Calderón asserted the following:

> In order to guarantee the honesty and transparency of those in charge of public safety, we are going to apply strict reliability controls to our peacekeeping forces, with special emphasis on ethics, discipline, and the quality with which they must carry out their duties. We want to do this throughout the country and with every police organization in Mexico, but as the saying goes, cleanliness starts at home. Therefore, just like our citizens, I demand an honest, clean, reliable police force for the residents of Mexico, and I know it will not be easy, but we urgently need to guarantee it. I am entrusting this to Ministry of Public Security. Let's begin with

Table 3.2 Perceived Likelihood That Someone Charged with Public Security Will Accept a Bribe

Question: "What is the likelihood of being able to bribe a ________?" (percentages reflect responses of "very likely" and "extremely likely")

	Category of Official		
	Someone in the Prosecutor's Office	**Police Officer**	**Judge**
Mexico	56%	65%	58%
Paraguay	56%	58%	55%
Argentina	50%	57%	46%
Brazil	39%	52%	36%
Ecuador	44%	52%	47%
Dominican Republic	44%	49%	38%
Venezuela	42%	46%	40%
Bolivia	32%	45%	34%
Guatemala	37%	45%	37%
Honduras	35%	41%	38%
Costa Rica	37%	39%	23%
Peru	30%	38%	36%
Uruguay	30%	37%	25%
Panama	36%	33%	27%
Nicaragua	32%	33%	33%
Colombia	28%	30%	24%
Chile	19%	22%	20%
El Salvador	19%	20%	22%

Source: Latinobarómetro, http://www.latinobarometro.org/. Emphasis added.

> our police agencies. My office will promote a quality police to protect and safeguard the Mexican people; we will adopt international standards for the certification, training, and specialization of public order forces (Calderón Hinojosa 2007).

In short, there are two reasons why the police are not trusted to perform their duties in Mexico: (1) their low level of professionalization, which breeds growing public distrust; and (2) the corruption and impunity pervading public security institutions. The lack of trust in Mexico's law enforcement institutions relates, not to a lack of material resources or force size, but to the qualitative weaknesses of police agencies, especially the lack of integrity and professionalism among the personnel who make up these institutions.

THE MILITARIZATION OF PUBLIC SECURITY

There are several reasons why President Calderón has turned to the Mexican military to ensure domestic order. By virtue of its national organizational reach, the Mexican military has traditionally been the institution most prepared to address major domestic threats and crises. Its involvement in such matters was virtually unavoidable, given law enforcement's institutional inability to perform the task and the citizenry's low level of trust in the police.

> In Mexico, soldiers serve as a temporary remedy to the problems caused by the lack of an administrative bureaucracy and law enforcement leadership.... In this country, the police have a negative reputation, due to the near absence of education of its members, their inefficiency, and corruption (Rico 1997, 86).

Moreover, there is a widespread perception that the armed forces are the only public institution capable of instilling trust in the Mexican population. Social acceptance and recognition is a component that should not be ignored, and it is one that undoubtedly influenced top-level political decision makers. As documented by a 2004 Ipsos Bimsa poll, the army ranked among the most trusted public-sector institutions in Mexico (see table 3.3). The public's positive opinion of the military has remained unchanged in recent years (table 3.4).

Table 3.3 Public Opinion Ratings of Public-Sector Institutions in Mexico

Question: "Do you have a very good, good, bad, or very bad opinion of ________?"

	Public Perception		
Institution	**Very Good**	**Neutral**	**Bad/Very bad**
Church	64%	21%	12%
Federal Electoral Institute (IFE)	61%	26%	9%
Army	**60%**	**26%**	**7%**
National Human Rights Commission (CNDH)	50%	27%	15%
Mexican Social Security Institute (IMSS)	33%	27%	36%
Office of the Federal Attorney General (PGR)	33%	32%	27%
Supreme Court (SCJN)	33%	32%	23%
Federal Legislature	19%	28%	43%

Source: Ipsos Bimsa 2004. Erubiel Tirado provided the database. Emphasis added.

Table 3.4 Percentage of Mexicans Holding a "Good" or "Very Good" Perception of the Mexican Armed Forces, 2004–2007

	2004	**2005**	**2007**
Positive perception of the military	60%	72%	69%

Source: Ipsos Bimsa survey, April 26–May 1, 2007.

Figure 3.1 Public Perception of Military Career Versus Other Careers in Mexico

Question: "Would you recommend a career in ________ to a member of your family?"

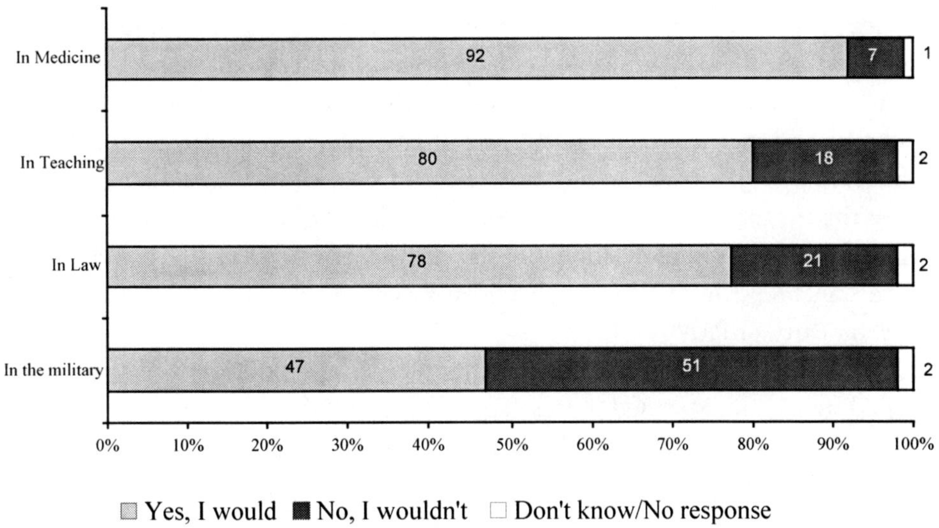

In sum, Mexican society exhibits a marked appreciation for its military and tends to favor forcible solutions, associating values such as discipline and order with the army (86.5 percent). Similarly, 45 percent of the Mexican public feel that the primary mission of the armed forces should be crime fighting and combating drug trafficking, far above the 16 percent who identify defending national sovereignty as the military's main mission. The legitimacy of the process of militarizing public security obeys both the wide social acceptance of the armed forces and the use of the army to combat drug trafficking, given that 74 percent of the population feels the army helps "a lot" or "somewhat" to reduce drug trafficking and drug use in Mexico.

That said, public regard for the military does not necessarily translate into a strong endorsement for a military career. In the same survey in which 78 percent of respondents indicated that military personnel "do not cause them to feel fear," 51 percent reported they would not recommend a career in the military to a family member (figure 3.1).

THE MEXICAN ARMED FORCES: AN ATYPICAL MILITARY INSTRUMENT

The uniqueness of the Mexican armed forces goes beyond its origins, composition, and traditional subordination to the political system. To the keen observer, its nature and missions are the distinctive features that separate it from its counterparts elsewhere in Latin America.[3] Throughout its short institutional history (just over nine decades), the Mexican armed forces have been oriented toward managing domestic problems. Furthermore, in the current state crisis, marked by a breakdown in public security and ineffectiveness on the part of law enforcement agencies, the military has seen its role expand to an unprecedented degree. It is somewhat paradoxical that this expansion of the military's domestic role has occurred during Mexico's supposed democratic consolidation and the election of two successive presidents (Fox and Calderón) from the country's longest-surviving opposition party, the National Action Party, or PAN.

It is important to take note of the dual roles—political and technical—filled by Mexico's armed forces. The country's defense sector comprises two cabinet-level ministries: the Ministry of National Defense (SEDENA, which includes the army and air force), and the Ministry of the Navy (SEMAR),[4] directed, respectively, by a division general and an admiral.[5] Again, this suggests the interweaving of the political (defense policy) and military (technical) spheres embodied by the armed forces.

To put it differently, in Mexico it is men in military uniform who establish policy for this sector, without any intermediary political power.[6] The absence

---

3 For more in-depth information on this topic, see Moloeznik 2005a.

4 Until December 31, 1939, Mexico had a single defense agency, which incorporated both the army and the navy. On that date, the navy separated, becoming first a department and later a ministry, as of December 31, 1940. Both agencies are members of the National Public Security Council, a think tank whose purpose is to establish and articulate national security policy. See Article 12 of the Ley de Seguridad Nacional, Diario Oficial, January 31, 2005.

5 Pursuant to Article 29, Section I of the Ley Orgánica de la Administración Pública Federal, SEDENA is in charge of "organizing, managing, and preparing the army and air force." Pursuant to Article 30, Section I of the same Act, SEMAR is in charge of "organizing, managing, and preparing the navy." See Instituto Nacional de Administración Pública 2000, 102 and 122.

6 Moreover, the armed forces are largely seen as an unblemished institution. More than 70 percent of persons interviewed indicated that the Ministry of National Defense should be headed by a member of the military, versus 17 percent who said it should be a civilian. See Ipsos Bimsa 2007.

of civilian authorities in defense matters means that the military enjoys substantial autonomy. Furthermore, there is no integration or common doctrine among the branches of the armed forces. There is no high command or joint command; there are few joint training exercises or operations on record; and there seems to be no organized logistics carried out according to common criteria.

Regarding the military profile and capabilities of Mexico's armed forces, it is fairly clear that Mexico is currently unprepared to face a situation of international conflict. In the unlikely event that the armed forces became involved in a foreign conflict, they would have to undergo an in-depth reorganization in order to rise to the challenge (Garfias Magaña 2005, 1). Other sources seem to confirm this assessment; according to Jane's Sentinel Security Assessment (2005, 3): "It is difficult to conceive the Mexican Army as a conventional combat force.... In practice they have served as a sort of national constabulary." And according to General Gerardo Clemente Vega García, former minister of national defense under President Fox, "The Mexican army and air force is not a war machine" (El Universal, May 16, 2004).

What then, in practice, are the main responsibilities and expectations for the Mexican military? Figure 3.2 provides a schematic illustration of major military priorities with regard to the structural organization of the Mexican armed forces. Though national defense features prominently, a broad array of domestic missions appears to dominate the military's agenda. SEDENA's main planning document, the Operation and Development Plan, suggests that the military's primary mission is internal: "The characteristics and size of the Mexican army and air force must respond to issues arising from our domestic situation, contributing to the development and well-being of Mexican society" (SEDENA 2001, 4). This point is reiterated throughout the Operation and Development Plan, as well as in other official documents pertaining to the military's missions and priorities. For example, the current program for the Ministry of National Defense outlines a variety of domestic missions and responsibilities that have a primarily inward focus:

> The armed forces, in strict compliance with their general missions, aid the competent civilian authorities in large domestic endeavors in order to timely and effectively respond to drug trafficking and organized crime,

Figure 3.2 General Missions of the Mexican Army and Air Force

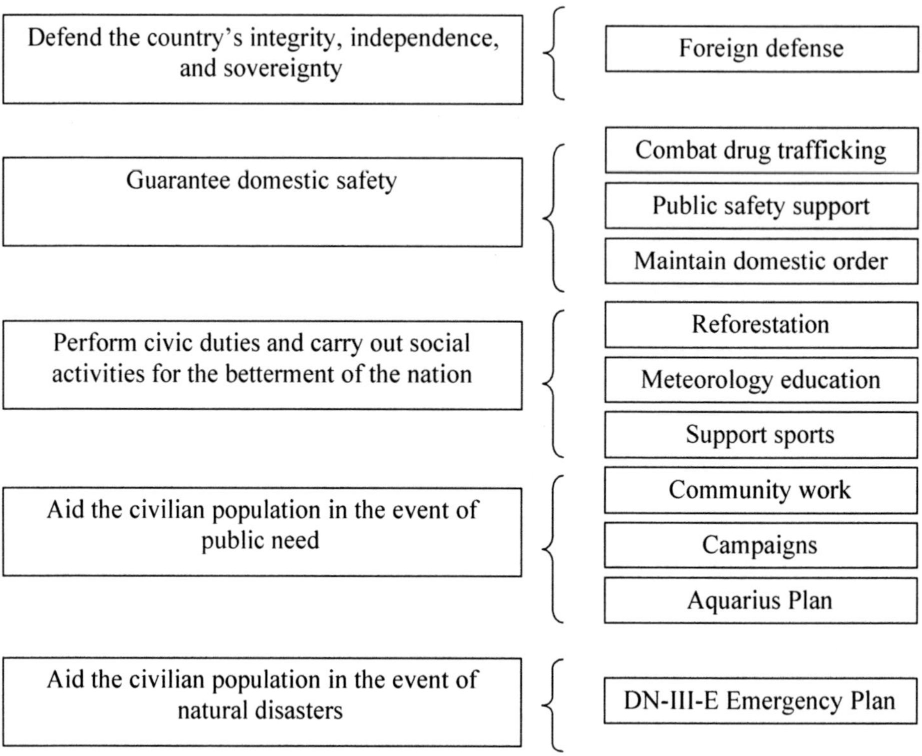

Source: Secretaría de la Defensa Nacional. 2005. See also Article 1 of the Ley Orgánica del Ejército y Fuerza Aérea Mexicanos and later revisions, Diario Oficial, December 26, 1986, and January 23, 1998.

natural disasters, environmental deterioration, as well as to support public security forces and supply its contingent to guarantee the country's strategic systems, and in social enterprises to improve the conditions of underserved populations (SEDENA 2001, 3).[7]

7 The fact that the chief missions and duties entrusted to the military are primarily land-based means that the army plays a particularly prominent role in these efforts.

Among the military's wide array of domestic concerns, combating drug trafficking, and organized crime more generally, rise to the top. One indication of this priority is force deployment; the Operation and Development Plan specifies assigning soldiers to these missions (SEDENA 2001, 35).[8] The prominence of drug trafficking and organized crime as military priorities can also be inferred from the document that regulates long-term national policy development in Mexico, the National Development Plan:

> There are risks and threats in imminently internal factors which, in combination with other external factors, result in activities such as illegal drug trafficking, organized crime, terrorism, and environmental deterioration.... Drug trafficking and organized crime are one of the main sources of violence and lack of security for the population, and a threat to institutions. They cause corruption, deterioration of image, loss of confidence and prestige both domestically and internationally, affecting our sovereignty and damaging our international relations (Poder Ejecutivo 2001, 128, 130).

The SEDENA Operation and Development Plan echoes the sentiment of the National Development Plan, since it acknowledges that:

> Drug trafficking has harmful effects on human health and national development. Mexico is affected by domestic production and international trafficking of drugs. These actions tend to endanger our country's political, economic, and social structures and weaken the credibility of institutions. They lead to family disintegration and increase crime rates. On the foreign front, drug trafficking affects sovereignty and damages international relations (SEDENA 2001, 2).

Concern about organized crime, especially drug trafficking, is also reflected in the National Security Act, which defines the following as national security threats:

8 See also PGR 2002, 17, which highlights the involvement of SEDENA and SEMAR.

- Acts intended to commit espionage, terrorism, rebellion, treason, genocide, against the United Mexican States within national borders;
- Acts that prevent the authorities from acting against organized crime;
- Acts intended to hinder or block military or naval operations against organized crime;
- Acts against aviation safety;
- Any act intended to commit the trafficking of nuclear material or chemical, biological, and conventional weapons of mass destruction;
- Illegal acts against maritime navigation;
- Any action funding terrorist actions and organizations;
- Acts intended to hinder or block intelligence and counterintelligence activities; and
- Acts intended to destroy or render unusable infrastructure of a strategic nature or essential for the provision of utility and public services (Diario Oficial, January 31, 2005).

Additionally, an overwhelming majority of SEDENA press releases focus on military actions to combat drug trafficking. As noted in a 2005 SEDENA communiqué, the military plays a crucial counter-drug role:

> Mexico's objective is to permanently eradicate the planting, growing, and trafficking of illegal substances, using a strategy that includes the use of the armed forces in the fulfillment of its constitutional missions, taking advantage of their organization, discipline, education, and training. To that end, the army and air force shall partake in this great effort in two fundamental areas: the eradication of illegal crops and the interception of drug shipments by land, air, and sea (http://www.sedena.gob.mx/comunicados/2005).

This is not to say that the military's sole focus is organized crime. They also have key missions in support of domestic and public security, including preserving domestic order. On this issue, a specific objective in national defense preparedness is: "to guarantee the capacity of the army and air force to respond to situations that threaten the nation's social stability and peace" (SEDENA 2001, 9).

Figure 3.3 Public Perceptions of Key Army Priorities

Question: "In you opinion, which of the following activities ought to be the army's number one priority?" (percentages)

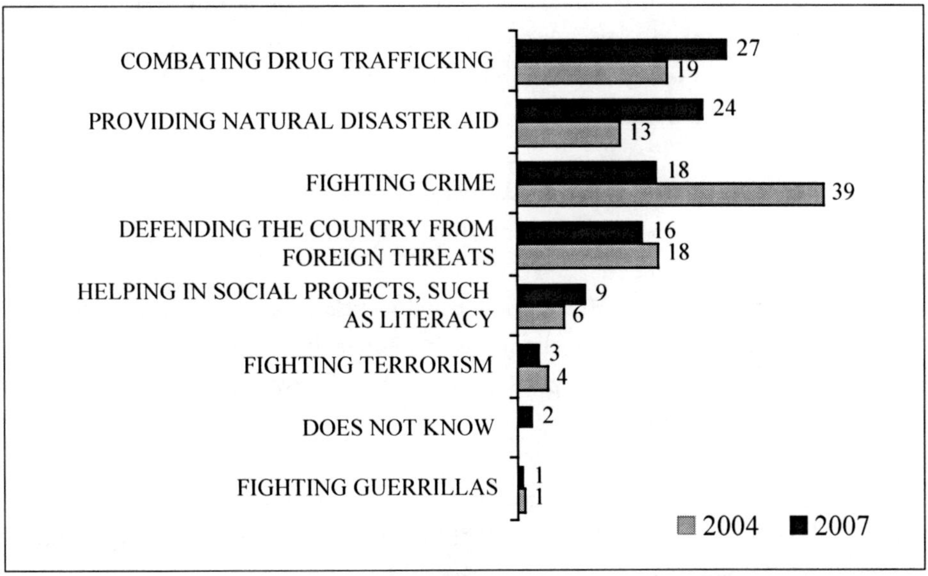

This capacity to respond in case of national instability and violence also covers combating armed opposition movements, such as the guerillas and insurgents that sometimes arise in Mexico. There were cases of such groups in the 1990s: the Zapatista National Liberation Army (EZLN), the Popular Revolutionary Army (EPR), and the Insurgent Popular Revolutionary Army (ERPI). Counterinsurgency becomes the antidote to state violence in counteracting armed uprisings against the political system. SEDENA's Operation and Development Plan also identifies a role for the military in coordinating and promoting the National Public Security System (SNSP) as detailed below:

> As a member of the National Public Security Council, the Ministry of National Defense (High Command) shall aid in the search for strategies that make it possible to combat crime more effectively, together with their Sector Commands in each state and regional Public Security Council (SEDENA 2001, 36).

The military is also responsible for controlling guns and explosives by enforcing the Federal Firearms and Explosives Act. Given that "illegal gun trafficking has recently emerged as a modern-day threat to the safety and security of the state, undermining social structures and promoting the commission of violent crimes against individuals, property, and national assets," SEDENA's organizational chart includes a Federal Department of Firearms Registration and Explosives Control, with duties that elsewhere are reserved for domestic law enforcement authorities (SEDENA 2001, 37). These duties are:

- To maintain the Federal Arms Registry;
- To control the possession and carrying of firearms pursuant to applicable laws and regulations; and
- To monitor, control, and supervise activities related to firearms, ammunition, gunpowder, fireworks, and chemicals that either alone or in combination could be employed as explosives, pursuant to applicable laws and regulations (http://www.sedena.gob.mx/index4.html).

The public seems to agree with the military's prioritization of these various concerns. Only a small portion of the public (below 20 percent) considers that national defense from foreign threats should be the military's top priority (see figure 3.3). Furthermore, public support for making drug traffickers a top military priority increased from 19 percent in 2004 to 27 percent in 2007, providing some endorsement for President Calderón's strategy of heightened military involvement in the war on drugs. However, we should also note that public support for the military's role in fighting crime as a top priority fell from 39 percent in 2004 to 19 percent in 2007. Increased public support for the military's role in providing aid during natural disasters probably reflects the military's prominent role in responding to the devastating effects of the 2005 hurricane season in Mexico.[9]

---

9 In August 2005, the Mexican military participated in relief efforts in the United States following Hurricane Katrina. In early October 2005, tropical storm Stan flooded the Mexican states of Veracruz, Chiapas, Oaxaca, Tabasco, Puebla, Hidalgo, and Guerrero, killing 15 people and displacing 370,000. In all, some 1.5 million people were affected. Later that month, Hurricane Wilma caused severe flooding in Quintana Roo and Yucatán, killing 7 people, affecting more than a million, and displacing approximately 300,000 people in Cancún alone.

As other authors in this volume have indicated, the scope of the military's duties is so broad in large part because of the institutional weakness of domestic law enforcement agencies. But it is also important to underscore the extent to which domestic law enforcement agencies have become "militarized" through the incorporation of military agencies and personnel into their organizational structures, as discussed below.

THE MILITARIZATION OF DOMESTIC LAW ENFORCEMENT

The trend toward the militarization of domestic public security functions is evidenced by the prominent role given to the military and to military personnel within domestic law enforcement agencies. Supreme Court decisions paved the way by establishing that the three branches of the military "may participate in civilian activities to protect public safety, in support of civilian authorities" (Suprema Corte 1996). This enables military institutions and personnel to play a significant role in domestic law enforcement activities by adopting roles normally reserved for civilian personnel.

This can be seen at the federal level in the National Public Security Council, the highest coordinating body within the National Public Security System (Moloeznik 2005b). The military's prominent role in the Public Security Cabinet contradicts the notion that its public security role is a temporary remedy to address exceptional circumstances and the recent surge in high-profile criminal activities. According to the Office of the United Nations High Commissioner for Human Rights in Mexico, "In 1996, the government invited the top military officials in the country to join the National Public Security Council, thus bestowing upon the armed forces a direct role in making public safety policy. The administration of President Vicente Fox increased the involvement of top Mexican army, air force, and navy officials in said policy, by means of the inter-institutional coordination groups for each of the Mexican states" (UNHCHR 2003, 44).

The Mexican army and air force also established a special auxiliary corps which—though nominally under the command of the president—is technically, operationally, and administratively dependent upon the Ministry of National Defense. This special auxiliary corps is bestowed with the specific mission of providing support to civilian authorities at all levels of government: "in activities to restore public order and security, to fight drug trafficking and organized crime or against acts that threaten the security of the nation" (Poder Ejecutivo 2007). According to a declaration by the joint forces high command on February 19, 2007: "The military assists all three levels of government in guaranteeing and preserving the public security demanded by society for their well-being and the protection of their property" (http://www.sedena.gob.mx/index4.html).

Militarization is also evidenced by the massive participation of military personnel in the staffing of domestic security agencies. On January 6, 2005, President Fox charged the Ministry of Public Security (SSP) with "analyzing and assessing government policies and actions regarding public safety within the scope of action of the federal executive branch." Under Article 3 of the same decree, the SSP would have the following duties, among others:

- To establish criminal policy in coordination with the agencies of the executive branch, so as to formulate plans and jointly execute actions that serve as deterrents to crime; and
- To define the instruments for evaluating and monitoring public security policies, strategies, and actions (*Diario Oficial*, January 6, 2005).

Nonetheless, a substantial integration of the armed forces into the SSP could be seen with entry of more than 5,332 military personnel as auxiliary forces for the Federal Preventive Police (PFP), the ministry's main operational component. It is important to note, however, that this pattern of integrating the military into domestic police forces is not limited to the federal level. According to Alvarado and Davis (2001, 130), by 1999 an overwhelming majority of Mexican states (twenty-eight of thirty-two) had named mid-level military officers to domestic law enforcement positions. In addition, military-to-police ties are now enhanced through mixed operations centers, which combine law enforcement and military personnel, as well as through the military's advisory and support involvement in the hiring, selection, training, and education of law enforcement personnel.

In short, there has been a significant and sustained trend toward an increased role for the military in Mexican public security functions, in terms of both its operational mandate and its relationship with domestic law enforcement agencies. Though this pattern has developed over time, it became particularly apparent at the outset of President Fox's term with the appointment of General Rafael Macedo de la Concha as attorney general, and it continued through the massive military deployments of Operation México Seguro in June 2005. Thus the Calderón administration's use of military force in several states and municipalities was not a new development, nor was it solely a function of the escalation of drug-related violence. It would seem that this progressive militarization has been driven by other factors, factors that elicit significant concern for democratic governance in Mexico, as discussed below.

THE POLITICS OF MILITARY AUTONOMY IN MEXICO

As noted above, both the Fox and Calderón administrations turned to the armed forces to handle law enforcement issues, such as public security (or the lack thereof), public order, and social peace. The massive military deployments initiated under the Fox administration, especially for Operation México Seguro, have continued into the Calderón administration, with an estimated 45,000 troops deployed nationwide in 2008 in intensified efforts to contain drug cartel violence. While these deployments have a clear operational objective, there is a subtext to the process of militarization in Mexico that relates to the country's recent political development. It must be remembered that the increased role of the military has coincided with a process of regime transformation—a shift from seventy-five years of single-party rule under the Institutional Revolutionary Party (PRI) to two successive administrations by the PRI's longtime political opposition, the National Action Party (PAN).

Evidently these are the political costs of the Mexican armed forces' loyalty to democratically elected presidential authorities. In exchange for their loyalty, the branches of the military have gained significant prerogatives and privileges (while avoiding some much-needed structural reforms), thereby consolidating the political autonomy of the Mexican armed forces. One trade-off is a lack of legislative oversight of military activities, in contrast with the overwhelming majority of other countries in the region (Follietti 2005, 57–60). The Mexican Congress is limited to assigning budget appropriations to SEDENA and SEMAR, with absolute discretion in the areas of investment and increases in institutional expenses for three purposes—creation of new units, purchase and replacement of equipment, and logistical reserves for their maintenance—since it is the military branches themselves who make defense policy decisions (Tirado 2006, 14).

A second trade-off is the sustained increase in resources allocated to the military, as evidenced by the consistent increase in the number of personnel, particularly in SEDENA, at a time of erstwhile budget tightening (see table 3.5). Enhancing

Table 3.5 Number of Military Personnel in Mexico, 1994–2006

	Number of Military Personnel		
Year	SEDENA	SEMAR	Total
1994	168,773	48,170	216,943
1995	171,952	53,128	225,080
1996	179,038	53,128	232,166
1997	182,328	54,247	236,575
1998	182,328	53,566	235,894
1999	183,296	53,729	237,025
2000	182,329	55,223	237,552
2001	185,143	49,165	234,308
2002	188,143	50,026	238,169
2003	191,143	47,304	238,447
2004	191,143	47,316	238,459
2005	191,143	46,280	237,423
2006 *	191,143	45,770	236,913

Source: Fox Quesada 2006, 604.

* Data for 2006 are current through June of that year.

the military's domestic mission and its budget thus appear to be, to some extent, measures to ensure political harmony.

This can be verified by looking at the expanding numbers of military personnel, particularly in the army. SEDENA personnel, most of them members of the army, totaled 102,975 in 1980, 124,497 in 1985, 151,178 in 1990, and 171,952 in 1995. By 2006 the number had risen to 191,143. This increase results from the multiple missions assigned to the military in all three arenas of safety/security: national, do-

Table 3.6 Budgeted Expenditures (millions of pesos)

Budgeted Expenditures by Agency			
Year	SEDENA	SEMAR	Total
2001	22,031.1	8,852.5	30,883.6
2002	22,596.6	8,846.4	31,443.0
2003	24,203.4	9,201.4	33,404.8
2004	23,846.3	8,844.4	32,690.7
2005	25,271.0	9,528.8	34,799.8
2006 *	26,031.9	9,163.5	35,195.4

Source: Fox Quesada 2006, 294.

* Data for 2006 are current through June of that year.

mestic, and public. In contrast, the navy is experiencing a reduction in personnel in all its branches and services (Secretaría de Marina 2000, 20; 2002, 10).

The growth of the military is also evident in the gradual but steady increases in military budgets, especially for SEDENA though less so for SEMAR (see table 3.6). In addition, SEDENA, SEMAR, the Ministry of Public Security, and the Office of the Federal Attorney General have been exempted from the reductions in salaries and operational expenses which took effect in fiscal year 2007.[10]

In addition to the overall expansion of armed forces personnel, there is also a substantial number of high-ranking officers overseeing Mexico's military forces (see table 3.7). Indiscriminate promotions have distorted the military's hierarchal structures, with a disproportionately high number of senior officials in relation to the number of enlisted men. One option to address this problem is to retire high-ranking officers,

10 See "Decreto que establece medidas de austeridad y disciplina del gasto de la Administración Pública Federal," *Diario Oficial,* December 4, 2006. The exemption is set out in Articles 10 and 12 of this decree.

Table 3.7 Number of Generals on Active Duty, 2007

Rank	Number
Major generals	32
Brigade generals	195
Brigadier generals	295
Total	523

Source: Response received on March 4, 2007, to a request to the Institute for Public Information Access (IFAI), February 19, 2007, document No. 0000700030907.

Table 3.8 Monthly Income of Mexican Military Personnel (in pesos)

Rank	Gross Income	Net Income
Secretary	$228,599.10	$154,976.56
Undersecretary	$211,734.95	$143,677.60
Public official	$203,600.00	$138,365.06
Major general	$196,474.00	$133,590.64
Brigade general	$152,700.00	$104,408.00
Brigadier general	$113,608.80	$78,368.44
Colonel	$85,512.00	$60,129.71
Lieutenant colonel	$50,900.00	$36,816.11
Major	$37,666.00	$28,072.31
First captain	$31,558.00	$24,794.57
Second captain	$28,504.00	$22,939.11
Lieutenant	$7,701.00	$6,620.66
Second lieutenant	$7,096.38	$6,620.66

Rank	Gross Income	Net Income
First sergeant	$5,533.88	$5,219.26
Second sergeant	$5,262.65	$4,974.77
Corporal	$4,416.98	$4,207.76
Private	$4,053.38	$3,865.25

Source: Ministry of National Defense, http://www.sedena.gob.mx.

but there are few incentives for them to leave the service. An officer who favors improving conditions for retired personnel offered the following:

> Funny thing is, now we have two armies: the active-duty army, where brigadier generals make $99,000 pesos per month; brigade generals, $130,000; and major generals, $160,000, Meanwhile, an active-duty major makes more than a retired major general, and some of the officers who retired several years back receive extremely low pensions (Garfias Magaña 2004, 2).

In fact, there are two different armies in Mexico, and their differences expand beyond active-duty versus retired personnel. Rather, there is the army of the privileged few (top-level officials) who exercise command of the armed forces, involve the institution in law enforcement duties, and defend its autonomy, prerogatives, and privileges; and there is the army of the masses (the troops). The monthly income of the typical soldier, including a wage increase passed by President Calderón in early 2006, is less than US$500 per month (table 3.8).

Acknowledging this wage gap, President Calderón, supreme commander of the Mexican armed forces, declared a wage increase in February 2007, stating:

> This benefits package will mean that, for example, a private in the First Military Region, who previously received a 60 percent bonus, will now get a 90 percent bonus, increasing last year's salary of 3,500 pesos to 5,200 pesos, that is, a 46 percent increase.…Corporals will get a 45 percent

> increase, and so on down the line, so that a similar benefit can be enjoyed by all troop personnel and lower-income officers, lieutenants, and second lieutenants, whose wages were lagging seriously behind (http://www.presidencia.gob.mx/prensa/?contenido=29063).

It is interesting to note here that the members of the armed forces, "the people in uniform," share the abysmal inequities that characterize Mexican society as a whole.

CONCERNS ABOUT MILITARIZATION

The trend toward militarization ignites serious concern among academics and human rights organizations regarding the protection of civil liberties. A report by the United Nations High Commissioner for Human Rights in Mexico acknowledges that "the inefficiency and corruption of law enforcement agencies represents an obstacle to preserving public safety," and the UNHCHR encourages the government to "promote the progressive and verifiable substitution of the armed forces in public safety duties" (2003, 43, viii). To assign the military to missions and duties that are beyond its nature provokes a significant increase in complaints filed for alleged violations of basic rights:

> The armed forces appear year after year as one of the institutions with the most human rights violation complaints filed before the National Human Rights Commission. The complaints include both violations against their own members (complaints against internal actions would be one way to put it), as well as actions carried out against civilians, particularly during the aforementioned drug-traffic combating tasks (Cruzvillegas Fuentes 2007).

Another risk is institutional deterioration, including the risk of corruption. A group that calls themselves the Zetas offers an example here. The Zetas were deserters from the airmobile and amphibian units of the Army Special Forces (GAFE and GANFE, respectively) and from the elite forces of the Airborne Infantry Brigade. These individuals are trained in combating drug trafficking and terrorist threats, and they are proficient in using sophisticated communications equipment, all types of weaponry, and intelligence strategies. These groups were sent to Tamaulipas State

Table 3.9 Desertions from the Defense Ministry During the Fox Administration, 2000–2006

Rank	Number of Deserters
Colonel	1
Lieutenant colonel	9
Majors	38
First captain	50
Second captain	49
First Lieutenant	459
Second lieutenant	782
First sergeant	354
Second sergeant	2,239
Corporal	9,919
Private	109,318
Total	**123,218**

Source: Institute for Public Information Access (IFAI), March 26, 2007.

to arrest Osiel Cárdenas, head of the Gulf cartel, but they ended up being recruited into his inner circle as protectors, and—after Cárdenas's arrest—they took control of most of the cartel's operations.

The Zetas are arguably the best-known example of military corruption and desertion. Corruption and desertion are practically inevitable at the level of enlisted personnel, given the miserable compensation that members of the military receive. But there is also a disturbing number of desertions at the officer level. All told, over the course of the Fox administration, from December 2000 to December 2006, the Ministry of National Defense lost 123,218 of its personnel (see table 3.9). There is speculation that at least some of these individuals joined the ranks of organized crime.[11]

> Obviously not everyone who deserts from the armed forces goes and joins organized crime.... There is no doubt, however, that some of those more than 100,000 deserters during the last administration were recruited by organized crime.... If that were not the case, then the secretary general would not have announced ... that a bill will be submitted to Congress to modify the Military Code of Justice such that any member of the military, or deserter therefrom, who becomes involved in organized crime activities would be accused of the crime of treason against the armed forces (Fernández Menéndez 2007).

The scale of desertions—equal to a third of all military personnel—represents a very serious concern. Moreover, it is not clear that military defections are on the decline. During the first six months of Calderón's presidential term, the number of defections increased by a rate of roughly a thousand troops per month. In the words of Erubiel Tirado, a renowned expert on the subject:

> The structural degradation caused by this phenomenon and its consequences on the overall strategy of their drug-fighting campaigns was given the silent treatment institutionally.... The official handling of this grave phenomenon has been erratic at best. The authorities have admitted the existence of the problem due to pressure exerted from within (from human rights and other nongovernmental organizations, the media, and so on) and from without (foreign NGOs and the U.S. government), but responses are rather feeble and insufficient (Tirado 2006, 22–23).

This very serious situation can only be addressed by those in charge of the armed forces, and it does not suffice simply to penalize those who join the ranks of organized crime. Perhaps a better response would be to identify the root causes and address

---

11 Response received on March 26, 2007, to a request to the Institute for Public Information Access (IFAI), March 8, 2007, document No. 000700042407.

them, given that the cause could well be inappropriate or inadequate personnel recruitment, selection, and compensation policies.

CONCLUSIONS

Given its complexity, the process of militarization of public safety can be examined along several lines. First, we have seen a dramatic expansion of the role of the armed forces, empowered by the Mexican Constitution in matters of both national and domestic security. This expanded authority has been supported by the Supreme Court, which erroneously authorizes the military to become involved in public safety matters. Second, we have seen that assigning the military to a domestic security mission is a response to the poor institutional performance of law enforcement agencies, their high levels of corruption, and widespread social distrust of police. Third, the willingness of the high command to commit the military to public security duties leads to an increased degree of autonomy for the armed forces and preserves major privileges for senior officers (in comparison with other personnel), whose number might otherwise be reduced by a restructuring of the military. Indeed, during the Calderón administration, the government will likely choose to leave military reform off the table.

Since desperate times—such as Mexico has seen in recent years—often call for desperate measures, the involvement of the armed forces is understandable. The Calderón administration has insisted that the military's involvement is temporary, part of the initial phases of its effort to combat organized crime and drug trafficking, particularly in states and municipalities where crime bosses have established a strong and pervasive presence. The danger inherent in the Mexican government strategy is that its strategic objective will become diluted and the role of the military will be extended indefinitely. Achieving the rule of law for the long term requires a strategic framework that goes beyond operational tactics and approaches, one that sets a timeline for the military's involvement. Otherwise, there is a risk of prolonging their participation indefinitely in missions that are foreign to their nature and that contribute to their degradation.

While it is true that the Mexican armed forces have enjoyed a high degree of social acceptance until now, using the military in a public security role for which it is not well suited will ultimately undermine the public's goodwill. The best way to return the military to their barracks and to their natural duties and missions—the tasks that have earned them public support—is to make the military's involvement in public security unnecessary. To do so will require qualitative improvements in law enforcement institutions, many of which involve intangible factors such as professionalization, leadership, and transparency and accountability mechanisms to promote the overall integrity of the judicial sector. That is to say, Mexico must put in place a police doctrine focused on getting results and earning the trust of society. Then, and only then, will the militarization of public safety stop making sense.

REFERENCES

Alvarado, Arturo, and Diane Davis. 2001. "Cambio político, inseguridad pública y deterioro del estado de derecho en México: Algunas hipótesis en torno del proceso actual." In El desafío democrático de México: Seguridad y estado de derecho, ed. Arturo Alvarado and Sigrid Arzt. Mexico: El Colegio de México.

Amnesty International. 2005. "Mexico" (Hechos más destacados entre enero y diciembre de 2004), Informe 2005. http://web.amnesty.org/report2005/mex-summary-esl.

Barrón Cruz, Martín Gabriel. 2005. Policía y seguridad en México. Mexico: Instituto Nacional de Ciencias Penales.

Calderón Hinojosa, Felipe. 2007. "Estrategia integral para la prevención del delito y combate a la delincuencia." March 7. http://www.presidencia.gob.mx/prensa/?contenido=29337#b4.

Cruzvillegas Fuentes, Eréndira. 2007. Análisis del desempeño del Ombusman Nacional en México y su relación con la sociedad civil: alcances y desafíos a más de quince años de su creación. Mexico: CIESAS.

Fernández Menéndez, Jorge. 2007. "La pena de traición y las deserciones militares," Excélsior, April 30.

Follietti, Gilda. 2005. "Competencias constitucionales de los parlamentos latinoamericanos en el área de defensa." In Red de Seguridad y Defensa de América Latina (RESDAL), Atlas comparativo de la defensa en América Latina. Buenos Aires.

Fox Quesada, President Vicente. 2006. Anexo Sexto, Informe de Gobierno, September 1.

Garfias Magaña, Luis, General de División (Ret.). 2004. "El problema de los retirados militares." Mexico, September 29.

———. 2005. "Presente y futuro de las fuerzas armadas." Presentation at the III Simposio Internacional de Historia Militar de México. El Colegio de Michoacán, April 7–8.

Instituto Nacional de Administración Pública. 2000. La organización de la administración pública en México. Mexico: Noriega Editores.

Ipsos Bimsa. 2004. "Encuesta Nacional en Vivienda: Imagen del Ejército." Mexico.

López Portillo, Ernesto. 2002. "The Police in Mexico: Political Functions and Needed Reforms." In Transnational Crime and Public Security: Challenges to Mexico and the United States, ed. John Bailey and Jorge Chabat. La Jolla, CA: Center for U.S.-Mexican Studies, University of California, San Diego.

Lozoya, Jorge Alberto. 1984. El ejército mexicano. 3d ed. Mexico: El Colegio de México.

Moloeznik, Marcos Pablo. 2005a. "Seguridad pública y reforma policial en México: ¿Cambio o continuidad?" In Seguridad pública y reforma policial en las Américas, ed. Lucía Dammert and John Bailey. Mexico: Siglo Veintiuno/FLACSO Chile/ONU ILANUD.

———. 2005b. "La naturaleza de un instrumento militar atípico: Las fuerzas armadas mexicanas," Revista Fuerzas Armadas y Sociedad [Santiago de Chile], January–June. http://www.fasoc.cl.

PGR (Procuraduría General de la República). 2002. Programa Nacional para el Control de Drogas 2001–2006. Mexico: PGR.

Poder Ejecutivo Federal. 2001. Plan Nacional de Desarrollo 2001–2006. Área de Orden y Respeto. Mexico. http://pnd.presidencia.gob.mx.

———. 2007. "Decreto por el que se crea el Cuerpo Especial del Ejército y Fuerza Aérea denominado Cuerpo de Fuerzas de Apoyo Federal," Diario Oficial de la Federación, May 9.

Rico, José María. 1997. Justicia penal y transición democrática en América Latina. Mexico: Siglo Veintiuno.

Secretaría de Gobernación. 2005. "Tercera Encuesta Nacional sobre Cultura Política y Prácticas Ciudadanas (ENCUP)." Mexico.http://www.gobernacion.gob.mx/encup/.

Secretaría de la Defensa Nacional. 2005. "Organización de la S.D.N." http://www.sedena.gob.mx

Secretaría de Marina. 2000. "Plan de Desarrollo 2000–2006," Revista Secretaría de Marina-Armada de Mexico año 19, época 9, número 142.

———. 2002. Programa Institucional de Desarrollo 2001–2006. 4th ed. Mexico.

SEDENA. 2001. Programa de Operación y Desarrollo de la Secretaría de la Defensa Nacional 2001-2006. Mexico: SEDENA.

SPP (Secretaría de Seguridad Pública). 2007. National Public Security System. Mexico: Office of the Director of the Public Security Information System. January 31.

Suprema Corte de Justicia de la Nación. 1996. Semanario Judicial de la Federación y su Gaceta, novena época, tomo III, March.

Tirado, Erubiel. 2006. "La relación civil-militar en México y el déficit democrático de la alternancia política, 2000–2006." Manuscript.

UNHCHR (Office of the United Nations High Commissioner for Human Rights). 2003. Diagnóstico sobre la situación de los derechos humanos en México. Mexico: Grupo Mundi-Prensa.

Organized Crime and Official Corruption in Mexico

Carlos Antonio Flores Pérez

This chapter examines the nexus between organized crime and corrupt public officials in Mexico. Drawing on established studies of Mexico's drug-trafficking organizations, as well as original research and interviews with public officials, this essay provides a revealing illustration of the depth and breadth of official corruption in Mexico, as well as the interplay of political processes and organized crime structures. The recent atomization and proliferation of Mexico's drug cartels is, among other things, a reflection of the broader political transition to more decentralized and democratic governance.

ORGANIZED CRIME AND OFFICIAL CORRUPTION

Luis Astorga, a leading expert on drug trafficking as a sociopolitical phenomenon in Mexico, has identified at least four stages in the evolution of this illicit activity and in the ties of conspiracy between public officials and traffickers (Astorga 2002, 57):

- 1914–1947: The emergence of organized crime related to drug production and distribution and its subordination to local-level political powers.
- 1947–1985: The creation of federal mediating institutions between the political powers and criminal organizations. Relatively disciplined security institutions, framed within the bipolar logic of the Cold War.
- 1985–2000: The institutional breakdown of the security structures that mediated between the political powers and crime syndicates. Worldwide increase in drug trafficking. End of the Cold War and replacement of the political functions of key security organizations by public safety functions. Centralized control over drug trafficking in the hands of public officials charged with combating this activity. Loss of control over organized crime toward the end of this period.
- 2000 to the present: The Institutional Revolutionary Party's loss of hegemony. Displacement of those who maintained the conspiracy networks. Breakdown of the old rules, resulting not in a reduction of corruption but rather in

decreased predictability in the relationships between organized crime and public officials.

Across these stages there was a shift away from a *centralized-hierarchical* regime between public officials and organized crime and toward an *atomized-multidirectional* relationship. This chapter analyzes the evolution of that relationship and reviews some of the key developments that occurred in each phase. Among these, I contend, were the internal disputes among political elites during the presidencies of Miguel de la Madrid and, especially, Carlos Salinas de Gortari, which had major implications for the structure and organization of drug trafficking in Mexico. Another key development, also noted by other authors in this volume, is the army's growing involvement in combating drug trafficking.

In the late 1960s, drug use increased noticeably in the United States with the growth of the countercultural movement and the return of U.S. troops exposed to drugs during the Vietnam War. At the time, Mexico was an important supplier of marijuana and opium paste to the U.S. market, and the U.S. government, responding to public pressure, began to redirect that pressure to Mexico. In 1969 President Nixon launched Operation Intercept[1] in an effort to increase Mexican collaboration in the battle against drug trafficking (Ruiz-Cabañas 1993, 212).

The Mexican government's response was to increase its efforts to eradicate marijuana and poppy crops, and in 1975 President Luis Echeverría initiated the Permanent Campaign to Combat Drugs (Campaña Permanente de Lucha Contra las Drogas) which employed new technologies to locate and destroy illegal crops (Ruiz-Cabañas 1993, 208). Under the Operation Condor component of the Permanent Campaign, Mexico was divided into 13 zones and 344 surveillance sectors, advance outposts were built in crop areas, communications networks were set up, and the armed forces were assigned en masse to combating drug trafficking in several Mexican states. According to Ruiz-Cabañas (213), the Mexican government spent US$35 million and dedicated 2,500 troops, 250 federal police agents, and various state police forces to Operation Condor.[2] Astorga notes that the number

1 This operation virtually closed the border between Tijuana and San Ysidro, California, for three weeks in the fall of 1969.

2 Ruiz-Cabañas bases this information on Craig 1980.

of troops participating in Operation Condor ultimately rose to 10,000 under the command of General José Hernández Toledo (Astorga 2005, 115).

By the late 1970s and early 1980s, the Permanent Campaign—within which the army's Operation Condor now played a fundamental role—had obtained praiseworthy results. U.S. authorities reported that Mexican marijuana dropped from 75 percent of the supply in the U.S. market to 4 percent by 1981, and Mexican heroin decreased from 67 to 25 percent of supply by 1980 (Ruiz-Cabañas 1993, 213).[3] However, these achievements did not bring a permanent reduction in the amount of Mexican drugs available in the U.S. market, because, during these years, a centralized-hierarchical relationship was being forged between public officials and Mexico's organized crime syndicates.

To illustrate the patterns of organized crime and corruption in Mexico across the various stages identified above, I draw on interviews I conducted with former high-ranking government personnel from May to September 2004. The interview informants include a former top-level official from the Office of the Federal Attorney General (PGR); a former state attorney general; a retired Mexican army officer; a former undersecretary of public security with broad experience in penitentiary management; a former security adviser to the Office of the President; a member of a U.S. intelligence service, present in Mexico; and a former top-level official at the PGR who has also served as a state attorney general. The informants are identified in this chapter by the letters A, B, C, and so on.

EARLY MILITARY INVOLVEMENT IN THE WAR ON DRUGS

According to informant C and contradicting what most observers believe, Operation Condor was not the first important armed forces operation to eradicate illegal crops. Rather, C claims that the first major counter-drug operation by the military was Operation Octopus, which took place in Michoacán and parts of Guerrero in the late 1960s. C, who participated in that campaign as commanding officer of a unit, recalls that the most common illegal crop in that area is marijuana:

3 Ruiz-Cabañas draws this information from National Narcotics Intelligence Consumers Committee 1980, 91.

> In the past, the issue of drug trafficking … well, it wasn't really penalized or punished; there wasn't that much conflict. You would occasionally see … shipments escorted by the army in cars, on the highways, you know? You saw higher-ups, zone commanders … well, they were giving protection, and you could grow and transport marijuana freely.

C reports that the first major incident related to corruption in the army occurred in 1972 in the 51st Battalion of Apatzingán, Michoacán. The second-in-command of that battalion (a colonel) and his staff were arrested by the Mexican Secret Service. When asked if these activities were known to the superiors of the zone commander (a general), C replied:

> There are rumors that it came from the top, which is very likely. What is absolutely true is that the zone commanders, who were the maximum authority in the state … well, they allowed this type of situation.… At one point the zone commander there said to me, "Listen … do you know any *marihuaneros* [marijuana growers]?" I said, "Sir, I don't know about *marihuaneros*."… "You go and talk to them, we'll give them open roads from Nueva Italia to Guadalajara, for X amount."

Despite the centralization of power that characterized the Mexican political regime during the 1960s and 1970s, the imperfect control over the nation's territory is evidenced in C's recollections:

> We couldn't get into many areas because they were completely inaccessible, and our forces were really too small to go into those locations. There were places by Aguililla, for instance, a part of Michoacán, over by Caleta de Campos, with no roads—you'd have to walk in for three days—that were covered with marijuana. You could see whole fields, but you couldn't get to them. We had neither sufficient forces nor the desire to go in.

These statements confirm that even the government institution with the strongest presence, the army, was not always in full control. This imperfect territorial control appeared to serve the interests of some of the upper echelons of the military. This is illustrated by C's description of the internal army dynamics, which seemed designed to encourage corruption and worked to protect the drug trade. For example, soldiers had to cover many of their own operating and supply costs, even paying for transportation and bullets, which made collaborating with the criminals an attractive option. According to C: "You were working under so many limitations that you wound up saying, 'Fuck 'em,' or better yet, 'Okay, you son of a bitch, how much will you pay me?'"

This tolerance of organized drug trafficking contrasted notably with the government's campaign against political insurgents. When the political interests of the regime were threatened, the army's efficiency and capacity for action rose geometrically. Asked if the army's deficiencies undermined government efforts to combat insurgent groups, C offered a categorical response:

> The campaign against the guerrillas was well controlled. I went up against Lucio [Cabañas] and Genaro [Vázquez] in Ometepec, Guerrero. It was different because there we went out in companies.... There were resources and they knew how to distribute them.... At that time, the way we saw things, well, the *marihuanero*, I mean, there was no problem; but the guerrilla had to be beaten down.

CENTRALIZED HIERARCHY, CORRUPTION, AND STATE CONTROL

Despite the crime syndicates' ability to suborn high-level government officials with vast sums of money, it would be a mistake to assume that the criminals had the upper hand. To the contrary, government officials actually appeared to have greater capacity for controlling the relationship and subordinating the criminals than vice versa. At that time, the state's security institutions were strong, and non-state actors did not present a serious threat to the state's monopoly on coercive force. Hence the fact that state actors opted not to "beat down" the drug traffickers—and chose instead to profit from them—illustrates the leeway that state actors had to tolerate illegal activities or exert political and social control over them (Flores Pérez 2002, chaps. 3–4). The ability of the state to exert such control over a wide range of actors, from dissidents and guerrillas to drug traffickers, is precisely why organized crime opts to pay rents to the state.

A paradigmatic case was that of the Federal Security Directorate (DFS), which functioned as the political police from 1947 to 1985. The DFS was rewarded for its service to the state with near total impunity, granted from the highest levels of political decision making. Informant B attributes the institutional degradation of the DFS to this impunity, which led, according to B, to direct ties between the DFS and drug traffickers:

> When historical circumstances—such as the Liga 23 de Septiembre, the proliferation of kidnappings, the development of urban guerrillas—led to the creation of exceptional, extralegal powers to pursue these challenges and gave rise to the "dirty war," I believe *that* is where the problem began. The extra-legal power that emerges in security institutions induces extortion of criminals … and leads to the corruption of the institution itself. This is what led, finally, to the destruction of the Federal Security Directorate, where extortion certainly took place.

The conspiracy between many members of the DFS—some of them top-level personnel—and drug traffickers was a point upon which practically all the interview respondents concurred.[4] B perceives it as follows:

> In the final stage of the Federal Security Directorate, I believe there was a process of centralization … because of those discretionary powers. A process of centralizing the state's authority to deal with organized crime. The period in which the DFS reorganized into five regions [replacing state delegates with regional delegates] greatly facilitated linkages with criminal organizations.

Informant F corroborated this perspective:

> The Federal Security Directorate favored the spread of drug trafficking ever since the 1970s, even though the DFS was quite busy with leftist groups.… You have to remember that the DFS was composed of many individuals who had been in the military, and they had helped drug traf-

4 Astorga (2000, 101–102) also reports that high-level people within the DFS were involved in drug trafficking.

> ficking to prosper throughout Mexico. After the dissolution of the DFS, several commanders became major drug-trafficking figures.

Interview respondent A, who has held top-level positions in the Office of the Federal Attorney General, agrees that, in its day, the DFS exercised political control over drug traffickers:

> During the years of the Federal Security Directorate, they were the ones with political control. I don't think there was anyone who could oppose them.... And afterward, the Federal Judicial Police had a great deal to do in the control, naturally.

Hence, at least through the early 1990s, there was no criminal organization capable of exerting more pressure over government officials than the officials could exert over them. As powerful as organized crime syndicates may be, they could never break free from the control of representatives of the state. The terms of agreements between the two groups were dictated not by the criminals but by those in control of the political power structure. This is a fundamental characteristic of what I call the centralized-hierarchical model of organized crime.

According to the interviewees, criminals more often than not found themselves obliged to reach a pact with the forces of law and order, as, for example, when traffickers had to purchase "protection" from military zone commanders. C narrated a case (not reported in the media) in Tierra Blanca, Sinaloa, in the early 1980s in which a group of military men imposed a nonnegotiable agreement on a group of local drug traffickers:

> There was a well-known case there in Tierra Blanca.... It's said that [an officer, name withheld] went to see General [name withheld]. And he said, "General, there's a group of *narcos* [drug traffickers] here in Tierra Blanca who will put up a million pesos each for us to let them work." Then they called in this group of *narcos*, with their money ... and right then and there they're all arrested and killed.

Under the centralized-hierarchical regime that existed between public officials and organized crime, several factors combined to favor the expansion of drug trafficking in Mexico from the late 1970s to the mid-1980s. The first factor was increased U.S. demand. The second was the redistribution of drug traffickers, originally concentrated in Sinaloa, to other parts of Mexico following Operation Condor (Astorga 2002, 65; *Proceso* April 17, 1989). The third factor was a shift in South American cocaine traffickers' transshipment routes after U.S. forces intensified surveillance of their former entry points on the U.S. southeastern coast. The new routes went through Mexico, which necessarily required agreements between South American and Mexican traffickers. Until that time Mexican traffickers had dealt mainly in marijuana and heroin, but they now added cocaine to their inventory. The fourth factor is the increasing participation of Mexican security forces in the drug trade.

THE RISE OF COCAINE AND THE DFS

According to media reports and other sources consulted in this research, corruption in the Mexican security apparatus increased in the mid-1980s, at the same time that South American cocaine traffickers shifted their transit route from Colombia-Cuba-Miami to Mexico, bringing the cocaine traffickers into contact with Mexican traffickers. Honduran trafficker Juan Ramón Matta Ballesteros had contacts among important Mexican and Colombian groups. In late 1984, he put Gonzalo Rodríguez Gacha—"El Mexicano," an operative of Pablo Escobar's organization in Medellín, Colombia—in contact with Miguel Ángel Félix Gallardo.

The Colombians and Mexicans reached the following accord: the Mexicans would receive between US$3,000 and $4,000 per kilo of cocaine transported to the U.S. border (Boyer 2001, 54–55).[5] In later years, these terms were modified considerably, in favor of the Mexican organizations. However, already in the early 1980s the illegal income generated by the massive inflow of cocaine meant that Mexican organized crime groups had resources that far exceeded the budgets of federal agencies, making it very easy for them to escalate the level of corruption already present in the national security apparatus. By the mid-1990s, the profits from cocaine trafficking were between US$1.5 and $4.5 billion, and experts estimate that Mexican traffickers, thanks

5 Private sources support the accuracy of these figures. It should be noted that they could refer to the linkage between the Medellín cartel and the Mexican one headed by Miguel Ángel Félix Gallardo, since some cocaine trafficking already existed prior to this period, traveling from Colombia via Sinaloa. See Astorga 2002, 70, 146; Shannon 1989, 138–39.

to their association with the Colombians, received half of the takings (González Ruiz, López Portillo, and Yáñez 1994, 75–76).

By the mid-1980s, the Federal Security Directorate was the most powerful police force in Mexico. Having crushed the insurgent movements of the 1970s, the DFS now turned its attention full time to combating drug trafficking. The outcome, however, was completely contrary to official expectations. Instead of combating drug traffic, the DFS collaborated directly in its restructuring after it was disrupted by Operation Condor. Interview respondent B observes:

> My impression is that there is a centralization, where the central power of the DFS subordinates local powers and functions in coordination with the army. That is the impression I have.... The regional DFS delegates had de facto authority over local authorities, which supported a more coherent, functional structuring of the illegal drug market. It was a central authority. It was a guarantee.

These years marked the first stage of a broad centralization of control over the illegal drug trade, with the Federal Security Directorate playing a key role in extorting the criminal organizations involved in this activity. Diverse actors in Mexico's security institutions—including army generals and other high-level individuals—became intertwined with the interests of the drug cartels.

One example of this centralized-hierarchical relationship between criminals and prominent members of the government during the administration of José López Portillo is Mexico City police chief Arturo Durazo's pyramidal extortion scheme. Even beyond extorting the syndicates, he went as far as using police themselves in the commission of crimes.[6] By the mid-1980s, that centralized and top-down control was solidly in place among corrupt forces of law and order, which now had unprecedented amounts of illegal resources within reach.

Again according to respondent B, the institutional breakdown of the DFS took place as a result of the enormous leeway accorded to the police in the 1970s, when they were tasked with dismantling subversive urban movements:

---

6 Interviewee A mentioned that the amount of (presumably illicit) money found in Durazo's possession, some US$200 million, is small compared to the amounts in circulation and the fortunes that were made from drug trafficking in the years after Durazo.

> Agents of the Echeverría government, including the White Brigade, the DFS, and the military police … but especially the DFS, were given virtually free rein to engage in a "dirty war" against the guerrillas. The unlimited power they were granted leads them to confuse guerrilla safe houses with drug traffickers' warehouses.

Ultimately a rivalry arose between the DFS and the Office of the Federal Attorney General, the institution formally mandated to combat drug trafficking:

> They start to get involved, to blackmail the drug traffickers, and that gives rise to a conflict with the constitutional and legal authority of the PGR. During the López Portillo administration, Attorney General Óscar Flores decides not to participate in the White Brigade, he withdraws under the principle that all of the attorney general's agents must be subject to the law, and the White Brigade was not. He tries to take it into his institutional hands, to sideline the activities of the White Brigade and the DFS. In the de la Madrid administration, with García Ramírez, the Attorney General's Office would take a more active role. Miguel Aldana, director of Interpol in Mexico, and Mr. Ibarra of the Federal Judicial Police come into more open, more intense conflict with the DFS, which by then was deeply involved in the structuring of the drug traffic.

Interview respondent D confirms the competition between Mexico's security organizations to provide protection to the illegal drug trade:

> I believe that the political police, the Federal Security Directorate, along with Political and Social Investigations (Investigaciones Políticas y Sociales), didn't have a chance to reach that level until Toño Zorrilla was named head of the DFS in the de la Madrid administration. At that moment, they assume a power they didn't have before.... The only ones who could provide a counterweight to the Federal Judicial Police were the DFS, and that's what they did.

As informant D suggests, in the centralized-hierarchical model of relations between organized crime and the state, security forces compete among themselves for the best position from which to extort criminals. Notably, however, the criminal organizations seem to remain subject at all times to the centralized control of the state, which sets the conditions under which the illegal activities can develop.

The close ties between the DFS and drug traffickers were clearly in evidence during the de la Madrid administration (1982–1988), when José Antonio Zorrilla Pérez was director of the DFS. In November 1984, authorities "formally discovered" a massive marijuana plantation on the El Búfalo ranch in Chihuahua, which belonged to Rafael Caro Quintero of Sinaloa, one of Miguel Ángel Félix Gallardo's top henchmen.[7] The authorities destroyed between five and ten thousand tons of top-quality marijuana, in what the media called the biggest drug seizure in history.[8] What is most notable in this case, however, is the phrase "formally discovered." The ranch, located in the desert and easily visible from the air, employed some seven thousand workers. It is inconceivable that federal and state security authorities could have previously overlooked a plantation of that size and visibility. Moreover, the fact that DFS agents were arrested at the ranch erases any doubt that the DFS was providing protection to the drug traffickers (*Proceso*, May 22, 1989).

Shortly thereafter, in February 1985, Enrique Camarena, an agent of the U.S. Drug Enforcement Administration (DEA), was executed in Guadalajara, along with his Mexican pilot, Alfredo Zavala. Under increasing pressure from the U.S. government, Mexican authorities were obliged to act in order to quiet public criticism in both countries. Those who investigated the murders cast even greater doubt on the honesty of top-level officials in de la Madrid's administration. In the early 1990s, individuals in the U.S. witness protection program identified then secretaries of National Defense and the Interior of involvement in the decision to torture and murder Camarena and Zavala (*Proceso*, August 21, 1989, and March 29, 1993). The witnesses even alleged that General Juan Arévalo Gardoqui (National Defense) and Manuel Bartlett (Interior) were in the next room when Camarena and Zavala were being tortured.

Regardless of the degree to which high-level members of the executive branch were involved in protecting drug-trafficking organizations, one fact is incontrovertible:

7 Caro Quintero enjoyed political backing from early in his career. He was a bodyguard of Sinaloa Governor Leopoldo Sánchez Celis and served as best man at his son's wedding (Proceso, April 17, 1989).

8 http://www.pbs.org/wgbh/pages/frontline/shows/drugs/cron/.

when arrested, Caro Quintero had a badge identifying him as an agent of the Federal Security Directorate, given by its general director, Zorrilla Pérez. Zorrilla also authorized this type of documentation for Ernesto Fonseca Carrillo, who was later co-indicted for the murders of Camarena and Zavala. The DFS director's office extended similar credentials to Miguel Ángel Félix Gallardo himself (*Proceso*, May 22, 1989).

Another murder tied to the DFS is that of the reporter Manuel Buendía on May 30, 1984, just a few months before the El Búfalo case and the murders of Camarena and Zavala were made public in the early days of the Salinas administration. Unclear and contradictory evidence obtained through public investigations assigned material guilt to Juan Rafael Moro Ávila, head of the motorcycle corps of the Special Brigade of the DFS, and Zorrilla Pérez was identified as the intellectual author of Buendía's murder (*Proceso*, June 26, 1989).[9] According to the national media, Buendía was murdered to prevent him from going public with information about high-level government corruption linked to drug trafficking. An official in charge of the early stages of the murder investigation claimed that his team had been blocked when evidence began to point to officials even higher up than Zorrilla (*Proceso*, October 24, 1994).

These various incidents, which demonstrate the high level of corruption within the Federal Security Directorate and the DFS's broad participation in the illegal drug trade, culminated in the dismantling of the DFS in August 1985. As interview respondent B noted, it was its evident corruption that led to its breakup: "the Federal Security Directorate was the axis of the state's security system, and corruption was so extreme that the institution had to disappear."

The dismantling of the Federal Security Directorate ended the first phase in the relationship between organized crime and public officials, which we have framed as a centralized-hierarchical arrangement. It should be noted, however, that the centralized-hierarchical model did not end with the end of the de la Madrid administration. As I discuss below, the Salinas administration introduced a new centralized hierarchy of state protection for drug trafficking.

---

9 It should be noted that a source close to the principals in the case offers an alternate version to the official one resulting from the investigation.

SHIFTING POWER DYNAMICS WITHIN THE CENTRALIZED-HIERARCHICAL MODEL

According to newspaper reports and confirmed by my sources, the agreements established between Colombian and Mexican organizations underwent major modifications in the early 1990s. As noted above, under the deal reached in the mid-1980s Mexican traffickers were to receive US$3,000 per kilo of cocaine transported to the U.S. border. Between 1989 and 1991 Mexican traffickers changed their terms, demanding payment in kind from the Colombians—30 percent of the cocaine to be transported through Mexican territory. By 1993 the Mexican traffickers had forced the Colombians to cede 50 percent of the cocaine transported through Mexico for sale in the U.S. market (Boyer 2001, 68–71). One informant emphasized the different roles filled by the Colombian and Mexican organizations: while the Columbians sold a product, the Mexicans delivered a service. For the Mexican drug-trafficking structure, the priority has been to guarantee protection for shipments of cocaine—the drug that revolutionized the profitability of drug trafficking—coming from South America and passing through Mexican territory. The proper development of this protective service, and therefore its profitability, necessarily required broad protection from the governmental structure. Interview respondent A points out:

> "I control the market." That is the established rule. Now that can only be established by the use of public force. It has to be directed, an activity directed from the Attorney General's Office, to establish the lines of command in the market. Otherwise you cannot do it; it's a prerequisite.

Respondent A points to the case of a Colombian drug trafficker arrested while bringing a shipment of cocaine into Mexico. According to this trafficker's confession, 500 kilos of his 600-kilo shipment belonged in equal shares to the Colombian and Mexican organizations. The remaining 100 kilos were the property of the arrested trafficker himself, drugs he was compelled to sell to Mexican organizations immediately upon his entry into Mexico because, he declared, the rule was that if Colombians tried to transport drugs through Mexico themselves, they would be arrested or executed. Informant A considers that this rule could not be enforced unless the Mexican drug-trafficking syndicates had broad support from the state's public security forces: "That's how the rule was established in 1990, and that rule can only be established if you have true political control, if you're working at the level of a confederation of Mexican cartels, as they established jointly with the state."

A new centralizing process took place after the heads of the existing organizations were ousted in order to impose discipline upon the various criminal groups and force them to accept the new agreement. According to the testimony of one interviewee:

> First, they toppled Félix Gallardo, all the ones who had control, and they establish a new control. The new control is established by creating the Gulf cartel, with Juan García Abrego, and reformulating things with the others. Why is Amado Carrillo released from prison within eight months in 1989? Because there was an agreement, an agreement at the top. He accepts the new rules, and the rules were based on political control.[10]

This same source indicates that the arrangement was likely imposed by the president's brother, Raúl Salinas de Gortari. This claim is corroborated in a report by Swiss Attorney General Carla del Ponte, who in the mid-1990s investigated Raúl Salinas for money laundering. According to José Manuel "Alex" Ramos—a Colombian drug trafficker and collaborator of Pablo Escobar Gaviria and Gonzalo Rodríguez Gacha (head of the Medellín cartel's cocaine transit operations through Mexico)—the relationship with Raúl Salinas began in 1987, the year Carlos Salinas was selected as the PRI's presidential candidate. During this period the Colombians purportedly paid protection quotas directly to Mexican public officials and collaboration payments to their criminal counterparts in Mexico.[11] However, Ramos's testimony notes that their

---

10 According to a secret report of the General Staff of National Defense, in September 1995, Amado Carrillo's release was granted by then deputy attorney general Javier Coello Trejo, in exchange for US$2 million delivered through Rodolfo León Aragón, then chief of the Federal Judicial Police (Estado Mayor 1995).

11 The following is excerpted from del Ponte's report: "Raúl Salinas de Gortari met with me to inform me that they needed financial support for the political programs of the upcoming elections, and in exchange we would get protection everywhere in Mexico and we would have other facilities such as passports, U.S. visas, and possibly airplanes. He said that Carlos was the candidate, that there was no doubt, but that they needed money for that. For instance, government officials could confiscate airplanes of other drug smugglers if they didn't pay for protection. The planes could be reloaded and we could take them over. Back at the hotel, I told Raúl Salinas that I was going to meet with Gacha. The agreement was that each time the plane reached Mexico, we would have to pay $US300,000 per landing."

maneuvering room in Mexico was noticeably reduced once the new president took office and named security officials who subordinated the traffickers to the central power.

With Salinas's election, a new form of operation was established but still in the centralized-hierarchical model. Under the new arrangement, organized crime appeared to be more diffuse because it was more carefully covered up. But in fact it operated on a much larger scale, which was more profitable for both the Mexican traffickers and the political structure that protected them. Also, with the Federal Security Directorate gone, the center of control shifted to the Office of the Attorney General, with control established through specific individuals in the PGR, as interview respondent A points out:

> As in every business of this type, control has to be tightly contained to avoid scandal. That is, you can't have the whole Attorney General's Office involved, only a sector of the office and a subgroup of cities. It wasn't generalized. Of course, it was important to control some key sectors, like the Federal Judicial Police, the deputy attorney general for drug trafficking, because that is what allows you to establish control.

Informant F corroborated this when discussing the distribution of "*plazas*" within the PGR, specifically regarding the state-level appointment of PGR delegates:

> A federal deputy attorney general appointed by the president was selling the delegate posts for money, some *plazas* costing US$3 million, like in Ciudad Juárez and Tijuana. To pay for the prestige of representing the PGR as its delegate in those places, a person had to pay $3 million to the deputy attorney general through his subordinates, such as the director of the Federal Judicial Police. In addition, the deputy attorney general demanded a monthly payment, which was collected each month by his most loyal subordinates using one of the office's planes. Whether the deputy attorney general sent money to his boss (the president) is unknown, but it is believed there were gifts or benefits passed on to the top.

Respondent A reports that in order to maintain the structure within the PGR that provided protection to drug traffickers and to ensure that the conspiracy between public officials and criminals did not come to light, top political decision makers constantly changed the leadership of these institutions to prevent discovery of the scope of the protection the drug cartels enjoyed.[12] During this period, and conforming to the centralized-hierarchical model of ties between criminals and public officials, the state was able to regulate drug trafficking just as it could regulate any legal activity. Though a degree of balance had to be maintained between the various criminal factions, some groups benefited more than others. Those groups with the most to lose were traffickers who had made agreements with other political groups, agreements that conflicted with the preferences of the main decision-making structures.

Reportedly, the Amado Carrillo and Juan García Abrego organizations enjoyed stronger government protection during the Salinas administration. According to several informants, both organizations enjoyed protection from the highest levels. Yet, in the interest of maintaining a certain equilibrium, more marginalized criminal organizations were allowed to participate in the business, though to a lesser degree. These second-tier players were the ones who had established relationships with political figures who, though many still held positions in government, had seen their power decline with the arrival of the Salinas team.

Respondent D pointed out that, during this period, the incarcerated members of certain drug-trafficking groups received similar privileges from prison authorities, who provided them with better living conditions than were enjoyed by the rest of the prison population, let them leave the prison to spend time with their families, and permitted them to run their businesses from inside the prisons. When this informant was asked whether there were confrontations between imprisoned members of different drug-trafficking organizations, he replied:

> No, there was no confrontation between them. Nor did anybody try to confront them. Everybody knew that a war inside the jail would be terrible. They were all armed. Officials in the periods prior to Salinas had allowed weapons to be brought into the prison.[13]

---

12 The source suggests looking at the number of people rotated through the position of attorney general, which is higher than the turnover found in other institutions of the Salinas cabinet.

13 This interview respondent provided fascinating commentary on the pervasive corruption in the prison system: "Everything was for sale, and it continues to be.... In [a Mexico City penitentiary] they rent out the spaces for conjugal visits. We're talking some thirty rooms, rented out at an average of

One of my sources recounted the favors that Javier García Paniagua, then secretary of what is now the SSP in Mexico City and in charge of Mexico City's jails, bestowed on Miguel Ángel Félix Gallardo. In exchange for periodic payments from Félix Gallardo, García Paniagua allowed him to leave the prison intermittently and to continue some of his operations from jail:

> Félix Gallardo's situation was so special that … he would leave the prison to visit García Paniagua at his office.… He wasn't transported there in a prison vehicle, and the person driving him wasn't in uniform.[14]

Even so, this relationship does not necessarily imply a strictly hierarchical-bureaucratic structure. In the centralized-hierarchical linkages established during this period, it is possible that the drug kingpins were not always under orders from members of the political class or under government protection. Nonetheless, the powers at the top maintained the capacity to suppress any organization that was unwilling to bow to their directives. Informant F outlined the way in which the government would exercise control over the delinquents:

> Yes, there were agreements that delineated the acceptable limits of criminal activities. The military controlled certain groups involved in drug trafficking; the PGR and/or Federal Judicial Police controlled other groups involved in drug trafficking; and local police chiefs controlled the smaller criminal groups—kidnappers, smugglers of luxury items or cars, and so on. If any individual got involved in an activity that was already

---

30,000 pesos a month.… Who gets the money? It's split four ways. One part goes to the Secret Service; some to the mayor of Mexico City; some to the director of detention centers and the prison warden; and a quarter is divided among the technical personnel and the guards. That's the way it's always been.… For instance, let's say I'm a prisoner and I rent out the whole ground floor … ten rooms. I have my bodyguards there, my own dining room. I take down a wall to make a larger bedroom, put in a king-size bed, and so on. Nobody's ever going to search it. My visitors can come in without any hassle. They can even park in the prison officials' parking lot. They can come in any time, any day. My people can live in the prison with their families. That's how it works. The only law here is: money makes the dog dance."

14 After Operation Condor, a significant part of Félix Gallardo's criminal organization moved from Sinaloa to Jalisco, birth state of García Paniagua, who in addition to being the son of General Marcelino García Barragán, former national defense minister, was also head of the DFS, a member of the cabinet, and chairman of the PRI during this period.

> covered by another individual or group in favor with the authorities, then the individual who did not have their blessing would be told he could not continue to operate. If he persisted, he would be imprisoned or executed by the rival group.

At the next tier were high-level officials in the security institutions who were specifically charged with guiding the state's protection of criminal activities. They had some flexibility to privilege certain organizations, but they were also required to maintain balance among them to prevent inter-group conflicts. However, these officials were not immune to reprisals from the drug traffickers.

> The corruption attributed to Deputy Attorney General Ruiz Massieu or the director general of the Federal Judicial Police involved the sale of *plazas* and maintaining the balance.... For instance, [an official who had been director general of the Federal Judicial Police] was not controlled by Amado. He sold *plazas* and also trafficked in cocaine. There is an arrest warrant out for him, but he was selling *plazas* ... and received money for them, but he wasn't controlled by any group, because that's another characteristic. Even [another official who was also director general of the Federal Judicial Police] had to maintain the balance because if the other groups—the Arellanos, for instance—saw that he was working only with Amado ... they would cut him down, because that would mean they would be focusing all their energy towards only one side.

On several occasions, these officials sent some like-minded subordinate to serve as a contact with the drug traffickers and to work directly with them. One source mentioned the case of federal judicial police agent Alcides Ramón Magaña, "El Metro," who was chauffeur and aide to Amado Carrillo:

> For instance, El Metro ... starts out as a guy who works on stolen vehicles but isn't even necessarily corrupt. Then [an operations director of the Federal Judicial Police] sends him to be a driver for Amado, and he accepts. You see how it starts, with a little bit of corruption. Then they keep them on the payroll, and being on the payroll they are integrated into operational commands and are promoted.

However, the "integration" was not unilateral. While some lesser officials are under the direct orders of the drug traffickers and their eventual promotion depends on the services they can provide to advance that illegal trade, other officials during this period found themselves in a situation of relative equality with the drug traffickers. But it was only the very top political echelons that could guarantee the continued operation of the business through the hegemonic management of the forces of law and order, and even the top drug traffickers had to reach agreements with them.

Together, the preceding testimonies shed valuable light on the mechanics of the centralized-hierarchical model from 1988 to 1994. Under the conditions of this model, drug trafficking is protected through a system that greatly benefits the upper reaches of the power structure. However, the lower the hierarchical level of a public official and the smaller his political influence, the higher the likelihood he will be considered just another cog in the machine—and ultimately replaceable. The objective of those high in the power structure is to protect the illegal activity, even at the expense of the participants. Though some groups are privileged, the need to maintain some balance between the different organizations may dictate that individuals who break the rules must be done away with. The lower levels in the security institutions, and sometimes individuals at higher levels, can be sacrificed. This is the mechanism that explains the presence of conflicts between police institutions and between the police and the cartels. One can appreciate that, under these conditions, public officials and criminals can clash among themselves or with their respective counterparts, using violence and/or legal coercion to gain influence or to increase their share of the benefits derived from the illegal activities.

The system worked well for high-level corrupt officials, who reaped substantial financial benefit. For these high-level decision makers, clashes with lower-level officials and/or criminal organizations gave the impression that they were actually waging an effective war against criminal gangs. During this period the media reported on murders that supposedly were the product of disputes between rival criminal organizations competing for hegemonic control. However, one source said that, for the most part, these executions were not the result of a war between organizations but rather a punishment meted out to individuals who broke the rules. Also, contrary to the usual media coverage, this same source downplayed the danger government officials face if they refuse to participate in corruption:

> Most times, your refusal to participate means you'll have to leave your position, because if you don't accept, they might go to one of your superiors, who is willing to play along. If he does accept, he'll make life impossible for you or simply say you have to leave. But it doesn't get any worse than that.

Public officials involved in drug trafficking are more likely to be killed for not complying with unwritten rules of the business. Asked what actions of a public official could result in execution, respondent D observed:

> What can happen? You can take money to do something and not do it, either because you don't want to or because it can't be done at that moment. Quite apart from the fact that you have to return the money, your life is in danger. And there have been deputy attorneys general jogging around the park in Mexico City who got gunned down. There have been prison wardens gunned down in front of their homes. It could also happen that you take the money and do the "favor," and when you leave the job they demand that you return the money, even though you came through on your part. And if you don't return it, you die. If you don't share the money you received, you're in danger from your superiors or your colleagues. And finally, if you do a favor and someone from a different group—not a rival group, just a different one—asks you to do the same favor for him and you refuse, you're also putting your life on the line.

It should be mentioned here that during the years of PRI hegemony in Mexico, outgoing government officials generally rotated to another, similar position or retained sufficient contacts in government that it did not behoove criminals to demand the return of monies paid in the past. This changed with Mexico's democratization beginning in the 1990s, and the operating logic of the ties between criminals and officials has changed as a result.

Arguably, this shift began with the administration of Ernesto Zedillo, who took steps to dismantle the drug-trafficking protection structure that had been built up during the Salinas years. One of Zedillo's measures was to name an attorney general from a party other than the PRI. Another was the army's incorporation into intelligence tasks that, it was anticipated, would lead to the arrests of drug traffickers. Further, the Federal Law against Organized Crime was passed during the Zedillo administration, which included provisions for a witness protection program that aimed to encourage informants from within the criminal organizations to testify against other members. It was also during the Zedillo administration that SIEDO (the Organized Crime Investigations Unit) was created. This elite structure within the PGR was specifically designed to dismantle the ties of corruption in the state's security apparatus.

Such measures allowed for certain advances in dismantling the corrupt networks protecting drug traffickers. Indeed, several high-level military figures, even some who had been deemed "untouchable"—were indicted for protecting drug traffickers. Division General José de Jesús Gutiérrez Rebollo, former head of the National Institute to Combat Drugs (INCD), was imprisoned in February 1997 (on two 75-year sentences) for protecting the Amado Carrillo cartel. In March 1997, Brigadier General Alfredo Navarro Lara began serving a 15-year sentence. Brigadier General Jorge Mariano Maldonado Vega has been in prison since January 1998. Brigadier General Mario Arturo Acosta Chaparro and Division General Francisco Quirós Hermosillo were imprisoned in September 2000 after having been found guilty of providing protection to Amado Carrillo.

President Salinas's own brother, Raúl Salinas, who some informants identify as the architect of the political protection network for drug trafficking that was built up between 1988 and 1994, was arrested in 1995 on charges of masterminding the murder of José Francisco Ruiz Massieu, general secretary of the PRI, governor of Guerrero, *and* Salinas's brother-in-law. Raúl Salinas was also accused of money laundering by Mexican and foreign authorities.[15] Because he was accused of the same crimes in Mexico and abroad, the foreign authorities ceded the investigation and formal charging to the Mexican authorities—who proceeded to exonerate Salinas, over the objections of the Office of the Federal Attorney General.[16] In early 2005, following the assassination of Raúl's and Carlos's brother, Enrique Salinas de Gortari,

15 Swiss authorities discovered million-dollar accounts held by Raúl Salinas in that country's banking institutions and began their own money-laundering investigations. The official report presented by Carla del Ponte in late 1998 highlighted, according to newspaper reports, the former president's brother's participation in building the agreements that guaranteed protection of drug traffickers. http://www.jornada.unam.mx/1998/oct98/981024/transfirio.html.

16 http://www.jornada.unam.mx/1998/may98 /980521/exculpan.html.

in December 2004, a French warrant for the arrest of Raúl Salinas on charges of laundering drug money (issued on June 29, 2004) was made public, and the French office of Interpol sent a communiqué to all affiliated police forces for the arrest of the former president's brother (*Proceso* 2005).

Mario Villanueva, former governor of Quintana Roo and former member of the Zedillo cabinet, is in prison for his role in protecting the Amado Carrillo cartel (*Reforma* 2001). Another governor from that era, Jorge Carrillo Olea, was pressured to resign following his impeachment by the Morelos state legislature. He had been accused of protecting well-known drug traffickers from the Juárez syndicate, including Amado Carrillo himself. Although Carrillo Olea was never arrested or charged, some of his key subordinates in the security apparatus in Morelos were found guilty of protecting gangs of kidnappers operating during Carrillo Olea's administration.[17]

Amado Carrillo's organization, which enjoyed protection from high-level officials in the federal and state governments during the Salinas presidency, suffered important reversals during the Zedillo administration. The testimonies presented above indicate that the protection network had been established with the blessing of the central powers, who were in control of all lower-level authorities. But with the end of the Salinas administration, the central protection structure gave way, and the effect filtered all the way down to those who occupied local-level positions. The information presented above enables us to appreciate the impact that the loss of centralized protection had on the cartels. To wit, in 1997 Amado Carrillo was found dead, apparently the victim of inadequate medical care following plastic surgery.[18]

The other organization that had enjoyed substantial government protection during the Salinas period was the Gulf cartel, headed by Juan García Abrego. Without this protection, the syndicate's structure deteriorated rapidly, and García Abrego was arrested by Mexican authorities and extradited to the United States, the grounds being that he was a U.S. citizen and had violated Mexican immigration laws (PGR 1998, 91–92).

---

17 Among those arrested were former state attorney general Carlos Peredo Merlo and the head of the state judicial police, Jesús Miyazawa. See PGR press release o68/98, March 8, 1998, http://www.pgr.gob.mx/cmsocial/bol98/mar/b0006898.htm.

18 http://www.jornada.unam.mx/1997/jul 97/970710/presunto.html.

Under Zedillo, the Office of the Federal Attorney General issued arrest warrants against two officials who had headed the Federal Judicial Police during the Salinas years. One, Rodolfo León Aragón, was charged with protecting drug traffickers;[19] the other, Adrián Carrera Fuentes, was arrested and sentenced to six years in prison for money laundering.[20] Such actions damaged the central control of the drug trade that had been established in key positions of the state apparatus. Though the central structure collapsed, many of its participants sought to continue operations through local agreements. It should be emphasized once more that the centralized control of drug trafficking by top-level public officials was dependent on the capacity of political decision makers at the highest levels to command the main security institutions of the Mexican government as they chose. Once this central protection structure gave way, the focus shifted to local agreements, which constituted a gradual shift toward an *atomized-multidirectional* model in the articulation of relationships between public officials and organized crime.

A DECENTRALIZED MODEL OF ORGANIZED CRIME–STATE RELATIONS

The centralized-hierarchical ties established during the 1988–1994 period sought to avoid the notoriety that characterized the conspiracy links established in the early 1980s. Therefore, the powers that were capable of establishing the rules and ensuring compliance with them were not formally involved in the operation of the drug trade, and it was their designated subordinates who guaranteed drug traffickers' operations through the protection networks. Under these conditions, the drug kingpins did not appear to be linked to the upper echelons of power, but de facto they were subordinated to the general operating conditions imposed on them by political actors. Failure to adhere to these conditions would lead to their exclusion from the drug trade. This

19 Rodolfo León Aragón, director of the Federal Judicial Police from 1991 to 1993, and some of his subordinates, were subject to arrest warrants issued by Federal Judge Olga Sánchez Contreras. Nine of these warrants were annulled by the First Collegiate Tribunal in August 2004. www.eluniversal.com.mx.

20 Adrián Carrera Fuentes was arrested by the PGR in March 1998 for crimes against health [drug trafficking], money laundering, and bribery in 1994 and 1995. In his statement, Carrera Fuentes admitted receiving more than a million dollars from the Juárez cartel between 1992 and 1993 to protect drug shipments from Colombia (La Jornada, September 1, 1998, and October 14, 2000). He later entered the witness protection program.

is the factor that led to the portrayal of drug traffickers as independent forces capable of unilaterally infiltrating the government apparatus, especially security institutions. Their almost limitless economic resources and their capacity for violence suggested that it would be very difficult to subordinate them to a single political entity, no matter how powerful. However, the protection agreement under which drug traffickers operated did have to be established from the top down, given that only a centralized structure for the exercise of violence—the state—could ensure compliance with the rules under which the illegal activity would function—price setting, protection payments, and so on. As one source pointed out:

> Whoever was capable of establishing the model controlled everything.... He said, "these are the rules." And those were the rules. And that's how things worked from 1988 to 1994.

To be in charge of the national security structures whose mission was to combat drug trafficking also conferred the ability to build a broad, efficient, and stable network of protection for the drug trade. For this structure to be profitable and for the drug trade to survive despite pressure from the U.S. government and negative public opinion, it was necessary to maintain the illusion that these very same institutional structures that were actually protecting the cartels were committed in their battle against drug traffickers. The disputes between lesser-ranking officials of various federal or state agencies, their arrests for participation in drug trafficking, and the execution of some of them sustained a public image of a continuing war by the state against drug cartels and against the traffickers' supposed attempts to infiltrate security institutions. According to the testimonies of my informants, the upper echelon of decision makers protected drug trafficking as a whole, even if this contravened the interests of certain officials and criminal organizations. However, when the central control structure gave way, no institutional figure or member of the political class had sufficient executive power to force the different parties to observe fixed rules, not even informal ones, or to adhere to conditions set under the previous arrangement. The new protection agreements were established with local authorities or with relatively marginalized federal officials. In this context it was difficult to establish general operating rules for the drug trade. No current public figure had sufficient institutional coercive capacity to force the drug kingpins to accept his conditions. Therefore, with the dissolution of the centralized structure of protection, the rules and agreements would have to be more fluid, as is postulated in the atomized-multidirectional model.

Agreements between public officials and criminals are necessarily precarious. The clandestine nature of such ties and the fact that they imply extortion by officials do not favor institutionalization or permanence. In general, their continuance is the product of the correlation of forces at a given period. When state institutions can significantly regulate the actions of various social actors, it is often the officials (in an abstract sense) who have the capacity to mobilize public resources to establish general (informal) rules under which the illegal business operates. This does not depend on personal qualities, but rather on the possibility of employing institutional resources—in this case, coercion—for a different purpose than the officially established one. Thus, when the political regime in Mexico permitted the centralization of all federal or local security and justice structures and also guaranteed the exercise of power without checks and balances, the institutionalized power was able to impose its informal rules on organized crime. When the political regime changed, the capacity to exercise centralized control was weakened, and that modified the relationship between public officials and criminals. This is the fundamental factor that leads to a shift toward the atomized-multidirectional model in the late 1990s.

Even during the Salinas administration, criminal groups and public officials were already seeking ways to obtain additional benefits over and above the informal rules imposed from above. One of the informants noted:

> Every important *narco* wanted to control his own governor. And the governor who needed resources for his campaign, well, he was amenable.

Thus, the ties of conspiracy between public officials and criminals lost the centralized nature that had characterized them through the mid-1990s and continued into the following years. As one source observed with regard to statements in the national press concerning the protection that top-level authorities in one state provided to drug trafficking and other organized crime activities:

> Look, I'm talking about the city government where I live, in [state], where I worked as an undersecretary, where the drug trafficking, the protection of drug traffickers and car thieves, was controlled directly from the

> governor's office and the state government. It was in all the papers. I know for a fact it's true.

According to some observers, when Vicente Fox was preparing to assume the presidency in 2000, his team deliberately opted not to gather intelligence that would have provided a detailed view of the relationships of corruption in the federal and state political structures it would soon govern. This choice was made in the interest of maintaining a smooth transition between administrations. According to informant E, who had a privileged perspective on the transition process:

> The previous administration didn't provide any specific report on progress in the investigation of drug-trafficking gangs.... They left the case files in the Office of the Federal Attorney General, and they turned over the files on active cases, including ongoing investigations. But there was no government report as such.... It was a transition in which the incoming Fox administration, and Fox himself, did not want a violent transition or increased conflict. So he didn't ask for more investigations, he didn't ask for more detailed reports. He didn't ask for independent investigations. We just stuck to what they wanted to tell us.

According to this source, nor did the incoming administration request intelligence information from the United States:

> What the U.S. agencies told us was that they had no faith in the police and that there was complicity in some manner or another at very high levels, given that all the information ... they turned over to the Mexican government was very quickly known to the drug traffickers.... [But as to specific names], there were none, and we didn't ask. Fox didn't want to ask. He didn't ask the United States. We could have gone to the Americans and asked them what information they had on ... and I brought it up many times, but the Fox administration refused to do it. President Fox refused to do it.

Another source able to observe the transition at close hand stated there was an evaluation of the general aspects of public security and popular perceptions of the issue. He even referred to the adoption of a strategy to combat organized crime, but he made no comment on specific allegations of corruption of given individuals. He agreed with E in that the new government did not attempt to obtain alternate intelligence data, as from the U.S. agencies:

> The truth is that, during the transition, U.S. officials maintained their distance in terms of foreign policy.... During this period, as always, they were very reserved in making comments about internal politics in Mexico and the cabinet changes that would come.

All of this leads us to believe that the incoming authorities had a limited understanding of the political structure that protected the drug trade. This was confirmed early in the Fox administration when a notorious trafficker, Joaquín "El Chapo" Guzmán, escaped from a maximum security penitentiary. The Fox administration was apparently unaware of the level of corruption in the prison system and of the fact that "connected" prisoners could buy almost anything, including their freedom. The Fox administration's strategy of combating drug trafficking and organized crime is apparent in its tendency to rely ever more heavily on the military for this task. Under Fox, most Mexican security institutions had high-ranking military people in top leadership positions, reflecting the common belief that, despite some evidence to the contrary, the armed forces remain the strongest—and least corruptible—institutional pillar of the regime. One of the risks of involving the armed forces in the fight against organized crime, especially drug trafficking, is the potential this offers for increasing the level of corruption within the military.

It is very difficult to determine to what degree the protection structure still exists in federal security institutions. One source spoke about broad levels of protection that local security institutions provide to drug traffickers and hinted that this relationship is tolerated by high-ranking federal officials. Nevertheless, the conditions that characterize the new political environment seem to show a shift toward the atomized-multidirectional model in the structuring of linkages between public officials and criminals, and the disappearance of the earlier centralized-hierarchical structure. Paradoxically, the instability to which the Office of the Federal Attorney General was subjected during the Salinas administration and the pruning it has suffered since then have undermined its institutional capacity to centrally regulate the conditions under which the drug trade operates, as it used to do, according to informants' testimonies. Interview informant B explicitly states:

> You can't talk about the state's ability to regulate anymore. I think there have been important efforts—one must be fair—to reestablish certain institutional bases.... But the institutional command was deteriorating long before the transition to the new regime.

Several events since the presidential transition in 2000 have demonstrated a notable change in the correlation of forces between officials and criminal elements. There is evidence that the conspiracy has endured.[21] However, it is increasingly evident that the more important crime bosses are less disposed to unquestioningly accept the tutelage of officials in government. In August 2004 the deputy attorney general for the investigation of organized crime stated that the Gulf and Tijuana cartels, headed, respectively, by Osiel Cárdenas Guillén and Benjamín Arellano Félix, were concocting a plan to storm the La Palma federal prison and spring two cartel members (*El Universal* 2004a).[22] Two months earlier, this same official declared that these crime syndicates were offering more than US$2 million for the assassination of the attorney general (*El Universal* 2004c). In October 2004, in an unprecedented act, Osiel Cárdenas declared to a national television network (from a cell in La Palma) that the Attorney General's Office was combating drug cartels *selectively*, and only targeting certain groups (*Reforma* 2004).

In 2005, the execution of two drug traffickers being held at the La Palma penitentiary exposed the breakdown of the controls that supposedly made La Palma a high-security facility.[23] The PGR indicated that a broad network of corruption existed in

21 For instance, the 65th Army Infantry Battalion detailed to Guamuchil, Sinaloa, was dismantled in October 2002. General Ricardo Vega García, minister of national defense, admitted that 48 of the 600 members of the unit had links with drug trafficking (El Universal 2002).

22 There had already been an attempt in April to free Pablo Tostado Félix, who had links to Juan José Esparragoza, an important trafficker in Sinaloa (El Universal 2004b).

23 Several traffickers close to Joaquín "El Chapo" Guzmán Loera were murdered. One was his brother, Arturo "El Pollo" Guzmán Loera, killed on December 31, 2004; another was one of his lieutenants, Miguel ángel "El Ceja Güera" Beltrán, who was killed on October 6, 2004. Both were shot. See SSP press releases 284/04 and 405/04 (October 6, 2004, and December 31, 2005). www.ssp.gob.

the prison, and it detained several officials, including the warden (*La Jornada* 2005). Federal authorities decided to submit La Palma to military oversight, coordinated by the Ministry of Public Security.[24] Days later, it was decided to relocate several heads of notorious drug-trafficking organizations being held at La Palma,[25] and four days after that, possibly reflecting the drug kingpins' unwillingness to submit to the designs of public officials, six officials at the prison in Matamoros, Tamaulipas, were found executed within sight of that facility.[26]

The precarious position of public officials in the exercise of their official duties, including the subordination of criminals in their previous relationship, can be appreciated in the fact that the official designated to replace the warden at La Palma resigned just over a month after his appointment.[27] An official of the Ministry of Public Security claimed knowledge of a planned ground and air assault against La Palma, which he viewed as an effort to free Osiel Cárdenas and Arellano Félix (*La Crónica de Hoy* 2005). Whether one accepts that such a plan really existed, the various incidents related above are strong indicators of the shift from a centralized-hierarchical model to an atomized-multidirectional one.

The political confrontations that occurred throughout the Fox and Calderón administrations between various political forces, along with the breakup of several federal security institutions, naturally increases the attractiveness that local-level protection agreements hold for organized crime groups. They now have very strong incentives to enter into agreements with local officials or mid-level federal officials. The institutional breakdown that this implies, and the concomitant struggles for position that can be expected to emerge between different sets of allied officials and criminals—which are characteristic of the atomized-multidirectional model—bode

---

mx/application?pageid=pfp_sub_2&docId=2660.

24 SSP press release 018/05, January 14, 2005.

25 SSP press release 023/05, January 16, 2005.

26 SSP press release 027/05, January 20, 2005. The response of the authorities was to declare a maximum alert at all federal prisons and to place their immediate surroundings under military surveillance. SSP press release 029/05, January 21, 2005. It is noteworthy that Leonel Oceguera Jiménez, lawyer for Osiel Cárdenas and Benjamín Arellano Félix, was murdered the next day. The attorney had participated, along with the traffickers' family members, in marches in protest of the prisoners' relocation (El Universal 2005).

27 SSP press release 057/05, February 15, 2005.

very poorly for the consolidation of a liberal democratic regime in Mexico and may contribute noticeably to further eroding the Mexican state's hegemony over its national territory.

CONCLUSIONS

This chapter basically tells a story about the structure of corruption, as determined by the distribution of political power within the state. The relationship between organized crime in Mexico evolved into a highly centralized and hierarchical arrangement during the 1980s and 1990s. This transformation occurred in part because of shifting market dynamics as Colombian traffickers developed a thriving market for cocaine in the United States and established transit networks through Mexico. The fact that power within the Mexican state was highly centralized and hierarchical—thanks to the existence of a hegemonic party organization that governed virtually all political offices throughout the country—meant that the relationships between the state and organized crime reached the highest levels and were largely top-down. The gradual rise of Mexican criminal organizations required the explicit collaboration of high-level decision makers within the Mexican state. While the names and faces changed, the centralized-hierarchical nature of this relationship remained the same over the course of both the de la Madrid and Salinas administrations.

Shifting power dynamics and the gradual erosion of the PRI's political control began to transform the relationships between organized crime and the state. This has produced a more atomized and multidirectional set of relationships between organized crime groups and the state. While the links between organized crime and high-level officials persist, the current model of organized crime and corruption has proven more chaotic and less top-down. Criminals are more inclined to directly challenge the power of state actors in a way that was rarely the case under the centralized-hierarchical model. This suggests that the shift to democratic governance brings with it a more precarious situation, in which the integrity of the state is actually more greatly undermined.

President Calderón's strategy of outright war against the cartels is therefore an uncertain venture. Despite their decentralization, Mexico's cartels are extremely powerful, and their willingness to directly challenge the state has grown tremendously. The fact that they now infiltrate the state in a decentralized manner and from multiple directions makes it potentially more difficult to root out corruption.

Moreover, the feuds between different organized crime groups—which were once engineered practically by design by those at the top of the hierarchical-centralized model—now appear to be highly uncontrollable and a serious threat to the state's coercive capacity. The consolidation of Mexico's democracy hinges on the government's ability to regain the upper hand, not only in controlling organized crime, but ultimately eliminating its influences.

REFERENCES

Astorga, Luis. 2000. "Crimen organizado y organización del crimen." In *Crimen organizado y gobernabilidad democrática: México y la zona fronteriza.* Mexico: Grijalbo.

———. 2002. "The Field of Drug Trafficking in Mexico." In *Globalisation, Drugs and Criminalisation: Final Research Report on Brazil, China, India and Mexico.* Management of Social Transformations, UNESCO.

———. 2005. *El Siglo de las drogas: El narcotráfico, del porfiriato al nuevo milenio.* Mexico: Plaza y Janés.

Boyer, Jean François. 2001. *La guerra perdida contra las drogas: Narcodependencia del mundo actual.* Mexico. Grijalbo.

Craig, Richard. 1980. "Operation Condor: Mexico's Anti-Drug Campaign Enters a New Era," *Journal of Interamerican Studies and World Affairs* 22, no. 3 (August): 345–63.

El Universal. 2002. "Battalion Dismantled for Narcotics Links," October 15.

———. 2004a. "PGR Reveals Alleged Plan to Take La Palma," August 13.

———. 2004b. "Frustrated Rescue of 'El Azul' Lieutenant," April 14.

———. 2004c. "Capos Offer 2 mdd to Kill the Attorney General," June 16.

———. 2005. "Osiel Cárdenas Lawyer Murdered," January 21.

Estado Mayor de la Defensa Nacional, Antinarcotics Intelligence Center. 1995. "Avances en el análisis de la información sobre el narcotráfico en México." September 2.

Flores Pérez, Carlos. 2002. *Seguridad nacional y democracia en México: La redefinición de un concepto en un nuevo marco de convivencia.* Mexico: Universidad Autónoma Metropolitana.

González Ruiz, Samuel, Ernesto López Portillo, and José Arturo Yáñez R. 1994. *Seguridad Pública en México: Problemas, perspectives y propuestas.* Mexico: Universidad Nacional Autónoma de México.

La Crónica de Hoy. 2005."Yunes Confirms That Osiel Cárdenas and Benjamín Arellano Planned Air and Ground Attack against La Palma," January 27.

La Jornada. 2005. "PGR Places Former La Palma Warden and 4 Officials under House Arrest," January 9.

National Narcotics Intelligence Consumers Committee. 1980. *The Supply of Illicit Drugs to the United States from Foreign and Domestic Sources (UIT Near Term Projections)*. Washington, DC: U.S. Government Printing Office.

PGR (Procuraduría General de la República). 1998. "La lucha de México contra el narcotráfico. (Reducción de la Oferta)." Mexico: PGR. December.

Proceso. 2005. "Order from France: Capture Him!" No. 1494 (June 19): 10–16.

Reforma. 2001. "Former Governor Mario Villanueva Arrested, in Cancún," May 25.

———. 2004. "Osiel Accuses PGR of Blackmail," October 19.

Ruiz-Cabañas I., Miguel. 1993. "La campaña permanente de México: Costos, beneficios y consecuencias." In *El combate a las drogas en América*, ed. Peter H. Smith. Mexico: Fondo de Cultura Económica.

Shannon, Elaine. 1989. *Desperados: Los caciques latinos de la droga, los agentes de la ley y la guerra que Estados Unidos no puede ganar*. Mexico: Lasser Press Mexicana.

The Weaknesses of Public Security Forces in Mexico City*

Elena Azaola

This chapter outlines some results of an ongoing study begun in 2001 on the preventive police in Mexico City. A key goal of the study has been to give voice to police officers so as to understand their views, their perception of their job, and the obstacles they face when doing their work. The premises upon which the study is based are: (1) that police officers must know about and be willing to carry out any police reform project if it is to produce deep changes; (2) that if reform is to have the backing of the police, it must take their needs into account and respond to their problems; and (3) that to know and understand the problems that are most important for police officers, it is necessary to listen to their points of view.

The study included gathering and analyzing the testimonies of over 250 police officers in all ranks of the hierarchy. Half of these were obtained in interviews at police headquarters; the remainder comprises autobiographical writings by police officers of different ranks and career lengths that describe their lives as policemen.

The preventive (street) police in Mexico City totals seventy-six thousand officers. Half are considered employees of the Ministry of Public Security (Secretaría de Seguridad Pública, SSP). The other half (auxiliary and bank police) have an irregular status such that, although they are members of the force, their labor rights are not fully recognized and they operate autonomously and according to arbitrary and not very transparent criteria. Of the total, including auxiliary forces, 80 percent wear uniforms and 20 percent (the traffic police or *policía de vialidad*) dress in brown uniforms. Even though not all members of the traffic police have access to a patrol car or motorcycle, belonging to this force and wearing a brown uniform is considered a privilege, because these officers have the opportunity to extort people who have committed traffic violations. The income these officers receive from extortion far outstrips their wages.

*This chapter is based on a paper presented at the seminar "The Challenges of Criminality for Democratization and the Rule of Law in Latin America," Oxford University, June 17–19, 2004.

MAIN FINDINGS

It is well known that there is widespread dissatisfaction with police performance among Mexico City residents. It is perhaps less known that there is also deep and widespread job dissatisfaction among the police. There is a high level of uncertainty because norms are not consistently applied. There is also widespread vertical (inter-rank) and horizontal (inter-pares) distrust within the police, which constitutes a significant obstacle to their best performance. Because norms and procedures are not consistently applied, a parallel informal or paralegal regime governs relations within the force. Deplorable working conditions have also generated a sense of abandonment or lack of protection among police officers, leading to their growing loss of interest in properly fulfilling their duties. Another important problem is what the rank and file describes as a continual lack of citizen respect and recognition.

Several recurring themes emerged in the interviews conducted and autobiographical writings consulted during the course of this study. The first involves problems related to deficient working conditions. Another is the problem of corruption and the way in which police address the issue. Others were relations with police chiefs, negative self-images and citizen images of the police, lack of training and the problems that resulted, officers' perceptions of their treatment by the institution, and alcohol and drug consumption among officers. The following section draws on a small sample of the testimonies in discussing these issues.

Deficient Working Conditions

A set of issues that police officers often mention relates to deficient working conditions (low wages, long work shifts, lack of promotion). There is broad consensus on this point, though there are nuances depending on rank, seniority, or the sector or group to which an officer belongs.

Wages

There is broad rank-and-file dissatisfaction with wages, and officers of all ranks say that low pay promotes and even justifies corruption. They also affirm that poor police performance is linked with low wage levels:

> Our society doesn't place any value on this job. In any other country, a policeman is well paid, but a policeman is not well paid here, so he can't do his job properly.
>
> To decrease corruption, they would have to pay us a good salary. They pay us 3,000 pesos per two-week period, minus deductions.... This is not enough for a family.... Without a living wage, we look for another way to get ahead.... If we got a decent wage, we would do our work more carefully and we would not take a risk just for the 100 or 200 pesos that drivers give us.

Strange at it may seem, some police officers have even suggested that their employer should help them to find another job if they cannot pay them a better wage:

> I think a policeman should be helped, or the institution itself should help him, to find an extra job, to improve his living standard.... I would like to be called into the office someday and learn that they would find us another vocation other than this one of being a policeman, so that there would be more opportunities for the people who have a real service vocation.

The rank and file also express dissatisfaction because the rules and procedures that would make their jobs more secure are not consistently applied. There is a lack of recognition for their work, there are no other incentives and benefits, and many promises made to them are never fulfilled. Thus one major cause of discouragement is that police officers never know what they can count on:

> The main problem is a sense of resignation and disillusionment because they feel defrauded; so many promises, for whatever reason, are never fulfilled.... We need clear rules for this to work properly ... rules that prevent a corrupt officer from becoming a chief. Recognition from higher-ranking colleagues is very important when good work is done. We are lacking in self-esteem, to the point of sometimes entertaining thoughts of suicide because we feel that no one cares about us as human

> beings. We need people to listen to us and to take an interest in what is happening to us.

As these testimonies show, the problem is not just that policemen are poorly paid, but also that their efforts are not valued or appreciated and that they are not able to express their viewpoint. They repeatedly stressed the need for their superiors to listen to them and take their opinions into account. Indeed, they describe many situations in which a superior's failure to recognize good work discouraged them in future efforts.

Equipment and Uniforms

Police officers are almost unanimous in their discontent over their shoddy uniforms and the lack of equipment:

> We lack equipment because of corruption at the higher levels. They haven't given us uniforms for two years.... We have to buy our own bulletproof jackets. The quality of the uniforms is very poor, and we're not given good equipment.

Police do not receive the minimum equipment necessary to do their job properly. Worse, police officers are required to pay for much of what they do have, including access to a weapon, motorbike, or patrol car. They also must pay if they want to work in certain—less dangerous and more "profitable"—areas. According to the testimonies, police are also charged for bullets, flashlights, batteries, and patrol car maintenance, costs they choose to incur rather than forfeit their access to "extra income":

> We have many unmet needs. We have to buy our own flashlights, batteries, everything we need to patrol. We know we have to buy some things, but we can't afford to buy our own uniforms only to have them stolen.
>
> The top administrative ranks have not given us uniforms or official credentials for over ten years. The majority of criminals have better weapons

> than ours. We even have to pay for our bullets. They charge us 10 pesos, and most of the time we just shoot into the air to scare people.

It is interesting that the inadequacy of the uniforms is mentioned more frequently than the lack of equipment. This is because the uniform is a large part of what constitutes the police identity. Indeed, the identity of the police seems to be intertwined with or represented by the uniform, which is why police officers are offended when given a uniform of poor quality.

> I want to go on serving in this uniform and thus honor the name of the police.... This uniform is my life; I am not ashamed of being a policeman.... I love this uniform and wouldn't change it for anything in the world.

Work Hours

The police workday is a common cause of complaints from higher (superintendent) and mid-level ranks (officers and inspectors):

> We get no time for family or a social life.... We haven't had a holiday for over fifteen years. Many of us are single because we destroy any chance of having a family.... We don't get to see our children grow up. Sometimes we see what we gain, but we don't see what we lose: family and health.

> We get up at 4 o'clock in the morning and get home at 10:30 at night, irritable and exhausted.... Everything on the street is noise and confusion.... We just want to get home so we can relax. The family sees us from 11 o'clock at night until 4 in the morning.... We can't even enjoy our family.

> Chiefs and supervisors should only work eight-hour shifts, not the long hours that we do, because it feels horrible to fall asleep the minute we get into the patrol car.

> We never get holidays, never. We haven't missed one day of work in seven or eight years. If you've got a position in the structure, that means you can't miss work, get sick, nothing. If we get sick, we're fired.
> We're always at work at 5:30 in the morning, and we're there till 11 at night. So the people who run the ministry are exhausted. A mid-level officer is not allowed to go on holiday or take sick leave. This is an attack on the family, not only on the officer, and this breeds discontent among the commanders.

Although excessively long work shifts appear to be a greater source of discontent among the upper ranks, there are many reasons why it should concern policemen who are not in leadership positions. One reason is that their place of residence is not taken into account when sector or group assignments are given out. The failure to consider the length of a police officer's commute to and from work can extend his or her workday by up to four hours. Indeed, policemen are not allowed to request reassignment based on the distance between home and work. Another consideration that can prolong the workday is the fact that police officers are sometimes punished with between eight and thirty-six hours of arrest for minor infractions (such as not wearing their helmet) or based on an arbitrary decision by their superior. Even when police officers say that these problems have eased, they still claim that conditions are seriously out of compliance with clearly established rules and procedures.[1] Indeed, almost every policeman included in the study claimed to have been subjected to unjustified arrest.

The police also expressed unhappiness with the food served at police barracks or provided to them when they are working on the street. Another complaint was their inability to attend to their most basic needs while at work. Many policemen said their superiors were indifferent to their basic needs, and the same was true of citizens, who criticize them for eating in public—to the point that the police feel their humanity is not recognized:

---

1 Article 42 of the 1993 Law of Public Security of the Federal District, in force at the time of the study, states that "the arrest or detention suffered by a subordinate for significant misdemeanors or for accumulating five warnings in a calendar year" can last up to thirty-six hours. However, the law does not stipulate which kind of conduct deserves this punishment, which gives superiors ample margin for discretion.

> If you're a policeman, it's as though you're not human, like you can't go to the bathroom or eat. Citizens don't like it when they see you eating some tacos. When they see us eating, people shout at us, asking if that's what they're paying taxes for.
>
> There are no proper facilities at the barracks, no decent bathrooms, no dining room, no library.... The police wouldn't need to go out and get money to buy lunch if there was a dining room with even just coffee and bread. A person with a full belly would go to work happily.... If they want better security, they have to improve the barracks, the bathrooms, dining facilities. Otherwise, what condition are we in when we leave the barracks to go out on the street?
>
> There is something very fundamental: people have to realize that police are human beings, not robots. We can't work like robots.... Society doesn't take the trouble to think that we also think and feel, just like they do, that we are not made of steel, and that we are not supermen either.
>
> I would ask for more psychological support because sometimes we need to know that we matter to somebody.

The image of the robot, the machine, the superman emerges when police talk about their work conditions and their basic needs, and this clearly reveals their sense that they are treated poorly.

Promotions

Another leading cause of discontent is the failure to respect the procedures and norms that regulate careers and promotions. There is broad consensus about this within the rank and file (though not among the top ranks). Police testimonies frequently mention disappointment over a promotion not given even when all the stipulated requirements had been met. There are also references to innumerable arbitrary decisions that ignore the requirements in order to give jobs to family members, friends,

TABLE 5.1 Views of Working Conditions Among Police Officers, by Rank

Top Ranks	Mid-Level Ranks	The Rank and File
I've been on the job for 45 years, and I earn a good wage. I can't complain. Things have gone well for me, so what I have I owe to the police. I have not paid for my rise up the ranks; I earned it with my work. The regular policeman works an 8- or 12-hour shift, but we who have a post in the structure have no personal life. And because of my age and seniority, I hold on to this. I do my job carefully because it's the only thing that sustains me. If I retire, they give me a pauper's wage of 5,000 pesos, and I lose my rank. And do you know what this has cost us? Our life. It's harder to be a supervisor now because the rank and file don't show you the same respect as before. Arrests used to last 8 to 15 days, but not anymore. There used to be more discipline. They didn't know as much before, and now they read the regulations and know that arrests can only last 36 hours. They have lawyers advising them. We shouldn't let them be advised like this.	The street is a jungle; you have to cross yourself before going out. It's not our judgment but that of our supervisors that counts on the street, or we risk being arrested. For them everything is wrong. If they find us eating or if we go to the bathroom, you have to ask permission for everything. They don't care whether we get anything to eat or drink, they don't care what time we go home, so what rights has a policeman got? Only a few of us enjoy this job. We do it because we need to, because, as we say, where can we go at our age? I'd rather die here, go to jail, or get kicked out than be unemployed. We feel bad because there's no work security. If a new superior comes along, you might get fired or lose your position. Effort is not rewarded.	I took exams to get promoted, and they even gave a rank to people who failed. And those of us who passed were told there weren't enough posts. They tell me the same thing at every examination session. It would be better if they told me how much I have to pay for a rank rather than making me go around in circles. I've been in service for 22 years and have taken the exams several times. They always say the same thing: there are no open posts. They lower your morale and even lower your wages. They should be fair and not have preferences, because they promote their friends and their secretaries. It's traumatizing to be in service for so many years and always remain a lowly policeman. We're not given the chance to ascend by honest means. We have been here for so many years, and I haven't even been thanked. We don't even get the medals we used to receive every 5 years. Now they just give us 2 pesos more for every five years in service and 34 pesos as a "pantry" bonus.

Source: Interviews by Elena Azaola and Esperanza Reyes, Ministry of Public Security.

or recommended individuals, bypassing officers who have served for years without promotion.[2]

> There have been no promotion courses for ten years. I was promoted twice during the first eight years, but over the last ten years I have not been able to rise up through the ranks… There are so many obstacles, and you lose heart. When you prepare for something and you don't succeed, you get frustrated.… What has happened to all those promises?

> There are people who rise through the ranks because they have prepared themselves well, but others are promoted just because they're somebody's relative. Everyone wants access to a motorbike or a patrol car, but only the "chosen" get a chance. There are no places left for us except the mounted police or the foot patrol.

Various police testimonies mentioned a loss of motivation because of repeated failed attempts to make the rules work as they should; a lack of trust and a sense of insecurity when rules exist but are not obeyed; and a sense of apathy and paralysis caused by these situations. Table 5.1 compares opinions about working conditions according to rank.

Corruption

This section looks at the different explanations policemen give for corruption and examines some of the corrupt practices in which they engage. The simplest explanation offered for corrupt behavior is the low wages paid to the rank and file:

> Policemen are corrupt because what they get paid is not enough to live on.

2 At the time this study was undertaken, these norms and procedures were in the "Rules for the Establishment and Operation of the Career Civil Service of the Federal District Police" (*Gaceta Oficial del Departamento del Distrito Federal,* February 28, 1994).

> If they paid us a good wage, corruption would be solved. What happens now is that the fines we collect ourselves make up for salary we don't get.

In contrast, some people think policemen enter their profession because they intend to make money through corruption:

> They use the uniform to get rich; 95 percent of policemen come in with the idea that they will get rich.

Others blame corruption on the lack of institutional support police receive from the very outset of their professional careers. Some policemen mentioned that they came into close contact with corruption from the first moment they started basic training at the police academy:

> The instructors themselves were part of the hated corruption because some unethical teachers would sell exams and ranks, and some instructors would let people off when they were arrested—if they were paid enough.

> We went to the shooting range three times, but we weren't given any bullets. The teacher told us that if we wanted to shoot, we would have to pay him for the bullets.... This is when I realized that it is in the police academy itself that the spirit of corruption among the police takes shape.

However, others said corruption began when they were assigned to a specific sector or group:

> You get to the sector and your superiors begin to ask you for money. They force the police to get money off people. There are policemen who say that if they go out with five pesos, they have to come back with a thousand; that's what they say.

> As soon as you set foot in the sector, you get asked for money for everything: the uniform, notebook, not to get sent here or there, not to have to do this or that job, and most of all, for a patrol car.... As soon as you get there, everybody's got a hand out, asking for money. I pay if I've got it, because it's to my benefit.... There is consent at all levels.

The preceding excerpts from the policemen's own testimonies make the corruption issue blatantly clear, as are the elements common to all of them: the ease with which people admit their own and others' participation in corruption; the absence of legality as the frame of reference; and the acceptance of a parallel order or paralegal regime that governs the institution. One additional and striking commonality is the policemen's apparent sense of the inevitability of corruption, hence their failure to question it and their ultimate acquiescence. Some women police officers said they also participate in corruption:

> There is more corruption among the men than among us women.... We don't ask for money, but we accept it if it's offered. What happens is that we are not offered it as openly and unashamedly, because some of us get offended and kick up a fuss, though others don't.

Police who have held administrative posts also mentioned cases of corruption:

> There are a lot of irregularities. For example, according to a staff list, I had 1,200 policemen in my charge, but there were really only 200. The others were seconded to politicians, and I didn't even know them or have their files. The Mexico City government itself would grant them leave and would send them out with journalists, former presidents. It was a crime of diverting human resources.... Some were seconded for as long as fifteen or twenty years. I never knew where they were, but they had a rank and received a wage.
>
> Previously, some journalists and artists received the rank of police officer and would be paid a wage corresponding to their supposed rank. The wives of the police chiefs got rank and salary as well. So there were artists that were captains, colonels, and so on.

These statements demonstrate how ties of corruption link institutions through informal agreements that speak to the dominance of a paralegal order. This system operates on the basis of personal and political connections that include the upper and middle management of the police organization. In other words, at the margins of existing laws, a number of police have abandoned their public security functions in order to protect the private security of civil servants and their family members, members of the governing party, friends, or journalists. On the other hand, there are groups within the police—such as the motorcycle or vehicle patrols—that are especially envied since these assignments are seen as providing the best "income." Assignment to these groups is reserved for relatives or people recommended by the chiefs.

> Patrol car duty brings in quite a lot of money.... Some colleagues opt to repair their own patrol cars or buy parts when the cars break down, because if they wait for them to get fixed through official channels, they stop earning.... They know that it's better to invest their money in the institution than in any other business.... In the police, if you invest you can reap juicy benefits, although some of the fault lies with the public, with people who don't report the corrupt practices.

> We pay 100 pesos not to come to work, 500 to ride in a patrol car. I could go on like this, listing the infinite number of corrupt practices that exist within the institution of the police.

Some policemen hold their chiefs responsible for corruption. Several mentioned what is known as "The Brotherhood" ("La Hermandad") among the chiefs:

> The top ranks are part of a power group, the so-called *hermandad*, that doesn't allow trained young policemen to take leadership posts. They say that the high posts have cost them years of service and money too, and they don't think somebody should rise up through the ranks without paying the price. They own this ministry, and between them they rotate across sectors with the help of a godfather (*jefe halcón*). There have been sector chiefs who have been removed for corruption but, instead of being punished, they were simply relocated to another sector.

> The famous *hermandad* has to end. That mafia does so much damage to the institution and does nothing except to rotate through posts.... But a chief has never been fired; that really would be a notable thing.

> We all go into the force wanting to be good policemen, but our aspirations are cut short by some chiefs who, instead of supporting us, send us out to work so that they can demand kickbacks from us.

> All of us who have been career officers get caught up in the game of receiving money [from the people] and giving money to the commander in exchange for privileges.... It's a chain that reaches all the way to the top.

The preceding excerpts point to a second reason for corruption, one that is at odds with the suggestion that corruption is the result of inadequate wages paid to the rank and file. These quotations suggest that corruption appears because of the pressure that the top ranks put on lower-ranking officers to raise money for them. This behavior pattern is also seen as immutable, even though most of the interview respondents report that, in one way or another, they are victims of such a system. Others mention that ranks can also be bought and that many people became chiefs by paying for the post:

> There are still personnel whose ranks were given or bought during past administrations.

> That is the first link in the chain of that old corruption; everything has a price.

> Here you can ascend via your wallet, by buying posts. I have never had the chance to do that because you also need connections in high places, and I've never come across any influential people.

A third form of corruption is to earn money by protecting criminals:

> One thing that facilitates corruption is fear, because when we get a criminal, we know who they are and we know they'll get out and maybe offer us money in the future.... And since wages are really low and we don't get promoted, well, sometimes we take it.

Still another source of corruption involves the distribution of benefits. For example, there is a lottery system for helping police get homes, but the system does not operate on the up-and-up. Several policemen testified that it is often the police chiefs who win the lottery:

> Here the police don't ever get houses, but they say there are police chiefs who have three or four apartments that they got by "winning" the lotteries.

Another corruption problem that is frequently mentioned is the management of the police savings bank, a problem that has not been resolved despite having been the subject of a criminal investigation and prosecution a few years ago.

An additional approach to explaining police corruption stresses the willing participation of the citizenry in corrupt practices, although in some cases the emphasis on citizen responsibility appears to be an attempt to exonerate the police. In addition, some police gloss over corruption, saying it is not that they extort, but rather that citizens give them "gifts" to show gratitude and appreciation for their services:

> Corruption is often the fault of citizens who offer us money to sort out a problem. Other times it is a gift because they are grateful for our work.... So we don't know if it's right or wrong to accept what citizens give us out of gratitude.... I don't think there is anything wrong with it; it's not as if we extort them.

> People think that all police officers are corrupt, but corruption starts with the citizens because it's easier for them to speed up their business and save time by "greasing the wheels" with cash. The government allows many things. Corruption is rampant, and since we don't get good social benefits because of the economy, the policeman allows himself to be corrupted.

> I would like to ask citizens and the media: why are they so keen to put the blame on us if there is corruption everywhere in this country? [Even] several government authorities and leaders have stolen money from the Mexican people.
>
> There are others who steal millions and get immunity. But when a policeman steals four pesos, he is persecuted.

The preceding statements are cause for great concern because they seem to suggest the following: If the politicians can steal, why shouldn't the police do the same? If politicians can engage in corruption with impunity, why shouldn't the police benefit equally? Pointing out that others are corrupt seems to be an attempt to justify or minimize police corruption.

There is also a widespread view that it is not possible to put a stop to corruption or even to address it with any degree of success:

> Corruption within the police is an evil that cannot be rooted out.... At the rank-and-file level, as long as a policeman is efficient, corruption should not be seen as a negative.
>
> People say that if we were better paid, we'd stop extorting bribes. I don't think so; there would still be extortion money, plus the higher wage.

Finally, some policemen suggest that corruption is not just part of the relationship between police and citizens, but that it also profoundly alters the relationship that police officers have among themselves:

> There has to be discipline, but corruption breaks the chain of command because we can't look at our chiefs in the same way after we've given them money and they've accepted it. If I am going to apply corrective measures to someone for not doing their job and if the chief has received money from that person, then he will not be able to apply that corrective measure because the subordinate will not respect him anymore. That is how the chain of command is lost, because of corruption.

Thus corruption not only alters or subverts the relationship between police and citizens, but it also irremediably distorts relations among police officers. The statements collected in this chapter suggest that most policemen cannot escape corruption, a fact that both discredits them in public opinion and undermines police self-confidence. If chiefs ask their subordinates to pay "dues" and the latter, in turn, ask citizens to do the same, if someone is suspected of having bought their rank or post, if everybody knows about their colleagues' corrupt behavior, then nobody is immune and nobody can trust anybody else or be trusted by anyone else. This is perhaps the greatest weakness afflicting the police.

This being the case, corruption is probably more damaging to the police than to citizens. In other words, it is clear that policemen cannot escape corruption, which leaves them exposed, makes them vulnerable, and weakens their capacity to carry out their duties properly. It is as though they are unable to act other than from a position of vulnerability, a state that does not allow them to escape corruption—their own, that of their chiefs, and that of their peers. In such a situation it would appear that the only way to counteract this vulnerability is to subscribe to a tacit pact that obliges policemen to protect themselves and cover up for one another. This pact, however, can at best establish a precarious equilibrium, one that is under constant threat of breaking down. This explains the growing numbers of policemen who have been reported, are being investigated, or are in prison.

As regards corruption among the citizenry, the procedures in place to ensure compliance with traffic laws appear to be so ineffective that it seems to be to everyone's advantage—even if only in the immediate term—to break the rules and then seek a resolution through corruption. What is needed to address this problem is a set of procedures that encourages the public to obey traffic laws and also allows for the reestablishment of trust between the police and the citizenry.

Image and Self-Image

One issue that has received little attention in the literature is the self-image of the police. This issue is highly relevant, however, when trying to understand the way the police view themselves and think they are viewed by others. It is also important to determine whether perceptions differ, as, for example, between how officers view the police before and after entering the force and between how they think they are viewed by citizens and how they, in turn, view citizens. This set of "images" can tell us how police feel vis-à-vis everyone else, the perceived constraints on their work that are a result of their image, and the way in which this affects their performance.

Policemen's views on these issues can help us understand how they relate with others once they have adopted the policeman identity. Their views also help us integrate a subjective dimension (self-perception) with objective reality (relations with other agents or sectors). As we know, these two dimensions constantly interact with and condition each other.

Self-Image

Most of the statements presented below address the question of how individuals viewed the police before they entered the institution and how they see it and themselves now:

> Just hearing the word "police" would leave a bad taste in my mouth.... I thought that all these people did was to rob or extort people who had the misfortune of falling into their hands. Six years on the other side has not changed my idea of the police much. There is no end to the justifications, some very valid, others less so. But what is certain is that the police as an institution does not work as it should.

> Before I joined the force, my opinion was the same as the one many people have today. I thought that being a policeman was the worst thing, that policemen were crooks, extortionists. I thought it was degrading to be a uniformed police officer, that they were undereducated people. I was against the police in every way. After I entered the institution, I was insulted, attacked, even beaten by people who think just like I used to think.

> For civilians, the police have always been a source of fear, repression, beings from another world, illiterate, drunks, drug addicts, thieves, and on and on. I didn't think any differently then. When I saw an armed officer, I would think he was going to stop me so he could rob me or detain me in the police car.

> Before I joined the police, I thought they would be really rough during training, that they would make fun of me for making a mistake or because I'd not done well.

> The idea I had was that the police lacked academic training, which was apparent in the way they spoke; that they were careless about their appearance; that they were thieves and all the other labels society puts on us—abusive and even murderous.

> Before becoming a member of the police, I thought that being a policeman was degrading, that it was a job that was unworthy of the sacrifice I'd made to get my degree.... When I used to see policemen on the street, they never symbolized security. Instead, they inspired mistrust. However, economic need forced me to overcome my prejudices and seek admission to the mounted regiment.

> Initially, I had a deplorable and very negative idea about the police, perhaps because I had never had any dealings with them, or maybe because of their reputation for corruption and arrogance. But now that I've experienced the harsh conditions that a good police officer has to face, I realize how wrong I was.

> In my opinion, 80 percent of policemen are unhelpful, and only 20 percent want to serve society.

These statements provide insights to how policemen see themselves and how they feel they are seen by others. Taken together, some of the characterizations—policemen described as thieves, abusive, arrogant, ignorant, dirty, alcoholic, corrupt, rude, drug addicted, aggressive—illustrate the predominantly negative view people have before entering the organization. In some cases, that image became more positive with membership, and a majority of officers report that their perception changed somewhat. In other cases, policemen say that entering the organization did not change the negative image they held previously but only corroborated that image. It is relevant to ask what kind of relationship the police can establish with the citizenry on the basis of this self-perception, or even how they are able to perform with such a poor self-image. The following section addresses these questions.

Citizens' Image of the Police

Having looked at how policemen view themselves and how they think others view them, we now look at how policemen view citizens and what they have to say about the created image of the police:

> Everyone, from the highest politician to the lowliest citizen, uses the police as their shield for hiding the bad things they do. They say we are corrupt when, in fact, it is the citizen that is corrupt. The first thing he does is offer us money to get rid of the problem after he breaks the law.
>
> Citizens make demands of us, and I get angry because people complain, for example, that I'm a drunk. But they themselves don't start by changing things. It's not just the police who are corrupt, but also the citizen who is willing to bribe us. Corruption is bred out of necessity. Citizens do not support us; they shout at us, throw stones at us.
>
> I would like society not to stigmatize us because of our humble origins. It's true that we lack a certain economic status, but we do have a strong fighting spirit and enough courage to give our lives for someone that we don't know.
>
> I'm perfectly aware, I know the problem that surrounds us because of the pressure citizens submit us to.... I think everyone knows that we, the police, don't get support from any side. Everyone calls us thieves, conmen.
>
> As regards the citizenry, my experience, like that of my colleagues, is of aggression—insults and the classic threat that they'll have me put in jail just for doing my job. But even despite all this, I have a good view of society since, in the end, we're there to serve it.

> When we try to establish order, they insult us. They have no idea what it's like to spend eight hours standing at an intersection.... There are crazy people on the street that insult us for no reason. Sometimes you get into arguments with people... Sometimes you have to yell at people.

> According to society, we're the scum of the earth because they say we are evil and corrupt. It does not occur to them that we are part of that same society, and we are as corrupt as it is. The whole of society has lost its values.... It's not worth talking to a society that is more corrupt than we are.

In the view of the police, citizens are also arrogant, corrupt, and incapable of respecting the rules. It is as though the police feel they have become scapegoats, that they must purge the evil others do. Their anger comes across in many ways. They feel scorned, made to look ridiculous, abused. Some even express a desire to get revenge on the citizenry. Others are more resigned, as if they had no choice but to tolerate citizen abuse. Whatever the case, at least in the abstract their relationship with the citizenry seems to be characterized, if not by confrontation, then by fear of being insulted, scorned, and mistreated. It seems as though policemen have to engage in a dual battle when they go out on the street: one is the battle to combat crime, prevent accidents, and maintain order; and the other is to combat the citizens' distrust. Given the way citizens regard them, the police may have less motivation to offer them protection and security.

Institutional Image

The following statements refer to the way in which police view the institution to which they belong and how they see themselves as members of that institution, as well as how they believe they compare with other police organizations throughout the world:

> We are at a disadvantage internationally, but only in terms of equipment and facilities, because in terms of courage, aptitude, what we call esprit de corps, we are at the level of any other country, if not in first place.

> I don't think we can compare with any international institution because we are so far below any you might mention, not because we have a low opinion of ourselves, but because we know our place and must try to overcome our situation and improve, so that someday we can be counted among the best police forces in the world.
>
> The SSP is among the best public security forces in the world. What we lack is better training to optimize our performance, legal support when we carry out our duties, and a better quality of life for police officers through better salaries and benefits.
>
> I think that there are some serious deficits in the police corps in Mexico, not only economic deficits—infrastructure that would enable us to be better equipped, trained, to be professionals when combating crime—but also deficits related to culture, conscience, commitment, loyalty, and honesty.

These opinions contrast markedly with those in preceding sections. Although they recognize the institutional shortcomings that put police at a disadvantage in relation to counterpart institutions in other countries, there is also recognition of the strengths of the institution. Many of the testimonies highlight what policemen consider to be their greatest virtues: bravery, commitment, and esprit de corps, which for some compensate for the material insufficiencies and place them on par with police forces abroad. However, the elements that still dominate in the statements are the very high levels of tension and distrust between citizens and the police. Statements about how citizens devalue or denigrate them are a constant in their self-portrayals. What is clear is that whatever position the police adopt to confront that reality (identifying with the image that denigrates them, rebelling against it, alleging that this image is better applied to corrupt citizens, or expressing hope that police-citizen relations will improve in the future), their ability to perform their duty and to provide citizens with security and protection is currently compromised.

CONCLUSIONS

This chapter has focused on many of the obstacles that preventive police in Mexico City face in their efforts to fight rising crime. Among the most important obstacles are deficiencies and weaknesses in the police organization itself, which have become more apparent of late as demands on the institution increase. Regarding the challenges that crime fighting poses to democratization, it is clear that the consolidation of democracy and the rule of law requires more solid and better managed organizations, ones that enjoy higher levels of trust and credibility.

It is important to remember that in Mexico City there has been no comprehensive police reform process, but there have been gradual modest improvements in the right direction. Civilian control over police has been achieved to some extent, though efficient police administration is still lacking.

In terms of human rights accountability, this is an issue that is just beginning to emerge on the institutional police agenda, and the organizational changes to implement it have not yet been carried out. Only in the last decade did public institutions begin to supervise compliance with human rights. Human rights violations are the focus of many complaints against the police, and this is an area where there is strong police resistance to enhanced regulation.

Finally, we must keep in mind the difficulty involved in reforming an institution that has seventy-six thousand officers. There are immense obstacles to improving working conditions and developing incentive programs for officers. At the same time, constant changes in the leadership undermine serious efforts to create consistency. Designing new policies calls for high-level expertise, and the lack of experts in this area has been a liability. As for corruption, there has been a complete collapse of the mechanisms and procedures to ensure accountability at all levels of the organization. And there is no strategic plan in place to combat the culture of corruption and the transcendence of a paralegal regime within the Mexico City security forces.

Mexican Law Enforcement Culture: Testimonies from Police Behind Bars

María Eugenia Suárez de Garay

> *Order, security, police, and everything else aside: this could be the public's slogan regarding the surge in violence: But the louder they shout, it just means the more they have to hide.*
>
> —Yves Michaud.

This chapter presents results from several years of research on a still largely unexplored topic:Mexico's law enforcement culture. The relative obscurity of this subject is not surprising given that Mexico's police forces only recently attracted a high level of public attention —or, more precisely, notoriety— brought on by mounting frustration with corruption, brutality, inefficiency, lack of internal and external controls, and a general lack of professionalism. Casual observers offer an oversimplified assessment of the current state of affairs, seeing only a lack of will on the part of the police to implement radical reform. However, a more serious analysis of the various problems affecting law enforcement institutions in Mexico suggests that the problem is far more complex.

Analytical efforts to address this complex topic must be situated in an interdisciplinary "space" where the fields of communications, sociology, and anthropology intersect. It is in multiple disciplinary arenas that representations of identity are built and staged, and in which individuals talk about themselves and others. The police officer emerges from this space with a complex and multilayered identity that responds to and is shaped by often competing demands and expectations. In many cases, there is a divide between "what is preached" and "what is practiced," such that we can identify a distinctive law enforcement culture—with its own logic, language, and rules of conduct—that shapes the individual attitudes of police officers. This culture blends dual attributes: legal/extralegal, formal/informal, and visible/invisible. As Elster notes, institutions are not monolithic entities that convey and then carry out decisions from above (1996, 156). Rather, institutions are spaces in which culture also plays a role in determining behavior. Such spaces—or, more precisely what some might call practiced place[1]—are inhabited by "parallel" knowledge and practices which are not written down, but that derive from years of accumulated interaction and experience within police institutions (Vallespir 2002, 13). Law enforcement culture becomes another place in which to consider the various configurations and relationships that coexist within every social order and the margins of indetermination, negotiation, and even unvarnished opposition between social subjects. In other words, the culture within police institutions reflects many of the larger cleavages, tensions, and constraints within a given society.

How can we access the symbolic content of the police culture? How can we access its complexity? An analysis based solely on media reports would restrict us to stories of death, blood, and pain (Reguillo 2004, 261), which lead the citizenry to conclude that Mexico's police are a scourge in society. On the other hand, drawing only on statements by police officials would mean disregarding many of the harsh realities presented by the media, which has been so important in the production and reproduction of the understanding shared among the citizenry (Conde and Rodríguez 2002, 93). In this chapter, I attempt to tease out the complex of elements that constitute police culture by drawing on various representations culled not only from media accounts and official doctrine but also from interviews with the subjects themselves. In the process, their testimonies elucidate the patterns and practices that produce and reproduce police culture, and illustrate the tension between formal and informal logics and the points at which they intersect.

POLICE CRIMINALITY

As Donnelly and Shirk discuss in the introduction to this volume, Mexican citizens have witnessed a seemingly endless pattern of crime and violence over the last decade: the settling of accounts among rival crime syndicates; murders of suspected drug dealers in prisons, while other traffickers are broken out of jail; a trail of murders of women in Ciudad Juárez; and thousands of robberies, rapes, and kidnappings across the country every day. Official discourse about the increase in criminal behavior has implied a polarization between "us" (the good citizens) and "them" (the criminals) (Stanley 2001, 242), which in some cases has led citizens to "take the law into their

---

This essay first appeared in Spanish in *Politics & Society* [Universidad Complutense de Madrid] in 2005.

1 The concept of *practiced place* was developed by Michel de Certeau (1996, especially part 3).

own hands." A particularly bloodthirsty expression of such vigilantism occurred on November 23, 2004, when more than three hundred residents of San Juan Ixtayopan, Tláhuac (a municipality in Mexico's Federal District) burned two men alive and severely injured another after the three were allegedly caught photographing children outside a neighborhood school. Not only were these "criminals" not intending to kidnap the children, as the parents claimed; they were agents from the Federal Preventive Police who reportedly were investigating drug trafficking. Their explanations went unheard. Videotapes confirm that while they were being beaten, the three men did indeed identify themselves as police officers.[2]

This incident brings to mind Carlos Monsiváis's dictum: "If we do not take justice into our own hands, we will have neither hands nor justice" (1999, 36). Yet the public perception that the state has failed in its duties to society is clearly exacerbated when the institutions charged with protecting and preserving public security are the very forces that undermine it. Mexico's law enforcement institutionsare the principal protector of society but also tarnished by the commission of criminal acts and violence against that same society (Suárez de Garay 2004a, 32). The events in Tláhuac reveal the profound hatred of what the police represent and thus help explain the viciousness with which the police were beaten and murdered. These events also uncover the other face of the collapse of the public security system: the breakdown of the police. Even when attempting to "fix" a problem, the police are always under suspicion of responding to the "other side of the coin" in the set of double attributions, where illegality trumps the legal structure (Vallespir 2002, 13).

The foundation of the current police structure has evolved over more than seven decades of authoritarian rule, during which police loyalty to the regime was rewarded with the virtual impunity the police now enjoy, to the benefit of both parties (López Portillo 2003, 152). Nevertheless, it is not only the political system that is responsible for the current situation. Mexican society, characterized to a significant extent by clientelism and corruption, also forms a part of the framework in which law enforcement institutions have developed. Therefore, the police cannot be anything other than a part of the socially constructed totality in which multiple social processes are articulated.

2 Neither the Mexico City police nor the Federal Preventive Police responded to the incident in a timely manner. It was not traffic that kept them from reaching the scene (as they claimed) but ignorance, fear, and incompetence.

What is specific to the police, however, is that they inhabit a space with defined public functions, especially those that directly involve exercising the state's monopoly over violence. Their performance of these functions produces and reproduces a set of representations in society that often work to the detriment of the police. That is, when the police carry out functions that diverge from those assigned to them by law, the result is a law enforcement culture where priority is given to illegal activities: covering up crime, abusing authority, and failing to serve the public.

Vignettes from the national press help illustrate the contradictions and dilemmas surrounding law enforcement institutions in contemporary Mexico:

- In April 2004, José Agustín Montiel, coordinator general of the Ministerial Police of Morelos, was arrested, charged with directing a network of corrupt policemen that provided protection to the Juárez cartel (El Universal, April 12, 2004). Montiel was already under investigation in the death of a subordinate and because he was identified as a protector of drug traffickers in the criminal proceedings against Marco Antonio Yépez (Reforma, April 7, 2004). In response, Morelos Governor Sergio Estrada Cajigal, who had appointed Montiel to his post in the Ministerial Police, ordered the dismissal of all state ministerial police. They were replaced by 552 police academy graduates, agents from the Federal Preventive Police, and members of the military (El Universal, April 12, 2004).
- On June 14, 2004, the headline of the weekly Milenio Semanal read: "The kidnapping business, operated by police." Milenio reporters covering the II Congress of the Pan-American Federation of Private Security, held in Cancún on May 13, 2004, reported that "empirical data and specialized studies confirm that Mexico is the country where most kidnappings for ransom are committed and also the leading country worldwide in terms of participation by police and former police in the official judicial protection of kidnappers."
- In Jalisco, during that same month, State Attorney General Gerardo Octavio Solís stated that 120 members of his agency were the subject of an ongoing investigation (Público, June 20, 2004). Solís noted that, though his agency submitted would-be agents to a series of filtering measures—including medical, psychological, and personality exams, as well as background checks—sometimes a person who appears to be a good prospect "goes over to the other [the

criminal] side."In September 2008, El Universal reported that, in the states of Coahuila and Tabasco, Mexican federal authorities arrested dozens of law enforcement officials who were suspected of working for major drug cartels. In the case of Coahuila, the September 7 detentions stemmed from the arrest of a group of five or seven drug-trafficking suspects in Torreón. A team of city officers who were apparently working in collusion with the suspects engaged in a shootout with federal authorities. At least one of the police officers died during the gunfire exchange, and the rest were captured. Afterward, Mexican authorities identified the thirty-five police officers as suspected collaborators with members of the Gulf cartel (Barboza 2008).

- In January 2009, a special report by the Mexico City Reforma newspaper revealed that a total of 759 police in sixteen states were arrested in 2008, and most of them had ties to drug trafficking, according to a tally by Reforma. The numbers include officers from tiny rural police forces all the way to the chief of the Federal Preventive Police force, Víctor Gerardo Garay Cadena. Reforma found that the state with the highest numbers of detentions was the state of México, where charges were filed against 445 municipal police officers and 91 state agents (Reforma 2009).
- That same month two former directors of Interpol Mexico were arrested on suspicion of working with organized crime groups. The two officials, Rodolfo de la Guardia García and Ricardo Gutiérrez Vargas, were among a string of public officials detained through Operación Limpieza, which targeted public officials who worked with drug cartels. Both Interpol Mexico officials were identified as close collaborators with Secretary of Public Security Genaro García Luna. (González 2008).

When corruption within Mexican law enforcement institutions is made public and punished, it suggests a certain degree of transparency and accountability. Yet it also likely increases citizens' perceptions of insecurity, because it reveals the pervasiveness with which law enforcement institutions are corrupted. With the country's law enforcement institutions in disrepute, it is not surprising that a Mexican police officer appears as a figure of multiple coexisting moralities, and one the public regards with little trust (Suárez de Garay 2004b, 81).

The power of the police lies in their access to an arena in which they can act not only with impunity but with the legitimate authority of the state. Police criminality may range from taking mordidas (bribes), an act in which both the police officer and the "upstanding" member of society are complicit, to involvement in corruption and abuse of power on a larger scale: the unauthorized use of firearms, torture, kidnapping, and drug trafficking, among others. Yet, as Flores illustrates in his chapter in this volume, police can also extend their privileges to others, as illustrated when police establish clandestine linkages with organized crime networks. Giving police protection to criminals is extremely profitable, but it also gives an officer access to the inner circle of police complicity, that institutionalized system of impunity that supports the criminal activities that, paradoxically, the police have the duty to control and prevent.

In this sense, police corruption must be understood within the framework of relations, functions, activities, behaviors, beliefs, and rules that govern police life, and not as the product of anyone's individual nature. To blame the individual denies the significant role that the prevailing police culture plays within the institution as a whole. It is precisely that law enforcement culture—itself a reflection of institutional design, material incentives, and general societal norms—that can make sense of police actions, behaviors, and the manner in which officers fulfill their duties. The subalternity, inequality, discrimination, and exclusion that police experience on an individual level, both within and outside of the force, converge in their participation in corrupt practices. In other words, the culture in which police agents are immersed invites them to violate the rules, norms, and laws they are supposed to enforce. When, for some reason, a police officer's complicity in corruption is revealed and punished, they bear the burden of responsibility for the larger system of corruption in which they are involved. As illustrated above, in some cases they wind up behind bars.

Unfortunately, there are no accurate data on the number of former police in prison in Mexico, nor complete information on the crimes of which they were accused. An alternate source of information is the media, but we must bear in mind that the media image is tailored to its audience and contains very little detail about police officers who participate in crime, nor about their experiences or the meaning they give to their actions. Clearly, we need other sources of information that can provide insight as regards the criminal behavior of law enforcement personnel, the law enforcement world, and the needs and expectations of the people who inhabit it. My ongoing research on former federal, state, and municipal policemen currently imprisoned in Guadalajara for kidnapping, homicide, illegal weapons possession, and drug trafficking has given rise to a number of reflections about criminal law enforcement networks. In this discussion, I will limit myself to some preliminary insights about the criminal police world. To this end, I offer three sets of commentaries that may shed light on the world of police criminality and, from narrations of specific police experiences, may reveal its underlying meanings.

Armed

Police are characterized as being armed. This is literally true, in that they are men with guns, their weapon being both a symbol and an instrument of authority in the law enforcement world. Being armed means holding power, having the capacity to elicit fear in others at the same time that it guarantees one's own personal security (Torrente 1997, 54). But police are also armed in a figurative sense. That is, as members of the institution, policemen recognize the set of appropriate role behaviors, develop work strategies and skills, and keep adjusting themselves to the rules and values of the team and the institution itself. These processes are not rigidly predetermined. Rather, they imply a transactional interaction between the individual and the situation through a sequence of professional, social, and institutional adaptations.

For each policeman this implies changes in attitudes, values, behaviors, ways of thinking, and ways of interpreting the law enforcement environment. Although one's individual history will always exert some influence, once a person enters the shared world of law enforcement, he or she must internalize the law enforcement culture in which they are immersed. It is this culture that one applies in their everyday actions, adapting, modifying, and adjusting it as necessary. It is precisely here that we may be able to grasp how police identity takes shape in the intersection of two individual and group processes.

"Ricardo" is the pseudonym that I use for one of several imprisoned police officers I have interviewed in order to gain insights into police corruption. Below, Ricardo, a former state policeman imprisoned for kidnapping, recounts how law enforcement opened the door to another world, to the unknown, and to the unforeseeable:

> *Why did you decide to become a policeman?*
> I didn't exactly decide. At that time I had a relative in the police force, and he offered to get me in. I'd never thought about it! I was attracted to it, just like everybody else, but working as a policeman had never crossed my mind. But when you're young, you see them carrying their guns,

driving their patrol cars, well dressed, wearing jewelry. We'd see them. I started working as a laborer, and I was earning just over minimum wage. That's when they asked me to join the police and told me to "go for it." And just for the heck of it, I went to see what would happen, and they accepted me because I was recommended by the person who told me to join up.

Did you go to the police academy?
Yes, I went for three months.[3] They focus mostly on physical training. They give us some general ideas on what the job is about, but nothing more. Then reality hits and you say, "It's not like I was told at the academy." No, it's really rough out there. And at the academy they try to instill camaraderie more than anything else, because at first we're all strangers. Sometimes I'd see a smart mouth and say "fuckin' psycho." But a friendship would grow up little by little. When I graduated they sent me to the homicide division.

And what did you think?
Well, frankly, I wasn't thinking. I was just trying to assimilate because I saw them working. I would only see "tough guys," only older guys, with moustaches, sour-faced. Fuckin' psychos! Evil people! But I blended in at work little by little, and they started to accept me, to teach me. They made me work hard, but that's the only way I picked up some street smarts.

Ricardo's testimony reveals much about the recruitment, training, and daily life of a police officer in Mexico. He joins the police not by vocation but because it represents a better employment opportunity. The decision to become a policeman is not only due to his loyalty to the individual who puts him on the police path, but also to a generalized perception in which the value of law enforcement generates its own ambiguity: everything is possible. Passing through the academy does not mean that a trainee totally assumes the role defined by the institution and becomes a person

---

3 Police training typically lasts longer in other countries of Latin America; admission courses in Uruguay last four years and three years in Chile. In Mexico training lasts an average of four and a half months.

without judgment. Rather, the experience provides him with some of the resources to do his job, protect the common good, and ensure peace and tranquility. Nonetheless, the academy also represents a space in which the recruit comes to recognize the importance of camaraderie and the signals that say which values and behaviors will gain the approval of others.

The most important socialization into law enforcement life comes with the transition from police trainee to police agent. New recruits are immediately incorporated into established networks. This stage involves a significant, sometimes radical change for the individual officer, drawing a hard line between what was learned in the academy and the real world of policing, between what is preached and what is practiced. Above all, it is a period when the new recruit, alongside other policemen, learns the values and formal and informal norms that allow him to evaluate the environment and interact with it. "Bernardo," a former municipal policeman imprisoned for abusing his authority, recounts how the tacit understanding comes about:

> *What did you become aware of [upon joining the force]?*
> I became aware of the corruption; I learned that you can get your share. You patrol where there's money; there are areas where they pay you to be around. There are priority neighborhoods; influential people pressure the government for us to be there. But in the poorer neighborhoods, it doesn't matter if people beat each other up in front of the families. It's the other place that matters! They'd give money to policemen; not to me because I was a newcomer. That was in the beginning. Later they started giving me money and they told me, "This is your share"—for doing nothing!
>
> *And what did you say?*
> When they weren't giving me any money, I said, "I'm in just as much danger as you, even without touching one red cent, and I stand to lose, too." I was there! Afterward, when they told me, "Your share is this much," I'd answer, "That's fine." Over time you realize why they got paid and why they gave some of the money to you. It's all corruption! There are many things people are not aware of!

For Bernardo, reaching active duty status represented a point of inflection—a "before" and an "after." The behavior of others exerted a direct effect on him and on his possibilities for becoming a "good" policeman. He learned that the experience gained by the force as a whole over the years means opting for a different survival strategy, one in which the police close ranks and signal that no action is necessary, even when what is at stake could carry important costs for the police organization itself and the community it serves. For the new recruit, it gradually becomes clear that others in the institution adhere to the institution's legitimate purpose system at the very same time that they are betraying it. When one learns to recognize the possibilities that discretionary power brings, the police officer not only gets to perform his job "outside the margins," but he can position himself in the interpersonal dynamics inside the institution. The policeman learns the informal actions that are inherent to law enforcement and that require his discretion. It is not easy to enter and exit the game; there are codes that mark the entrance and exit points.. Access to the underworld requires an officer not to show inexperience, not to show naiveté in the practice of law enforcement. Once an officer has mastered the ability to control the margins of autonomy, he or she can aspire to become a trustworthy person.

Meanwhile, there are other dynamics that lend to the power and identity of the police officer. In Mexican law enforcement culture, individual identities are still heavily shaped by the traditional gender scheme. "Gilberto," a former federal policeman serving time for homicide, talks about the stereotypes and empowering gender dynamics of becoming a police officer:

> One starts noticing that it is a different kind of job, absorbing. You become aware of and recognize its advantages. For example, I was not a ladies' man. I was quite reticent in that area. I felt I was unlucky when it came to women, because I was ugly! But women are attracted to a policeman. Most women are attracted to power.
>
> *Did you start meeting women?*
> Women all over the place! You start seeing pretty women, ugly women, all of them at your feet. You see everything from a different perspective and say, "I'm down with this!"

While there is a growing number of women in the Mexican police corps, their presence on the force remains small. Hence the central place that "being a man" holds in the construction of the law enforcement "us" significantly influences relationships within the police and police relations with others. Masculinity is expressed by adhering to a script about the meaning of being a police officer. Other men's approval of "manliness" constitutes an element of expectation-evaluation, which is expressed physically and in opposition to the "feminine." Paradoxically, exercising an identity-related activity of the law enforcement "us"—be it rudeness, coercion, emotional control—presupposes not only an authoritarian mentality but also the acceptance of authoritarian practices that are essentially repressive in nature and are ultimately harmful to the individual officer himself. However, when a policeman has been primed with those teachings and logics, it is difficult for him to assimilate the validity of the rule of law for himself. If one accepts diversity and equality as primary social values, the policeman finds himself unable to contribute—given the social function he performs—to the creation of a peaceful society and of respect for the law and the rights of others.

Captive

The police are also sometimes characterized as being trapped, cornered, and paranoid. This should be understood not only in a literal sense, as in the case of the incarcerated police whose testimonies appear here, but also in a more profound and complex sense that relates to their state of mind in an institutional context where they are caught up in the web of corruption and abuse of authority that surrounds them. The policeman is "captive" because he is subjected to an institutional authority that condemns him to a conspiracy of impunity. Over time, the police officer gradually acquires the shared identity that modulates the being/doing of corruption and, because he re-creates it in his everyday actions, exposes a story of a conscious or unconscious learning. This dynamic lends itself to an inclination toward self-preservation in the performance of day-to-day activities and a permanent need to "save one's skin." Failure to express (at least tacit) complicity with the culture of corruption that surrounds them—or even going beyond the informally accepted parameters of that culture—may result in negative consequences for an officer.

In any police force, policemen are judged by their performance, by their capacity to assume risks and maintain self-control. Where corruption is institutionalized, however, police are distinguished by their knowledge and the secrets they have, and by their ability to play on two teams at the same time. These distinguishing classifications become codes that structure the interaction among the police and facilitate or constrain their possibilities for advancement in a given direction. This does not mean that their relationships in the ranks are permanently of an authoritarian, discriminatory, or arbitrary nature, but the codes that underlie their interactions are to a great extent dependent on the law enforcement culture that surrounds them.

The testimony of "Luis," a former federal police officer imprisoned for rape, shows that the use of coercion and violence is for some officers an everyday fact of their professional life and, indeed, a life-long pattern:

> We're archaic. I never liked to be beaten, ever since I can remember. I lived with my aunts, and they used to beat me. I joined the air force, and they beat me. I joined the police, and I see beatings all the time. I don't like to see beatings, but I had to see them again. I worked in an office, and the commander would interrogate detainees in the room next to my office. All I heard was beatings. They [the detainees] wound up admitting to whatever the commander wanted. Exactly as it's done today!
>
> *Did you ever question the commander about it?*
> Yes.
>
> *And what was his answer?*
> He said I knew how things worked. That I could either help him by preparing official documents or help him "warm people up" [beat them]. Well, I decided to handle the paperwork. It's tough! But when your mind and your heart get hardened..... After all I lived through in the air force! At least the police detainees just get a single beating. There [in the air force], it's almost every day! Besides, I used to think, "Well, they're committing crimes; they [the detainees] know how things work here. What the heck? They should take the heat!"
>
> *Did the commander feel he was being confronted?*
> No, he enjoyed his job. You could see it when he arrived in the mornings. Smoking. He was a classic, with ostrich leather boots, slim waist, jeans, his shirt open to show off a big gold medallion, his gun tucked into his

> pants instead of in a holster. He seemed to enjoy himself from the moment he saw the detainees. Bring them in, remove their handcuffs, and take them into the room. And if he didn't like what a detainee said, he would work him over. If the detainee had money and they could reach an arrangement, he wouldn't beat him. Afterwards a rookie who came into the force mimicked his way of working. He made that guy's workload lighter!
>
> *And did he accept that you wouldn't work that way?*
> Yeah, he did. He always accepted my boundaries. In fact, I wonder if it was a good or a bad thing, but everyone knew where I was coming from. They were aware that I knew a lot about weapons. So if they had any problems with weapons, they would come to me and I would help them out. That's why they respected me. They trusted my knowledge and respected that I did not want anything to do with interrogations. I have to admit, though, that I did wind up beating people sometimes.

Luis's comments portray the domestic side of the strong arm of the law. Arbitrary rules usually create problems for both the law enforcement institution and individual policemen. More and more citizens are denouncing arbitrary acts by the police, which can lead to the sanctioning or even termination of the officer involved. Yet the traditional patterns obviously remain in place, with police using subterfuge to cover up their non-application or countervention of the law. Thus there is knowledge among the police about how to beat people without leaving marks. Certainly the physical marks of violence can disappear, but not so with the threat they represent. When violence, in its myriad forms, becomes a widespread and everyday practice among the police, its seriousness becomes trivialized. And policemen are encouraged to view their interactions with others as areas over which to have dominion, control, and power. That vortex is inevitably dragging Luis from a position as witness toward one of being an accomplice, even while he censures the excesses.

That is the way force becomes law and violence becomes an everyday police practice. But there is also a violence that affects the policeman himself. "You cannot be weak," the police say. But not even the strongest can completely avoid the isolation that is also experienced in the ranks and can be summed up in another frequent comment: "You are alone." This points, on one hand, to traditional response mechanisms whose association with illegality, impunity, and corruption paradoxically convert the policeman into a vulnerable individual perpetually exposed to social scorn (Suárez de Garay 2004a, 46). On the other hand, it underscores the price of being immersed in a law enforcement system that is, more often than not, dehumanizing and depersonalizing. That is, not only is there a perception of "being alone out there" but also of being alone "in here," within the police force itself. Factors that are strong in Mexican police culture—the ambiguities of police roles, contradictory functions, the demand that one is always at the disposition of another, and poor labor conditions—all convey the certainty that there is no institutional protection. The resulting vulnerability usually leads to indifference, a lack of interest in performing one's duty, and the motivation to act on one's own (Suárez de Garay 2004a, 469). "Joaquín," a former federal policeman imprisoned for kidnapping, speaks eloquently from his own experience:

> I start saying, "enough is enough." I was upset. My ideas about right and wrong had been lost. I looked at my police ID and saw my photo and said: "Okay, I'm going to work for you." I go to meet José [the person who does his "dirty work"] and I tell him, "Look for a drug joint." He says, "I found one." We arrived at a pool hall and went in. We took the drugs, the money, and the pool hall owners. We kidnapped them! We put them in the van and took off. I took out my cell phone and said to the guy we'd kidnapped, "Do you want to call somebody? Call before we get to the station." He called and said that they were screwed, that they'd been caught, that he didn't know who we were but that we were taking him in. "We're federal officers," I told him proudly. "And if we don't make a deal real fast, you're lost." He asked me, "Does a hundred thousand pesos sound good to you?" "Make it a hundred and fifty thousand." "Okay." We arrived at the station and agreed to meet at a McDonald's to get the ransom. I sent José to pick up the money; we counted it and let the guy go. That's how we got started. Putting the screws to people; it didn't matter who. We started working like that! Any place drugs were being sold, we'd get there and mess things up. I'd take them to the station and rip them off there. I was that much of a cynic!

And how did you manage to hold them near the station?
I'd tell them, "If you raise your head and they see you're in the car, I'll have to take you in to the authorities." And that's how I operated!

How can we discover the elements involved in that fragile tension that makes a policeman lean toward upholding the law or toward violating the law? Joaquín clearly decided to act as he did based on individual autonomy. At the same time, he understands that his individual decision is a distillation, a reflection of the institution of which he is a part, which closes in upon itself and weaves an internal chain of complicity. Acting autonomously, for one's own benefit, becomes a strong motivation and part of the code of police life, though this display of free will still follows rules imposed by the institution to which one belongs. Cases like Joaquín's let us presume that illegal and criminal activities are known to other members of the force. The fact that everyone is aware of the corruption to some degree, that everyone else is involved in things of this nature, contributes to strengthening personal loyalties within the force (Martínez 1999, 19).

In other words, in the police culture, the institution allows commission of crimes when they are committed within the corporate framework and are of functional value to the law enforcement apparatus, but these crimes are punished when the motivation is one of individual benefit, particularly when members of the force betray the institution when "acting on their own" (Vallespir 2002, 47). In this context, breaking the internal discipline of the institution usually brings reprisals, sometimes disguised in legality and sometimes not. These can range from being given tedious assignments to being denied access to information, resources, and supplies; to being assigned excessive and arbitrary work shifts and heavy workloads; and all the way to humiliating and aggressive treatment by their superiors and co-workers. The "behind bars" condition becomes materialized in a radical way when police are apprehended and incarcerated. Andrés, a former municipal policeman serving time for rape, talks about the threat that such a rupture represents:

Did they beat you?
Yes, and my partner too.

What did they do to you?
The put a black bag over my head. They handcuffed me and rolled me up in a heavy mat. They knocked me to the floor and hit me. That's one thing they did! The other one is that while I was handcuffed they sat on me and stuffed a rag in my mouth. They'd pour water on me constantly. I felt like I was drowning. They had me there for about three days, and for one whole day they handcuffed me to a stool in a corner, and each time I tried to turn my head or say something … they would hit me on the head with a big book.

What else could they have done to you?
They murder people! I don't know about my partner. Maybe because he was younger, only nineteen, they got him to sign some statement they drafted.

Did they make you sign too?
They said, "Sign it." I told them I wasn't going to sign and then the commander told his boys, "He doesn't want to sign; take him away while." And they would take me and torture me some more. I really hated one guy, an effeminate guy. You can recognize them right away. And he says to me: "Anyone who winds up in Station 14 is fucked." And he even told me, "I'll make sure you guys get royally screwed." I'll never forget that guy!

Was he also a policeman?
Yes, he was with the minis-terial police. I'm telling you, even if you're not guilty, those guys can make you guilty, even when you're not!

It is no secret in Mexico that such uses of police violence have been developing over decades. It is commonly accepted that if one is faced with police brutality, the best thing is to submit to the implicit rules. What is dramatic in Andrés's case is that, when he refuses to sign the declaration prepared by the same policemen who are torturing him and forcing him to declare his guilt a priori, he discovers how the group to which he belongs can abruptly turn its back on him. This is indisputably a part of the amalgam that produces, reproduces, and legitimates that other, hidden, parallel order that characterizes police institutions: order-disorder, where the police are authorized to apply those "other" laws.

Distrustful

When policemen find themselves armed and behind bars, they become highly distrustful. The skeptical and pessimistic mind-set shared by many policemen is based on the distrust modeled from police culture, where no one dares to question the set of encapsulated norms and codes. Experience teaches a policeman a calculated sense of risk, but that sense has not only to do with concern about self-protection in the field. He is cautious above all because he knows that there is no institutional guarantee, no automatic institutional support. Adaptation to the "conditions of being a policeman" turns an officer into an individual with no rights. Even when laws and police regulations provide certain guarantees, unwritten rules compel police officers to watch what they say. "Jesús," a former state policeman imprisoned for drug trafficking, recounts how the distrust takes shape:

> Neither the institution nor the government takes much care in selecting personnel. The police ask, "Did you finish junior high?" If you say "yes," they say, "Join up; we need policemen." They do a count and toss out the ones they don't want. There's no loyalty in the police. And you're joining an institution that you don't respect from the start, and then you realize that the institution doesn't even respect those inside it. Why? Because when legal processes or problems arise, they fire the policemen. That's how they shield themselves from responsibility; they don't even offer them legal help. The institution gets rid of them, and the local authorities prosecute them. And what happens? Well, you become disillusioned.... That's why many people join the police with the idea of earning a salary and then look for ways to make five or ten thousand pesos on the side, because you know beforehand that you can steal if you're in the police.

Jesús's statement highlights the ambivalent framework that characterizes the police. The pernicious police practices Jesús describes nourish the criminality found among the police. When a policeman becomes aware of the corrupt and rotten power system, he realizes he stands to lose more by demanding respect or showing indignation. In his interview, Jesús also talked about how police learn to use "cracks" in the law and discover the uses to which these loopholes can be put.

In that sense, a policeman's word is made meaningless from the start. In interactions involving people higher in the hierarchy, the policeman is subordinated, silenced, enclosed by a police culture where the law is not credibly applied. Having no incentive to perform his duties diligently, he will seek, even if half-heartedly, strategies that will place him in the quicksand of forced complicity and put his capacity for resistance to the test. That is the context that shaped the aspirations of "Alberto", a former federal police officer imprisoned for kidnapping:

> They make you hard-hearted. Why? They tell you, "You're going to do this; it's your job. If you don't do it, you don't get paid. Period." I learned what abuse of power was, I learned what lies are right inside there! Anyone who's there is deceiving himself. That thing about "I'm going to build my human potential, my social potential" ... no such thing! There's no future there! There are only two paths. One is when they lose their balls [testicles] because they take their gun and badge away, and they have to work as cab drivers, as bouncers, or at some job their dad, brother, or friend gives them. But that supposed interest of the institution in building physical, human, social potential and all that.... No way!
>
> *What's the other path?*
> The other way is to be smart. Like people say, start making personal decisions. That's why they say, "If he can do it, why can't I? If he does it and nothing happens, then I can do it, too." I actually stole and didn't even have a gun!

The framework Alberto posits is convincing. Acting autonomously, for one's own benefit, becomes a strong motivation and a highly significant code in police life, even though this display of free will still follows rules imposed by the institution to which the policeman belongs.

When an individual exploits the informal rules to excess, the very same knowledge that guides his conduct is redirected against him in its crudest forms. The institutional response to excess is punishment. But punishment doesn't end with the completion of a prison sentence, as confirmed by Mario, a former state policeman imprisoned for kidnapping:

> When I leave this place, I don't know what I'll do. It's the only life I know! I don't know what I'll do now. Drive a taxi—no. Perhaps I'll become a hit man. So many things come to my mind because I know that it's going to be hell starting over on the outside. I would really like to go back to being a policeman, but I know that's not going to happen.... Only if I get acquitted!
>
> *Would you go back?*
> I'd want to, but I know I can't. It won't be the same. I wouldn't feel comfortable in that place anymore. I'm not going to look at them in the same way, nor would they see me the same way. I'd do the same thing! How can I say this? When they [policemen who were in prison] are allowed back into the force, well, you don't look at them the same way, you don't trust them the same as before. They're branded! People who've been in here become marked and are no longer accepted, and I don't want that to happen to me. I would rather work as a hit man.
>
> *Why do you think that?*
> I don't know what I'm going to do because I got used to having a good lifestyle—going shopping and buying whatever I wanted. Going to Gigante [the supermarket] and buying whatever I wanted. I'd do my work and I was doing fine. I wouldn't go around shaking people down or stealing. I'd hassle people but just the small-time crooks and people like that.
>
> *But why work as a hit man?*
> Well, not as a hit man. For example, I wouldn't be a thief. I don't like that. I'm too much of a chicken to be a thief. That would scare me, you know?

> *But what about the other option?*
> I don't want to do that other thing, but it's that ... God forbid! I don't see it as a choice, but I don't know what I'll do outside. Maybe when I least expect it, a chance for a job will come up and I'll be okay. But I keep thinking about it because here [in prison] there's a lot of people who worked as hit men.

Mario's comments reveal how recognizable and lasting elements in the police environment re-create themselves as distrust and a shattered future when the policeman's perspective is from a prison cell. Mario's consideration of "killing for hire" as his future occupation should not be seen as signaling his individual deviance but rather as a perverse consequence of the way in which the police institution "complies" with the rules and excludes and marginalizes the "rotten apples" that have behaved "improperly."

This testimony confirms that the prevailing police culture achieves efficient control over officers' ideology, not only by instilling in them a conviction that things cannot be other than they are but also by appropriating the meanings that protect the institution in perpetuity. Whoever disturbs or transgresses the rules will be condemned to exclusion, marginalization, and oblivion.

CONCLUSION

It is easier to talk about abuse and corruption in the police world than to unravel their causes. The challenge of attempting the latter has led me to dig deep into the core of police culture in Mexico. Setting aside the sensationalism with which police matters are often treated, we must remember that the police are "manufactured" products created by Mexico's own society and culture. At the same time, the existing police culture is a system that communicates, reproduces, and evolves on its own, such that we must delve into the "spaces" within police institutions to better understand police themselves.

To gain an understanding of the practiced place of law enforcement, I have drawn on conversations with former policemen who live and have lived within it. This approach is necessarily limited, since it reflects a very special subset of police officers: those who have fallen from grace and who are therefore more able and disposed to share their insights into the netherworld of police corruption. Their accounts clearly do not reflect the experiences of all Mexican police, but they do provide important insights into the nuances within police culture.

By eliciting their views and experiences, I hope to contribute to an understanding of the multi-determined complexity that led them to where they are today: alone and imprisoned in a different context than they were before. The picture we see stands in contrast to the prevailing monolithic, harsh, and absolutist conceptions of law enforcement institutions typically held by outsiders. One promising approach is to position ourselves on the line of tension between an individual with rights and dignity and an individual who is subjected to subordination and domination beyond formal rules. Caught in between, a policeman may also be a criminal, violating the same rules and laws he is meant to observe and uphold.

Police are crucial for the construction of a democratic state operating under the rule of law. A police force that is above the law has no role in a democratic state. Nor is there a place for an authority that lacks leadership, feels no responsibility to those it is meant to serve, and is incapable of recognizing its own deficiencies. And there is no role for a government that imposes and institutionalizes a police regime that violates human rights. Hence Mexico cannot abide a community of police that, defenseless and deprived of alternatives, is pushed toward illegality (Azaola 2005). If Mexico is to overcome the acute problem of insecurity that affects the nation today, it must have a police corps that carries out its duties with diligence and good judgment and is guided by a sense of public social morality. Only under this circumstance will it be structurally possible for the police to carry out their duties in compliance with the values of individual rights and citizenship rights.

REFERENCES

Azaola, Elena. 2005. "Desde Tláhuac, hacia la sociedad que queremos: Notas para una agenda," Insyde en la Sociedad Civil 5.

Barboza, Roberto. 2008. "Caen mandos ligados a 'narcolista' en Tabasco," El Universal, September 6.

Cano, Ignacio. 2001. "Policía, paramilitares y escuadrones de la muerte en América Latina." In Violencia y regulación de conflictos en América Latina, by Klaus Bodemer et al. Caracas: Nueva Sociedad/ADLAF/HBS.

Conde, Mariana, and María Graciela Rodríguez. 2002. "Mujeres en el fútbol argentino: Sobre prácticas y representaciones," Alteridades [UAM-Iztapalapa, Mexico].

De Certeau, Michel. 1996. La invención de lo cotidiano: Artes de hacer. Mexico: Universidad Iberoamericana/ITESO.

Elster, Jon. 1996. Tuercas y tornillos: Una introducción a los conceptos básicos de las ciencias sociales. Barcelona: Gedisa.

González, María de la Luz. 2009. "Dictan orden de aprehensión contra dos ex directores de Interpol Mexico," El Universal, January15.López Portillo, Ernesto. 2003. "La policía en México: Función política y reforma." In Crimen trasnacional y seguridad pública: Desafíos para México y Estados Unidos, ed. John Bailey and Jorge Chabat. Mexico: Plaza y Janés.

Martínez, Beatriz. 1999. La policía en México. ¿Orden social o criminalidad? Mexico: Planeta.

Maza, Enrique. 2005. "Hay sufrimientos, pero no culpables," Proceso 1489.

Monsiváis, Carlos. 1999. "Notas sobre la violencia urbana," Letras Libres, año 2, no. 5.

Ortega, José Antonio. 2005. "Inseguridad e impunidad: Los principales obstáculos al desarrollo de México," Entorno, año 17, no. 197.

Reguillo, Rossana. 2004. "Subjetividad, crisis y vida cotidiana: Acción y poder en la cultura." In La cultura en las crisis latinoamericanas, by Alejandro Grimson et al. Buenos Aires: CLACSO.

------. 2009. "Detienen a 759 policías ligados al narco en 2008," Reforma, January 6.

Stanley, Ruth. 2001. "Violencia policial en el Gran Buenos Aires: ¿Necesita el neoliberalismo una policía brava?" In Violencia y regulación de conflictos en América Latina, by Klaus Bodemer et al. Caracas: Nueva Sociedad/ADLAF/HBS.

Suárez de Garay, María Eugenia. 2004a. "El territorio de la ambigüedad: Un acercamiento antropológico a los mundos de vida de los policías en Guadalajara, México," Etnográfica [Centro de Estudios en Antropología Social, Lisbon] 8, no. 1

———. 2004b. "¿Te acuerdas de allá afuera? La experiencia de los ex policías en prisión," Revista Renglones [ITESO, Guadalajara] 58–59.

Torrente, Diego. 1997. La sociedad policía: Poder, trabajo y cultura en una organización local de policía. Madrid: Centro de Investigaciones Sociológicas, Universidad de Barcelona.

Vallespir, Alejandra. 2002. La policía que supimos conseguir. Buenos Aires: Planeta.

Two Steps Forward: Lessons from Chihuahua

Daniel M. Sabet

INTRODUCTION

As Guillermo Zepeda notes in his chapter, the urgent need to professionalize the Mexican police has been recognized since the early 1990s. In fact, numerous elected officials and police chiefs have come to office promoting new policies and pledging to end the scourge of illegality and lack of professionalism that has plagued Mexican police departments. However, at least in the arena of public perception, it appears that few gains have been made in actually improving police integrity and professionalism. Recent research finds that both perceptions of corruption and self-reported corruption may even be on the rise (Paras 2006; Carrasco Araizaga 2003). This presents something of a paradox: On the one hand, police misconduct has gained national prominence, earned a major place on the political agenda, and been the impetus for new legislation and policies. Yet, on the other hand, there have only been limited successes in professionalizing police agencies.

The underdevelopment of Mexican police forces also produces a second paradox. Benjamin Reames estimates that Mexico has around three thousand police departments divided among federal, state, and municipal governments and further divided into preventive, transit, and investigative police (2003). One of the commonly theorized benefits of federalism is that state and local governments can serve as laboratories of democracy. Best practices can emerge in one jurisdiction and be replicated throughout others. Yet despite this theory and despite so many departments, at the present time there are very few Mexican police agencies that can be held up as models. Throughout the country, police lack proper equipment, training, pay, incentives, oversight and accountability, and even basic police procedures.

This chapter offers a case study of one of a handful of success stories in Mexican policing: the Municipal Department of Public Security (Dirección de Seguridad Pública Municipal, DSPM) of Chihuahua City, Chihuahua. I highlight the department's success in implementing and institutionalizing policies that have increased the professionalism of the agency. It would be tempting to conclude that the department is distinct simply because it has selected such policies; however, there is general consensus about what kinds of measures are necessary to improve the honesty and professionalism of the police. Professionalization efforts do not necessarily require innovative policies, simply the implementation of basic measures such as the creation of procedural manuals and regular in-service training. Where other departments have failed is not in policy selection per se, but in their inability to successfully implement and institutionalize such policies. Social science does not need simply to explain what approaches are effective in professionalizing the police, but rather how such policy reform comes about and the conditions that allow for reform.

Results from this case study suggest that such professionalization is rare because of a lack of continuity between governing administrations—both an institutional and a cultural phenomenon. While it is not the only distinguishing factor, the primary difference between Chihuahua and other Mexican police departments is that the former has obtained a degree of continuity between its three-year municipal administrations. As a result, numerous professionalization efforts have had a cumulative effect over time. Rather than taking two steps forward and one step backward, or simply standing still, continuity in Chihuahua has allowed it to slowly and consistently make real gains in police professionalism. This is not to suggest that the Chihuahua police force does not have several challenges ahead of it, and, in fact, this chapter also explores some of the limitations of the DSPM's reform efforts.

The data on Chihuahua's municipal police used in this chapter come from a variety of sources. They include interviews with the DSPM leadership, operational and administrative staff, eleven patrol officers from various ranks, and members of Chihuahua's civil society active in the area of public security, including members of business associations, academics, and journalists. Additional methods include observation of police performance during a "ride-along" and analysis of municipal and DSPM documentation. The research also benefits from summary statistics from two surveys conducted in 2006 by researchers at the Chihuahua campus of the Instituto Tecnológico y de Estudios Superiores de Monterrey (Nájera Ruiz 2006a, 2006b). These include a survey of 2,002 Chihuahua residents and a survey of 250 police. It should be mentioned that this chapter is part of a larger study by the author on police professionalization in Mexico and, therefore, includes references to data obtained in other research sites.

MEXICAN POLICING AND STRATEGIES TO IMPROVE POLICE INTEGRITY

It is worth reiterating that law enforcement in Mexico is divided by both geographical jurisdiction and function. Geographically, the police are divided into municipal, state, and federal police departments, each of which has different responsibilities. For example, the transport and sale of drugs and guns are considered federal crimes and, therefore, are under the jurisdiction of the federal police. Robbery, homicide, and assault, however, fall to the states and municipalities. Functionally, the police are divided into investigative, transit, and preventive departments. Investigative police, known as the ministerial police, are organized under the auspice of the public prosecutor (ministerio público) at the state and federal levels. They are responsible for investigating crimes and making arrests for violations of state law (fuero común) and federal law (fuero federal), respectively (see López Portillo 2002; Reames 2003). Transit police are responsible for enforcing traffic laws and are at times combined with preventive police forces. Preventive police make up the vast majority of Mexican police (in terms of both the number of police officers and the number of departments). Preventive departments operate at all three levels of government and are typically organized under the auspices of a secretary or department of public security. Their primary job is to prevent crime, conduct patrols, maintain public order, and be the first responders to crime. At the municipal level they are also responsible for enforcing municipal ordinances. (They are generally referred to in Spanish as the Bando de Policía y Buen Gobierno.) Chihuahua's DSPM is a municipal preventive police force of approximately 1,100 officers serving a city of 760,000 residents.

It should go without saying that police play a fundamental role in a democratic society. When the police fail to enforce the laws, protect individual rights, or act above the law, they undermine democracy and the rule of law. When citizens do not feel protected by the law or believe that police operate above it, a variety of normatively undesirable results can occur: citizens can ignore the laws, they can take the law into their own hands, or they can demand more draconian laws harmful to individual rights. Unfortunately, a casual review of Mexican newspapers would suggest that all of these consequences are on the rise.

As acknowledged by other authors in this volume, citizen distrust of the police is widely recognized both inside and outside of Mexican police departments. Studies of self-reported bribe payment consistently find that the police are the most common recipients of bribe money in Mexico. The biannual National Corruption and Good Government Index has found consistently that among a wide range of governmental processes, most incidences of reported bribe paying involve payments to transit police to avoid a towing or traffic fine (Transparencia Mexicana 2006). Perhaps as a result, the public consistently gives the police poor marks in surveys. They not only express a lack of confidence in the police but have less confidence in the police than in other governmental and societal institutions. In the federal government–conducted National Survey on Political Culture and Citizen Practices (Encuesta Nacional sobre Cultura Política y Prácticas Ciudadanas), respondents rated the police, on average, at 5.55 on a scale from 1 to 10, below every other group except political parties (5.3) (Secretaría de Gobernación 2005). In the annual national survey of urban areas conducted by the Instituto Ciudadano de Estudios Sobre la Inseguridad, respondents ranked local preventive police forces a 5.3 on a scale of 1 to 10, on par with other police agencies and slightly above political parties (ICESI 2006). Respondents to the academic Latin American Public Opinion Project survey rated the police dead last, at 3.3 on a scale of 1 to 7 (or the equivalent of 4.7 on a scale of 1 to 10).

Given these negative statistics, it is worth considering some of the policies commonly posited to produce a more professional police force and, in so doing, illustrate the absence of such characteristics among many Mexican departments. The first point of concern is who becomes a police officer. In professional departments throughout the world, candidate selection is the initial point of intervention to ensure an honest and qualified force. Drug tests, lie detector tests, psychological tests, background checks, asset verification, interviews with references, minimum age requirements, and minimum education requirements are all important screening mechanisms.

There have been numerous efforts to improve selection criteria in Mexico, and psychological and drug tests are now standard. A few agencies also require a high school degree, and some have convened citizen committees to assist in and oversee selection. The federal government has created a National Public Security Personnel Registry (Registro Nacional de Personal de Seguridad Pública) to ensure that incoming officers to any police force do not have a criminal record and have not been previously let go from a different agency. Nevertheless, even where selection criteria have improved, exceptions appear to be common. Due to a variety of factors—including a negative reputation, high risks, and low pay—Mexican police agencies report considerable difficulties in attracting a sufficient number of applicants to be highly selective. In many cases, new selection criteria (such as threshold scores on psychological tests and minimum education requirements) have to be relaxed in order to ensure a sufficient number of incoming cadets. The challenge of recruitment has been most visible at the federal level, where the Federal Preventive Police had considerable trouble attracting college graduates to fill an announced 8,000 positions in its intelligence units (Gandaría 2007a). As a partial result of its recruiting challenges, the Federal Preventive Police has filled more than half of its ranks with 16,000 transferred military personnel (Gandaría 2007b). The problem is reproduced at the state and municipal levels, without the ability to fall back on the military, however. A worst case scenario can be found in Tijuana, where the expansion of the police force from just over 1,500 to almost 2,400 during the three-year administration of Jorge Hank Rhon (2004–2007) allowed for the infiltration of organized crime elements into the force.

Additional factors important to building a professional department include a reasonable salary and financial benefits, reasonable work hours, the possibility to rise up through the ranks, sufficient training and opportunities for educational advancement, police equipment of sufficient quantity and quality to fulfill one's functions, and established police procedures. Mexican state and municipal policing generally does not score well on any of these criteria. Even in northern Mexico, where the police are generally better paid, there are departments where police agents work 24-hour shifts (with only 24 hours off) for a salary of roughly US$550 (5,500 pesos) a month. Select departments have witnessed some improvements in these areas. A handful of municipalities and states in northern Mexico switched to 8-hour shifts and pay around $850 (8,500 pesos) a month. In Tijuana, one of the country's most conflictive municipalities, line-level police earn $1,495 (14,949 pesos) a month. Nonetheless, these departments remain the exception rather than the norm.

Furthermore, in most departments, advancement is based primarily on personal connections, and top and middle management can be replaced following the arrival of new police chiefs. Even in departments that have made considerable advances in professionalization, leadership positions remain important patronage resources. In one northern Mexican municipality, seven mid-level commanders participating in a focus group all reported that they had at one time held a higher position in the force, and they estimated that all of the approximately 120 current commanders had cycled in and out of the department's leadership. Officials rationalize their failure to develop a meritocratic promotions process by arguing that it is essential that police commanders have the flexibility to appoint people they trust. However, such a lack of continuity has several negative side effects, including removing the incentive for a police officer to excel in his or her work with the hope of rising up through the ranks.

As Suárez and Moloeznik discuss in this volume, insufficient training is a major obstacle to professionalization. Although the quality of academy training is improving with policies such as the national academy's certification of instructors in key areas (handgun training, tactics, and radio communications, for example), pressure to get more police on the street has resulted in a reduction of training times. More fundamentally, in-service training and refresher courses are still relatively rare. As one interviewee stated, "policing involves perishable skills that you lose if they are not reinforced." Nonetheless, in most departments, police that do not have leadership positions might go years without receiving a course of any kind. It is not that courses are not offered. Rather, they are given on an ad-hoc basis and tend to be more oriented to the leadership than the rank and file. Instructors responsible for testing rank-and-file police in seven areas of policing as part of a federal program privately reported in interviews that many police fail to demonstrate proficiency in basic aspects of policing.

A constant complaint among police, discussed in the Azaola chapter, is the lack of equipment to do effective police work. In interviews, police regularly quip that the criminals are better armed than they are. In response to this traditional failure, in recent years governmental authorities have ramped up investment in equipment. For 2008, the federal government initiated an unprecedented subsidy program called SUBSEMUN (Subsidy for Municipal Public Security or Subsidio para la Seguridad Pública Municipal). Under the SUBSEMUN program in 2009, 206 municipalities received large cash infusions that significantly increased their annual budgets. While there is close to universal praise for the long-needed investment, critics worry that a one-time subsidy will not facilitate long-term planning or solutions. In fact, there is a tradition in Mexico of major investments at the beginning of an administration, only to be followed by neglect.

Finally, and perhaps most surprisingly, many departments still operate without clearly laid out police procedures and procedural manuals. Instead, as one interviewed police leader contended, police action follows the discretion and style of individual commanders. When supervisors are changed, so does the method of addressing security challenges. The product is inconsistent law enforcement, inefficiency, and errors that can violate individual rights.

A final major factor affecting police integrity is accountability mechanisms. Professional departments throughout the world have some means "to police the police." These generally take one of two forms: an internal affairs unit that is within the department, or an oversight agency that is outside of the police. This is unquestionably the area where the least progress has been made in Mexico (Varenik 2005). Despite the widespread perception of corruption, there is little day-to-day investigation and removal of corrupt officers. Departments frequently have some variation of an Honor and Justice Council (Consejo de Honor y Justicia) comprising the department's high-level leadership and tasked with ensuring police accountability. In practice, such councils lack staff, meet infrequently, and are burdened with a number of additional responsibilities. These factors ensure that investigating alleged police corruption is not a priority. Rather, anticorruption efforts are limited to a few departments who undertake nontransparent, large-scale, one-time purges in response to major scandals and political pressure. Examples include purges of state and municipal police in Nuevo León in 2007, the Nuevo Laredo municipal police in 2005, the Tijuana municipal police in 2008, and the Federal Investigations Agency (AFI) in 2007.[1] Ironically, professionals working in internal affairs offices complain that in many such cases fired police have successfully challenged their removal in court and been reinstated on the force with back pay.

This brief overview suggests that despite widespread knowledge of policy tools to increase professionalism, such measures are often not implemented or not implemented effectively in Mexican police forces. There appear to be a variety of reasons for this reality. At the most basic level, law enforcement officials are granted significant authority; they have considerable discretion to use that authority; and they are difficult to monitor. As a result, police can easily supplement their income by stealing from a crime scene, shaking down citizens, or accepting bribes from criminals. If one considers that police work in Mexico is generally poorly paid, highly stigmatized, offers little opportunity for advancement, and has limited oversight, then misconduct appears very likely.

There also appear to be collective action problems in reforming Mexican police. This is most evident in the inability to create a meritocratic promotion process.

1 For example, after a string of assassinations and executions in Nuevo León, state and federal authorities placed over 150 municipal and state officers into custody. Thirty-six were eventually indicted on corruption charges (*El Universal* 2007).

As Barbara Geddes (1996) has found in a different context, politicians who reject patronage lose a key resource for shoring up political support. Moreover, they obtain no counterbalancing benefit of good government, because everyone else continues to play by the rules of patronage. The same basic argument can be applied to police forces where political and police leadership refuses to give up the right to appoint their friends and trusted associates to key positions. Given their own limited ability to combat pervasive police misconduct problems single-handedly, officials have little to gain from surrendering such personal privileges.

Some authors, such as Ernesto López Portillo (2002), have pointed to historical factors, arguing that the police in Mexico have traditionally been exploited for the benefit of political leaders. A complementary historical view provided by interview respondents points out that, until the last couple of decades, Mexico simply did not have the crime problems it has today. Absent major trafficking and drug consumption problems, creating a professional force simply was not a priority. Now that such challenges have become urgent, the presence of organized crime has dramatically increased the incentives for police misconduct (Sabet 2007; Payan 2006). The drug trade is a multi-billion-dollar industry with sufficient surplus to buy off the law enforcement officials needed to ensure its success. As summed up by the often-used phrase "plata o plomo" (the bribe or the bullet), organized crime is able to dominate the relationship between briber and bribe recipient. Although a police officer might be able to shake down an isolated lawbreaker, an organized crime syndicate provides its members with leverage and protection in confrontations with the law. While corruption is a rational strategy under normal conditions, in the presence of an aggressive organized crime syndicate it becomes a survival strategy for some officers.

Theoretically, citizens and civil society should provide a counterbalance to the negative incentives within Mexican police forces and exacerbated by organized crime. Nonetheless, such a counterbalance has empirically not been forthcoming. Unfortunately, citizens also benefit from the ability to bribe police, avoid fines for traffic and other legal violations, and intervene in law enforcement on behalf of family and friends. Mexico vies with Paraguay for the highest rates of self-reported corruption in Latin America. Transparency International (2006) found that 31 percent of their Mexican sample reported that they or someone in their household had paid a bribe in the last year. When questioned about corruption, interviewed police officers and government officials frequently lay the blame on citizens, complaining that it is they who offer money, without police extortion. While such arguments fail to recognize an officer's own culpability, they do raise a valid point about the ambivalence of citizens in addressing corruption. As Suárez points out in this volume, it is difficult to separate police culture from the broader culture.[2]

An additional reason why citizens have not provided a counterbalance to organized crime and corruption is fear. Several prominent members of Mexico's civil society, including journalists, businesspeople, and members of associations such as the Chamber of Commerce and good governance groups, have been the targets of threats, disappearances, kidnappings, and assassinations. For example, in Tijuana the head of a citizen public participation committee who had been a vocal advocate of improved security barely survived an attempt on his life by organized criminal elements (La Frontera 2007).. In Hermosillo, Sonora, the refusal of a woman to pay a bribe to an officer landed her in jail on trumped up charges (Comisión Estatal 2005)..

Perhaps most importantly, however, citizens and civil society lack the tools to hold officials accountable. Ostensibly because of the delicate nature of security and investigation, law enforcement is able to avoid transparency and meaningful citizen oversight. The lack of information about police actions is demonstrated every time an officer is assassinated. Rather than eulogizing killed officers as heroes with marches in the streets denouncing organized crime, citizens are surprisingly silent. Unfortunately, at the news of an officer's death, there is always uncertainty as to why he was killed. Was he killed because he was carrying out his duty, because he was disloyal to a cartel that was paying him, or because he was supporting a rival syndicate? Thorough investigations are always promised, but the facts of such killings almost never come to light. The silence of citizens reflects both their lack of information and their sense of powerlessness.

Nor have scandals of police misconduct produced effective tools for citizen oversight. While north of the border such scandals have produced powerful citizen led investigation committees, such as New York's Knapp Commission (1972), the Pennsylvania Crime Commission (1974), or Los Angeles's Mollen Commission (1994), no such commissions or citizen oversight mechanisms have been forthcoming in Mexico. As a result of these factors, citizens have not provided a counterbalance to corrupting influences.

---

2 This is not to suggest that corruption is a hardwired component of Mexican culture. Interviewed police point out that U.S. tourists on vacation in Mexico are also more than willing to offer bribes.

In short, there are many reasons why police misconduct continues and policing fails to become a true profession. Nonetheless, it is still surprising that, out of over three thousand departments, more success stories have not emerged. There are, after all, reformers both within the police and among elected officials who have tried to overcome the collective action problems inherent in reform. Politicians and police leaders would benefit enormously from a reputation as a successful reformer. In addition, there are numerous honest police officers who are frustrated by the lack of professionalization within their own department. Most police would prefer to work in a department where they are well paid, have sufficient resources, and are viewed as professionals and respected authority figures.

In fact, numerous police chiefs and city mayors have come to office with the genuine intention of professionalizing the police. Some have made considerable gains. However, as alluded to above, those gains can be rolled back in successive administrations. It is one of the unfortunate aspects of politics in Mexico that each administration seeks to clearly distinguish itself from its predecessor, even when the predecessor is from the same party (Guillén López 2006). New city mayors do not necessarily honor agreements made by previous administrations, and they typically reappoint most top managers, who in turn change middle management. These appointments are filled by individuals known literally as "trusted people" (gente de confianza). As a result, it is not uncommon to hear members of civil society quip that municipal officials spend one year learning the job, one year working, and one year preparing for what they will do at the end of the administration. While some important advances might be achieved in a given administration, they risk being overturned in the next.

Based on the above discussion, it is possible to see the paradoxes that were identified in the introduction in a new light. Police leaders and politicians promising change often fail because of the collective action problems inherent in realizing reform, the threat of organized crime, and the exclusion of citizens from the policy arena. Three thousand police departments have only produced a few success stories because the efforts of one administration are often lost with the change in government.

TWO STEPS FORWARD IN CHIHUAHUA

Unlike many police departments in Mexico, the DSPM, a department of roughly 1,100 police officers, has managed to defy the odds and make major strides in the area of professionalization. Given that the DSPM is one of a handful of success stories in Mexico, it warrants a more thorough investigation. Below I discuss efforts to professionalize the DSPM through certification by an international policing accreditation agency and through improvements in training, promotion, and work conditions. This is followed by a discussion of selection criteria and accountability mechanisms, two areas where the DSPM still faces considerable limitations.

CALEA Accreditation

The most celebrated of the DSPM's advances is accreditation by the U.S.-based Commission on Law Enforcement Accreditation, Inc. (CALEA). CALEA is a 501(c)(3) nonprofit organization founded in 1979 as a joint effort by several prominent law enforcement executive associations. It certifies police agencies for maintaining a body of standards covering many aspects of policing and accepted by public security practitioners and experts. CALEA offers two levels of certification: recognition and accreditation. Obtaining accreditation is rigorous, time-consuming, expensive, and requires that departments comply with 459 standards. To date, around 870 police agencies have been accredited by CALEA, primarily in the United States. The DSPM, which obtained recognition in March 2004 and accreditation in May 2007, was the first—and to date the only—police force in Mexico to be accredited by the commission.[3]

The CALEA process has resulted in substantial changes in policing in Chihuahua. It has corresponded with what several officers referred to as a transition away from *policías empíricos*, or basing one's decisions on one's own personal experience, to *policías científicos*, working based on best accepted practices. Procedures might appear to be common sense; however, when neglected, they can open up considerable loopholes for abuse. For example, a common complaint made by arrestees is that

3 The state police in Coahuila has obtained recognition, and at least ten agencies are in the initial self-assessment stage. It should be mentioned that the DSPM also has ISO-9000 certification in several areas.

TABLE 7.1 Police Responses About Their Work Environment

Question	Responses				
	Strongly agree	**Agree**	**Neither agree nor disagree**	**Disagree**	**Strongly disagree**
Do you think that complying with CALEA will help improve your work?	46.53%	30.56%	13.19%	5.56%	4.17%
Do you think that the process for determining promotions is clear and fair?	10.140%	29.050%	25.680%	15.540%	19.590%
Do you think that the DSPM equipment is adequate?	8.160%	27.210%	21.770%	25.170%	17.690%
Do you think that the designation of patrol zones is fair?	26.350%	50.000%	13.510%	4.730%	5.410%
Do you think that the work hours are adequate?	55.100%	31.970%	4.760%	4.080%	4.080%

Source: Instituto Tecnológico y de Estudios Superiores de Monterrey, 2006.

personal belongings surrendered upon admission to detention facilities are stolen. As a result of CALEA procedures, an inventory of items belonging to the detainee is taken, items are placed in bags in front of the detainee, and the bags are stapled shut with the inventory list, which is then signed by the individual taking the items. If followed, such a procedure can reduce incidences of theft and give internal affairs investigators a tool to determine if personnel acted properly.

In addition to improving procedures affecting day-to-day police work, the department also had to improve its internal management and supervision. Police are now evaluated annually by their superiors. Policy was improved for determining pay and promotion. The DSPM was required to update facilities and create an Office of Citizen Attention (Subdirección de Atención a la Ciudadanía) to receive citizen requests for service and complaints about police actions. A high school education has become a requirement for entering cadets. All officers must receive annual in-service training. And, not insignificantly, all police have been provided with a copy of the manual governing their behavior and that of the institution. As a result, in the department's internal survey, 76 percent of the respondents felt that complying with CALEA procedures would improve police effectiveness (see table 7.1).

Training

When asked why Chihuahua has successfully professionalized, most respondents attributed the change to improved training. Although its facilities are modest, the DSPM's police academy, which was founded in 1964, has a longer history than most, and it is accredited by the National Public Security System (Sistema Nacional de Seguridad Pública) and the state education authority (Secretaría de Educación y Cultura). Accreditation by the former ensures quality police training, and by the latter, that graduates of the academy earn a recognized technical degree. In addition, certification as a technical school does not permit the police leadership to drastically reduce the nine-month training period (including two months of practical training) to meet immediate operational needs.

Perhaps more important, and less common in Mexico, is a CALEA requirement that all police must return to the academy for a one-week retraining each year on basic police tactics. As discussed above, in most municipal departments, trainings are conducted on an ad hoc rather than a permanent basis and rarely trickle down through the ranks. In addition, the department has been encouraging general education. Those with only a middle school education are encouraged to attend continuing-education high school classes, and a high school degree is now a requirement for promotion to a supervisory position. In addition, academic institutions have provided pro bono services to the police department, allowing 80 police to complete a technical degree in police investigations, 46 police and administrators to take a 180-hour certificate in leadership and administration, and 40 police to complete a course on basic computing. In addition, 15 officers are currently working on a bachelor's degree in law, and 3 are enrolled in a master's degree program in "citizen security."

Incentives

Although higher than some police departments, the salary for agents in Chihuahua is still low by many standards. The base salary for agents is US$674 a month (6,741 pesos) with modest increases for rank, years of service, and participation in units with specialized training. In addition, agents typically receive a 12 percent monthly bonus if they do not miss work and do not have faults on their record. Police also have access to medical coverage (beyond the standard state employee medical insurance), a pension, life insurance, and potential access to credit, an important incentive given that police in Mexico are not eligible for credit from Mexican banks. Further, the department plans to invest an additional US$3 million in improving incentives as part of the SUBSEMUN program. Among several requirements to obtain the substantial federal subsidy, municipalities must match a certain percentage and invest that amount in improving financial benefits. It should also be mentioned that the police have benefited from the creation of a Citizen Public Security Committee (Comité Ciudadano de Seguridad Pública Municipal de Chihuahua), which has mobilized community resources to offer access to housing credit and discounts on goods and services from local businesses.

The DSPM first attempted to create a police civil service (sistema de carrera policial) in 2001. However, as discussed above, there are serious collective action problems in doing so. The killings of two policemen in 2006 revealed that a high-level officer used on-duty police to provide private protection for a businessman with alleged ties to organized crime, suggesting that promotion was based on factors other than merit and honesty (Tiempo 2006). When surveyed in 2006, only 39.19 percent of the sample of police felt that the system for promotion was fair (see table 7.1). In response to the survey results, additional efforts made the process more transparent, including the participation of members of the citizen committee. Under the current system implemented in 2007, given a set number of years at one's current position and a minimum level of education, officers become eligible for promotion. Following their application, promotion is determined by performance at the conclusion of a two-week promotion course. Citizen committee members participate in overseeing the process, and course results are posted publicly. While the police officers interviewed for this study are not a representative sample, all but one of the eleven felt that the current promotion criteria were fair and had improved markedly.

While academics and citizens might be inclined to believe that improved accountability mechanisms are the essential factors to professionalizing the police and improving police integrity, interviewed police respondents argued that it is improved technology and equipment that allow for a greater sense of pride, specialization, and professionalism. Although survey respondents perceived a continued need for more equipment, Chihuahua has invested heavily in technology. The department has a modern dispatching system, a high-tech mobile command unit, twenty-eight cameras throughout the city, several specialized units such as a SWAT-like team, laptops in supervisors' cars, and a helicopter. In addition, police are assigned their own cars, carry designated guns, and are less likely to be abused through excessive or unrealistic work shifts. Officers work 12-hour shifts, followed by either 24 or 48 hours off, averaging a 42-hour workweek. In the department's internal survey, 76.35 percent agreed that the assignation of work zones was fair, and 87 percent felt that the work hours were fair.

In summary, Chihuahua has made major strides in a number of areas. As a result, police departments throughout northern Mexico are following the DSPM's lead. At the time of writing, at least ten other departments were in the self-assessment stage of CALEA accreditation. Of course, CALEA does not represent a panacea. As one interview respondent put it, "a lot has to come before CALEA, and a lot has to come after" in order for police departments to change. As the troubles in implementing meritocratic promotion criteria reveal, writing a formal policy and carrying it out in practice are two very different things. What has distinguished the DSPM has been its ability to implement such policies; and as a result of its efforts the DSPM has been recognized both nationally and internationally.[4] However, as the following section illustrates, this discussion does not imply that the department does not have considerable challenges ahead.

4 For example, the department received an award from President Vicente Fox in 2004; it was given an exemplary evaluation by the Altus Global Alliance; and its police chief is president of the Asociación Nacional de Jefes de Policía Municipal (National Association of Municipal Police Chiefs).

Selection Criteria

The DSPM has struggled to ensure the quality of incoming agents. In 2004, the former mayor of Chihuahua, José Reyes Baeza, was elected state governor. He brought with him the DSPM's police chief, Raúl Grajeda Domínguez, to lead the state police, which formed a new elite unit called the Intelligence Police Force (Cuerpo de Inteligencia Policial, or CIPOL). To fill its ranks, CIPOL pulled heavily from the police department that Grajeda formerly commanded, drawing over two hundred police away from the DSPM and leaving the municipality with a deficit of police that it had to fill in the short term. Unfortunately, attracting a sufficient number of new police to the department required relaxing acceptance criteria, and several interviewed police complained about the quality and the integrity of these junior police agents. While the DSPM has tightened up its criteria, requiring a high school degree and passing anti-doping, health, knowledge, sociocultural, and psychological tests, some damage might have already been done.

It should also be mentioned that raising the selection criteria has limited the department's applicant pool. With a goal of seeking to admit fifty-five cadets in the upcoming class, the department attracted roughly one hundred applicants but only forty-five acceptable candidates. This highlights the challenge noted early in this chapter. Because policing still has a negative image, departments have a hard time attracting adequate candidates. The finding suggests that departments such as the DSPM need not only to raise the criteria for entering cadets but also to complement the criteria with active recruiting efforts among targeted groups.[5]

Accountability Mechanisms

The DSPM has also been hesitant to directly address the problem of corruption. On the one hand, there are several mechanisms designed to ensure police accountability in Chihuahua City, including the State Human Rights Commission for (Comisión Estatal de Derechos Humanos), the Internal Affairs Office (Subdirección de Asuntos Internos), the Office of Citizen Attention, and the Honor and Justice Council. The State Human Rights Commission investigates alleged human rights violations and makes recommendations to the municipal government and the police. The Internal

5 It should be noted that more recently the DSPM has made some gains in recruitment. In 2009, the department reported that it only accepted onto the force 15.67% of qualified applicants.

Figure 7.1 Citizen Confidence in the Chihuahua City Municipal Police

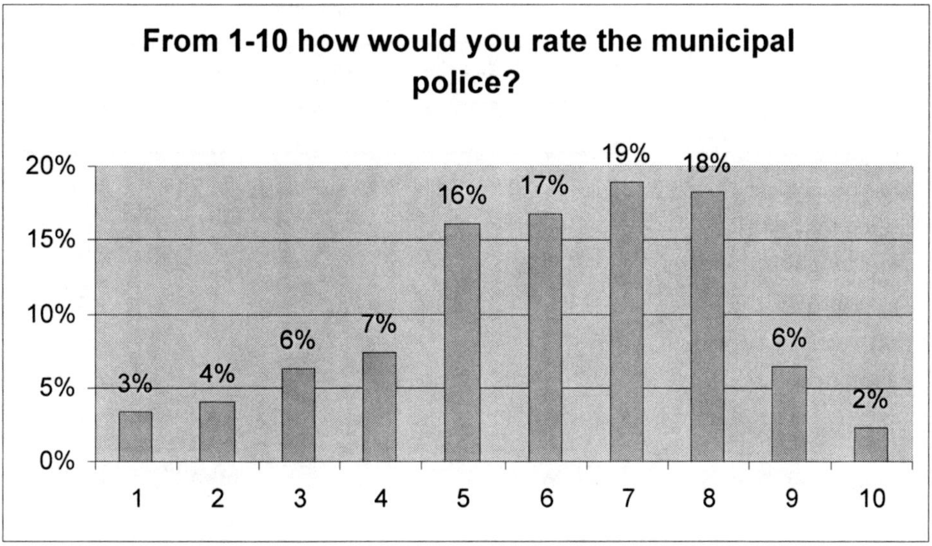

Source: Instituto Tecnológico y de Estudios Superiores de Monterrey, 2006.

Affairs Office is organized outside of the police department but is within the municipal government. It investigates any allegations of police misconduct and makes recommendations to the Honor and Justice Council. The Office of Citizen Attention is organized within the police department and receives both requests for service and complaints against the police. Working with police leadership, some complaints are addressed directly within the department and others are referred to internal affairs for investigation.

On the other hand, while there are many organizations, with the exception of the Honor and Justice Council, none of the other three agencies has the power to emit sanctions. Rather, this power is reserved for the Honor and Justice Council, which is made up of city and police officials. Unfortunately, according to the municipality, the Council emitted no serious sanctions against police officers in 2006, only four in

TABLE 7.2 Citizen Perceptions of the Police

	Responses				
Question	Yes, strongly	Yes, moderately	Yes, weakly	No	NA
Do you respect the police that work in your neighborhood?	33.67%	34.72%	13.59%	14.74%	3.30%
Do you trust the police that work in your neighborhood?	21.73%	32.22%	18.93%	23.73%	3.40%
	Yes			No	NA
Did you know that the municipal police is accredited by CALEA?	37.16%			60.39%	2.45%

Source: Instituto Tecnológico y de Estudios Superiores de Monterrey, 2006.

2007, and only three in the first half of 2008.[6] Theoretically, this could be a reflection of a clean police department; however, police leaders and officers acknowledge the continued problem of police corruption. The numbers also do not correspond with the ninety-four citizen complaints of extortion reported to the Office of Citizen Attention in 2007. Moreover, members of civil society expressed concern about infiltration by organized crime. Also, in early 2009, the arrests of high-level officials, including the head of the department's specialized units, also undermined citizen confidence. This suggests a lack of political will to address corruption directly and a

6 Número de Elementos Policíacos Sancionados por el Consejo de Honor y Justicia. 2008. Sistema de Indicadores de Gestión Municipal Administrativa. http://ras.municipiochihuahua.gob.mx/Default.aspx.

TABLE 7.3 Police Self-Evaluations

	Rankings on a Scale of 1 to 10										
	1	**2**	**3**	**4**	**5**	**6**	**7**	**8**	**9**	**10**	**NA**
In your opinion, from 1 to 10, how do you think citizens would rate the police?	0%	1%	1%	1%	14%	12%	18%	44%	5%	2%	1%
How would you rate the honesty in the DSPM on a scale from 1 to 10?	1%	3%	0%	2%	3%	6%	5%	20%	37%	14%	10%

Source: Instituto Tecnológico y de Estudios Superiores de Monterrey, 2006

hope that improving conditions for police training and the possibility for promotion will create sufficient carrots for good behavior even absent a credible stick.

In summary, the DSPM still faces several challenges, particularly in the areas of candidate selection and accountability mechanisms. Nonetheless, the department has won considerable recognition for the advances it has made in professionalization. These advances may be reflected in recent opinion polling conducted by the Instituto Tecnológico y de Estudios Superiores de Monterrey in 2006. On a scale of 1 to 10, residents of Chihuahua rate the police as 6, a modest advantage over the aforementioned national surveys (see figure 7.1). Trust and respect increase when survey questions relate to police assigned to a respondent's specific neighborhood. Sixty-eight percent of respondents strongly or moderately respected the police working in their community. Fifty-four percent strongly or moderately trusted the police working in their community. In addition, 37 percent of the sample reported awareness of CALEA accreditation (see table 7.2). While these numbers fall short of demonstrating full citizen confidence in the police, they do suggest greater public trust than is found in national averages.

For their part, the 250 police respondents, perhaps not surprisingly, rated themselves very well. They felt citizens would most commonly award them an 8 on a scale of 1 to 10 (see table 7.3). In addition, 71 percent rated the honesty of the police at 8, 9, or 10 on a scale of 1 to 10 (although 10 percent of the sample did not answer the question). Finally, when asked what moral values were the most essential to being a police officer, the most common answer, given by 26 percent of the sample, was honesty.

EXPLAINING CHIHUAHUA'S ADVANCES

Given the continued problems in so many departments, the advances in Chihuahua City beg the question, What makes Chihuahua City different? On the one hand, municipal and police leadership have instituted a number of policies and programs that have converted vicious cycles into virtuous ones. But why was Chihuahua able to successfully implement these and other policies? In other words, the question is not just what has been the effect of measures such as CALEA accreditation on Chihuahua's policing, but why was the DSPM able to achieve accreditation in the first place.

To begin to answer this question, it should be mentioned that Chihuahua City has two natural advantages over other locations in Mexico. First, the city and Chihuahua State are wealthier than many parts of the country and therefore have the ability to make greater investments in salaries, incentives, equipment, and administration. Second, until recently Chihuahua City had not been affected by organized crime to the same extent as many other cities in northern Mexico, such as the border cities of Tijuana, Ciudad Juárez, Nuevo Laredo, Reynosa, and Matamoros. Nonetheless, as will be discussed below, Chihuahua City has not escaped the scourge of organized crime, nor is it devoid of financial concerns. Moreover, these two factors represent insufficient explanations.

When asked when Chihuahua began to professionalize, senior police point back to 1992. According to one high-level officer with twenty-one years on the force:

> Since 1992 we have experienced a complete turnabout. We have better technology; we are more professional; we have paid more attention to our human resources, and CALEA has been the icing on the cake. When I joined the force, the chiefs didn't even know how to read or write. It bothered me because I had a high school education, and many of them didn't even have primary school—and they were the bosses.

In 1992, Patricio Martínez García was elected mayor, and he appointed Steven Slater, a former U.S. police officer from New Mexico, to head Chihuahua City's police academy. Slater brought with him the perspective of U.S. policing, and current police leadership credit him with making several small changes that have had long-term effects. Of particular importance was his focus on standardization. He initiated a process of standardizing police procedures and police trainings. In addition, he used his connections to attract U.S. police trainers to teach courses and promoted regular in-service training. Finally, he helped the department create specialized police units, such as the K-9 and special tactics units that continue to this day. As is the custom in Mexican politics, Slater would leave with the change in administration three years later, but his efforts would have a long-term impact. Here is where Chihuahua parts ways with other Mexican departments. Good leadership is not uncommon in Mexican policing. There have been a number of visionaries who have developed and implemented good programs and policies. However, as discussed above, such initiatives have too often ended with the change of administration.

In Chihuahua, however, rather than replace these policies, the DSPM built upon them. Interviewed members of the force all felt that the evolution of the police had been linear, that is, one of constant progress. In fact, the DSPM has experienced an unprecedented degree of continuity. To illustrate, Mayor José Reyes Baeza, who came to office in 1998, appointed Raúl Grajeda Domínguez to head the municipal police force. Grajeda's administration lasted six years and expanded over the terms of three city mayors from the Institutional Revolutionary Party (PRI), an unusual feat in Mexican local politics, even given the continuity of the party in power. Grajeda left the agency after the National Action Party (PAN) won the municipal government in 2004, and the new mayor, Juan Alberto Blanco Zaldívar, appointed Lázaro Gaytán

TABLE 7.4 ***Hypothesized*** **Lack of Continuity Across Administrations in Chihuahua City**

Timeline	1998–2001	2001–2002	2002–2004	2004–2007	2007–present
Party in power	Institutional Revolutionary Party (PRI)			National Action Party (PAN)	
Mayor	Reyes Baeza	Barousse Moreno	Cano Ricaud	Blanco Zaldívar	Borruel Baquera
Police chief	Chief 1	Chief 2	Chief 3	Chief 4	Chief 5
Policy	Policy 1	Policy 2	Policy 3	Policy 4	Policy 5

Source: Instituto Tecnológico y de Estudios Superiores de Monterrey, 2006.

TABLE 7.5 ***Empirical*** **Continuity Across Administrations in Chihuahua City**

Timeline	1998–2001	2001–2002	2002–2004	2004–2007	2007–2009
Party in power	Institutional Revolutionary Party (PRI)			National Action Party (PAN)	
Mayor	Reyes Baeza	Barousse Moreno	Cano Ricaud	Blanco Zaldívar	Borruel Baquera
Police chief	Raúl Grajeda Domínguez			Lázaro Gaytán Aguirre	
Policy		CALEA Accreditation			

Source: Instituto Tecnológico y de Estudios Superiores de Monterrey, 2006.

Aguirre to head the organization. Gaytán also managed to outlast an administration change and remains municipal director under the current PAN administration of

Carlos Borruel Baquera. While it is not impossible, it would be surprising to find another municipal police agency that has been led by only two men over a ten-year period.

Continuity has also occurred within the ranks of the police itself. Since legal reforms in 1993, the chief operations officers have come from within the ranks of the DSPM, ensuring that operations benefit from both institutional memory and local knowledge. The current operational director has led operations for the past four years—again overlapping two political administrations. In addition, the police statutes passed in 2001 outline something akin to a civil service reform for the police, allowing for a slow progress up through the ranks. Although leadership appointments can still be politically manipulated, such manipulation has to occur within a framework mandating a certain number of years on the force to be eligible for different ranks. As a result, all of the current police senior leadership at the rank of captain (coordinador) have served in the department for over twenty years.

There is even continuity in police-citizen interactions. In most Mexican police agencies, officers are rotated regularly and never patrol for long in the same area. Ostensibly, this is an anticorruption mechanism, designed to prevent police from extorting businesses for protection or developing commitments to criminal elements. However, there is a compelling counterargument to this policy: given constant rotation, the police never develop a relationship with the citizens they are protecting, never gain the trust of the community, and never develop local knowledge about crime problems. Most importantly for this discussion, citizens have no means to monitor individual officers in their neighborhood, because the police are constantly changing. In other words, constantly transferring leaders and police might not only fail to prevent misconduct, but it might prevent corrupt elements from being caught. As one interviewed officer commented about rotation policies, "If they are going to be corrupt here, then they are going to be corrupt somewhere else." Unlike most departments, however, Chihuahua's police have maintained their patrols in the same communities.

Finally and most importantly, there has been continuity in policy. To illustrate, the process for CALEA accreditation actually began during a PRI government, while Raúl Grajeda Domínguez was chief of police. Even though the accreditation process began under a different chief, a different mayor, and a different political party, the incoming chief Gaytán Aguirre continued the program of his predecessor and obtained accreditation. This is not insignificant. In the nearby cities of Mexicali, Baja California, and Hermosillo, Sonora, earlier administrations developed procedures and obtained the certification of ISO-9000, an international standard commonly used in industry and not specific to policing. Though in each case the initiative was much celebrated as a success of the administration, the following government simply allowed the certification to lapse. While the procedures developed at that time still exist on paper, they have not been updated, officers do not have a copy of them, and there is little emphasis on following them. It appeared likely that the same thing would occur in Chihuahua City. During his 2004 campaign, the PAN mayoral candidate criticized the accomplishment of his PRI predecessor, declaring that the police should obtain the "accreditation" of the citizens of Chihuahua rather than that of an international organization. Fortunately and to his credit, the new mayor was prevailed upon to allow the program to continue. Nonetheless, the episode reveals the pressure on political candidates to repudiate the achievements of their predecessors rather than ensure their continuity.

Tables 7.4 and 7.5 sum up the argument made here by contrasting what occurred in Chihuahua with what might have been expected to happen. Had the typical informal rules of Mexican local politics been followed in Chihuahua City, the past five administrations would have appointed at least five different police chiefs and initiated at least five distinct sets of policies. This hypothesized lack of continuity is illustrated in table 7.4. Chihuahua City, however, witnessed continuity in its police chiefs and its policies across different administrations and across different political parties. It is because of this degree of continuity that operational leaders can point as far back as 1992 to mark the beginning of the department's professionalization. It is for this reason that the advances made by an academy director seventeen years in the past are still viewed as important for the department's current development.

DISCUSSION

This chapter began with a question: Given efforts to improve the integrity of law enforcement and around three thousand different departments, why have only a handful of Mexican police departments managed to professionalize? To answer this question, I explore a case study of one of Mexico's few success stories, the DSPM of Chihuahua City. I find that the primary difference between Chihuahua and other municipalities has been continuity. As a result of continuity, Chihuahua City's DSPM has experienced a steady rate of improvement over time, something that has not occurred in other locations.

Unfortunately, however, continuity is something of a double-edged sword. In fact, continuity has traditionally been avoided in Mexican policing precisely as a means to reduce opportunities for police misconduct. By changing police chiefs frequently, it is hoped that they will not be corrupted during their short tenures; and by rotating police, it is hoped that they will not become co-opted by local criminal groups. In fact, the continuity of corrupt politicians, police chiefs, or police agents in their positions can produce a vicious circle that only ensures the continuation of police misconduct.

On the other hand, allowing for the continuity of good personnel, good policies, and good ideas allows for virtuous circles and an evolutionary professional development. So how does one separate out these two sides of the continuity argument? At its core, police professionalization means making an investment in the human resources of a police department. Departments would be better off prioritizing the continuity of personnel, policies, and ideas, while building sufficient accountability mechanisms to "discontinue" the individuals and policies that perpetuate police misconduct. In other words, there needs to be both continuity and accountability.

The importance of accountability mechanisms to solving the continuity dilemma points to a chink in the DSPM's armor. Although Chihuahua City's DSPM is a success story, it would be erroneous to overstate the gains made in the state of Chihuahua or to suggest that they cannot be eroded. The weakness of the department's accountability mechanisms is all the more salient given the increasing influence of organized criminal elements in the state. Since the beginning of 2008, the state of Chihuahua has become a major battleground between rival organized criminal groups resulting in more than 1,600 deaths in 2008 and nearly 900 by mid-2009.

Though Chihuahua City has avoided the worst of the drug-related violence experienced by its northern neighbor of Ciudad Juarez, it too has been heavily impacted. In the first month of 2009, four of its officers, including a district commander, were killed. Moreover, interview respondents expressed concern about organized criminal infiltration, and, in fact, the current state governor recently made the statement, "All the public security agencies are infiltrated—simply all of them" (El Diario 2008). These claims appeared to be supported when the head of the department's specialized units, along with two other officers, were arrested by federal officials. Time will tell if advances toward professionalism will help insulate the department against the increasing threat of organized crime. However, the weaknesses in accountability mechanisms and limitations of citizen oversight give reason for concern.

The drug trade and organized crime presents an additional challenge to the DSPM and municipal police forces throughout the country. Technically, even low-volume drug dealing and consumption are federal offenses that fall under the jurisdiction of the federal police. As a result, the DSPM is dependent on federal authorities to address an extensive problem that is at its core a very local police issue. Consequently, citizens are forced to watch drug deals occur with impunity as crime rates rise and allegations mount of local police turning a blind eye. At the end of the day, there is not an exact negative correlation between police professionalism and crime, and most citizens care first about crime rates and second about efforts to professionalize the police, viewing the latter as a means to address the former.

The rising crime levels and growing sense of insecurity played a roll in forcing the department's director Lázaro Gaytán to step down in late May 2009, after five years of distinguished service. As has happened in many of Mexico's conflictive municipalities, Gaytán was replaced by a retired military general Javier Aguayo y Camargo. While it is still too soon to determine with any confidence, the essential question for the future is whether Aguayo y Camargo and future administrations will build on the foundation created over the past decade or if the gains in professionalization will be rolled back by short term strategies focused on immediate security concerns.

REFERENCES

Carrasco Araizaga, Jorge. 2003. "Ningún avance in la policía mexicana," Proceso, October 12.

Comisión Estatal de Derechos Humanos. 2005. Recomendación No. 09/2005. http://cedhson.uson.mx/Recomendaciones/rec9.htm.

El Diario. 2008. "Todos los policías están infiltrados: Reyes Baeza," March 25.

El Universal. 2007. "36 Police Officers Jailed in N. León," May 16.

Gandaría, Manrique. 2007a. "Se han integrado 16 mil soldados del Ejército a la PFP," El Sol de México, May 22.

———. 2007b. "Reduce SSP a 3 meses el tiempo de capacitación para policías," El Sol de México, May 23.

Geddes, Barbara. 1996. Politician's Dilemma: Building State Capacity in Latin America. Berkeley, CA: University of California Press.

Guillén López, Tonatiuh. 2006. Gobiernos municipales en México: Entre la modernización y la tradición política. Mexico: El Colegio de la Frontera Norte and Miguel Ángel Porrúa.

Hernández, José. 2008. "Reporte de guerra al narco," El Heraldo de Chihuahua, July 7.

ICESI (Instituto Ciudadano de Estudios Sobre la Inseguridad, A.C.). 2006. Cuarta encuesta nacional sobre inseguridad/urbana. http://www.icesi.org.mx/documentos/encuestas/encuestasNacionales/ensi4_urbana.pdf.

La Frontera. 2007. "Atenta comando contra Capella Ibarra," November 17.

López Portillo, Ernesto. 2002. "The Police in Mexico: Political Functions and Needed Reforms." In Transnational Crime and Public Security: Challenges to Mexico and the United States, ed. John Bailey and Jorge Chabat. La Jolla, CA: Center for U.S.-Mexican Studies, University of Californa, San Diego.

Nájera Ruiz, Tonatiuh, ed. 2006a. "Diagnóstico Ciudadano de Percepción sobre Seguridad Pública." Mexico: Instituto Tecnológico y de Estudios Superiores de Monterrey.

———., ed. 2006b. "Diagnóstico Interno de Cultura Laboral." Mexico: Instituto Tecnológico y de Estudios Superiores de Monterrey and thel Comité Ciudadano de Seguridad Pública Municipal.

Paras, Pablo. 2006. The Political Culture of Democracy in Mexico. Mexico City: DATA Opinión Pública y Mercados.

Payan, Tony. 2006. The Three U.S.-Mexico Border Wars: Drugs, Immigration, and Homeland Security. Westport, CN: Praeger Security International.

Reames, Benjamin. 2003. "Police Forces in Mexico: A Profile." La Jolla, CA: Project on Reforming the Administration of Justice in Mexico, Center for U.S.-Mexican Studies, University of California, San Diego.http://repositories.cdlib.org/usmex/prajm/reames.

Sabet, Daniel. 2007. "The Border Bottleneck: Drug Trafficking and Incentives for Police Corruption." In Deceiving (Dis)Appearances: Analyzing Current Developments in Europe and North America's Border Regions, ed. Harlan Koff. Brussels: PIE/Peter Lang.

Secretaría de Gobernación. 2005. "Conociendo a los Ciudadanos Mexicanos: Principales resultados: Tercera Encuesta Nacional sobre Cultura Política y Prácticas Ciudadanos de la SEGOB." México: SEGOB. http://www.gobernacion.gob.mx/encup/terceraENCUP/Encarte_2005.pdf.

Tiempo. 2006. "La SIEDO debe aclarar identidad de Julio Porras," May 29. http://www.tiempo.com.mx/imprimir.php?id_n=7494&PHPSESSID=800b90e00fa0ee9bf97aae123138f217.

Transparencia Mexicana. 2006. "Índice Nacional de Corrupción y Buen Gobierno: Resultados 2001, 2003, 2005." http://www.transparenciamexicana.org.mx/documentos/ENCBG/2005/Folleto_INCBG_2005.pdf.

Transparency International. 2006. "Global Corruption Barometer." http://www.transparency.org/policy_research/surveys_indices/gcb.

Varenik, Robert O. 2005. Accountability: Sistema policial de rendición de cuentas. Mexico: Instituto para la Seguridad y la Democracia and Centro de Investigación y Docencia Económicas.

Public Security and Human Rights: Reflections on the Experience of Jalisco

Jorge Rocha Quintero

INTRODUCTION

The issue of public security in Mexico has gained great significance of late and has become one of the major topics on the federal government's agenda. However, there are serious concerns at the subnational level that the government's aggressive efforts to promote public security are endangering human rights and civil liberties. This study considers the implications of recent government efforts in the state of Jalisco, with a special focus on the greater Guadalajara metropolitan area, which has one of the state's highest crime rates, has been an important drug-trafficking area, and ranks high in terms of reports of human rights violations. I draw on the Jalisco experience to explore some core concepts guiding human rights theory and to illustrate the complexity and larger implications of human rights violations in Mexico.

The apparent contradiction between the protection of human rights and the actions and policies used to promote public security—that is, the false dichotomy between civil liberties and law and order—has been noted by scholars, activists, journalists, and others. One can read and hear in the local and national press, as well as electronic media, different social actors (business groups, the Catholic Church, and even some television personalities) vouch for the restriction if certain rights for the maintenance of personal security and the social order.

The logic underlying this perspective is an "exchange of rights," in which certain civil liberties and fundamental rights are traded (by necessity) for basic security. Unfortunately, this logic leads to the false conclusion that some rights are more important than others, and it ignores the integral relationship between our fundamental human rights and our right to security. An alternative perspective, proposed by Edgar Morin, emphasizes the integral nature and complexity of these rights, noting that any action regarding one right will have repercussions for the others (Herrera 2000).

THE COMPLEXITY OF HUMAN RIGHTS: MOVING BEYOND MINIMALISM

Some scholars assert the existence of a "hard nucleus" of core rights, whose protection is essential for the preservation of our humanity. This conceptual viewpoint suggests that there is an inalienable set of minimum rights that must be respected for all individuals, in any circumstance, time, or place (Gallardo 2000). This argument, though praiseworthy, suffers from two fundamental problems. The first is that there is no social or theoretical consensus about what minimum rights are necessary for the subsistence and development of the human individual. The determination of which rights belong to the nucleus of core rights is influenced by cultural and philosophical viewpoints, which differ within and across societal contexts. For example, in a capitalist system, a key fundamental right is the ability to accumulate and protect private property; in a Mesoamerican indigenous culture, collective rights would become part of this nucleus; and in farming cultures, the right to land would be essential. Hence, absent a consensus definition of the nucleus of core rights, those who hold political and economic power are usually the ones who ultimately define basic rights.[1]

The second problem with the assumption of a nucleus of human rights is that it focuses on the minimum level of protection of the most basic rights, rather than on the maximization of these rights. Hence the idea of a hard nucleus of rights not only ignores the possible progression or pursuit of a higher development of rights, it actually creates a definition of rights with a downward trend that takes us to the lowest common denominator (again, assuming we can identify some consensus as to what that might be). While it is true that most people would not cross the minimum line, it is a problematic starting point for a discussion of human rights because it necessarily limits our conceptualization of rights, and therefore circumscribes our reflection, evaluation, and ability to preserve those rights.[2]

Despite these problems, the presumption of a hard nucleus of basic rights is widely shared and has permeated the issue of public security in Mexico, where we have seen some trading of rights. For example, the right to private property has sometimes superseded the right to freedom of movement or freedom of association. Likewise, there have been cases where the physical integrity of some individuals has

---

1 A related problem is defining human nature, something that neither philosophers nor anthropologists have yet been able to do (Gallardo 2000).

2 An additional effect of the "minimum rights" logic is that it lessens the social responsibilities of big capital and government.

been violated in exchange for the physical integrity of others (cases of torture), in which rights are derived from social merit or power. This approach, then, takes us to a perennial paradox where the rights of some can only exist if the rights of others are violated. Who decides whose rights are respected and whose are violated? The answer depends on the particular political and economic forces present in a given society.

In short, rather than a universally accepted core of rights, there is in every society a much more complex panoply of rights that are interrelated and, though sometimes in tension, inseparable. As underscored by epistemologists like Edgar Morin, Alfredo Gutiérrez, and Guy Duval, social realities cannot be treated separately. That is, evaluating human rights protections in any society requires an understanding of the underlying social reality that determines both the existence and violation of human rights. Likewise, the rights in any society are linked to each other since they are observed or violated in concrete and specific realities. Some observers have postulated this same idea by asserting that respect for any given right implies, requires, and enables the respect of all others. Conversely, the violation of a given right constitutes a threat to the existence of other rights.

Such violations often appear in social conflicts that are symptoms of deep-rooted tensions. In Mexico, we can find cases where the complex integration of rights is manifested in a chain of human rights violations perpetrated in different types of social conflict. One clear example is the recent social conflict and human rights violations in Oaxaca, where unresolved social tensions resulted in violent confrontations between municipal police and members of the Popular Assembly of the Peoples of Oaxaca (Asamblea Popular de los Pueblos de Oaxaca or APPO). The first major conflict, on June 14, 2006, resulted in injuries, fatalities, and fifty arrests. Several violent incidents followed, including the death of U.S. journalist Brad Will of Indymedia.[3]

The state government managed to repress the APPO and restore order, but at the cost of numerous human rights abuses.[4] The government was able to undermine the

---

3 State Attorney General Lizbeth Caña García allegedly refused to prosecute a police officer who was photographed shooting at an independent activist journalist. The journalist died from gunshots following a clash between non-uniformed paramilitaries and unarmed APPO-aligned protesters. The killing of the journalist, Bradley Roland Will, a U.S. citizen, ultimately led the U.S. Embassy in Mexico to issue a public condemnation of the public security crisis in Oaxaca, spurring the outgoing administration of President Vicente Fox to deploy federal police in late October 2006 (Ross 2007).

4 This statement does not deny that there may have been excesses and violations of the law on the part of some members of APPO, and these should be prosecuted by law. However this does not justify

movement by arresting APPO's unofficial leader, Oaxacan political activist Flavio Sosa, who was lured to Mexico City in December 2006 on the pretext of official negotiations with Interior Ministry officials in the new Calderón administration. When Sosa arrived in the capital, he was arrested on charges of sedition and rioting (Reséndiz 2006). There was a simultaneous mass detention and deportation of rank-and-file APPO protesters, many of whom were arrested merely for participating in an APPO "mega-march" in downtown Oaxaca City in November. They were then transferred to a distant prison in the state of Nayarit, ostensibly to protect them from vigilantes. However, the deportations appeared to be part of a strategy of intimidation aimed at breaking a movement whose power lay in its ability to mobilize huge numbers of supporters. These serious abuses appeared to bear the stamp of Francisco Javier Ramírez Acuña, President Calderón's interior minister and formerly governor of Jalisco. Federal police were also involved in the state's strategy to crack down on APPO protesters while ignoring the vigilantism by progovernment paramilitary groups who were implicated in the deaths of several APPO supporters.

Although the government's strategy appeared to succeed in restoring order, sporadic protests, confrontations, and human rights abuses continued. On July 16, 2007, members of the APPO, teachers of Section 22 of the National Education Workers Coordinating Committee (CNTE), and social organizations in Jalisco embarked on a massive protest march during the annual celebration of the Guelaguetza festival.[5] When they reached the Cerro del Fortín, the venue for the festival, the protestors found it guarded by the state government's preventive police; the banking, industrial, and commercial auxiliary police; and Oaxacan municipal police. These security forces used tear gas and threw stones for three hours in an effort to stop the demonstrators. The outcome included the illegal arrests of people unrelated to the movement, extreme police violence, sixty people injured (including fifteen policemen and two others who were hospitalized in critical condition), and the burning of six buses, five private cars, and a water tanker. During the confrontation, the police assaulted reporters from several media outlets, including the national newspapers *Reforma* and *Milenio*, the local *Noticias de Oaxaca*, and the state government's Channel 9.

---

social repression, much less total inattention to the Oaxacans' underlying demands.

5 The Guelaguetza, held annually in June and July, showcases the unique expressions of Oaxacan folklore and culture.

National and international human rights organizations condemned the government's actions in Oaxaca in the strongest terms. On separate official missions to Mexico, the heads of Amnesty International (AI) and the Inter-American Commission on Human Rights (IACHR, part of the Organization of American States) collected testimony from victims who charged officials with committing and condoning police brutality, political assassinations, and illegal and arbitrary arrests in their continuing mismanagement of this simmering antigovernment rebellion centered in Oaxaca City. Neither AI Secretary General Irene Khan nor IACHR President Florentín Meléndez disputed the conclusion reached by Mexico's National Human Rights Commission (CNDH), which, in a report issued March 2007, blamed authorities with tolerating and carrying out rights violations that had led to some twenty deaths, mostly of antigovernment protesters, during the height of the Oaxaca conflict, from July to October 2006 (CNDH 2007). Amnesty International noted that this was not the isolated handiwork of rogue cops, asserting further that the physical brutality against protesters and the illegal detention of citizens were systematic and institutional. Among concrete recommendations, AI exhorted Mexican officials to implement a series of CNDH recommendations aimed at making government officials accountable for their handling of the unrest (Amnesty International (2007).

AI's report included testimony from victims who alleged that federal, state, and municipal police brandished guns at them, beat and kicked suspected antigovernment demonstrators, and threatened to rape, kill, and detain incommunicado persons believed to be associated with APPO. AI concluded that eighteen people, the majority of them antigovernment demonstrators, had been killed since the start of the rebellion in spring 2006, and that since that time authorities have failed to conduct "serious and impartial investigations into these abuses." Among other charges, the international human rights organization censured Oaxacan authorities for failing "to preserve crime scenes or gather and conserve evidence in a timely manner" and for selectively prosecuting suspected antigovernment protesters while turning a blind eye to the violence perpetrated by progovernment paramilitaries. The AI report describes a criminal justice system that intimidates victims, many of whom fear that filing complaints will draw reprisals. According to the report, state prosecutors were being manipulated by Governor Ulises Ruiz Ortiz and were reluctant to pursue cases that ran counter to partisan interests.[6] "The inertia of official investigations into reports of human rights violations stands in stark contrast to the burden placed on victims to identify perpetrators, get witnesses to testify and provide avenues of enquiry. This lack of due diligence on the part of investigators is a key obstacle to ending impunity which is widespread in Mexico's public security and criminal justice system" (AI 2007).

In a more diplomatically worded statement, the IACHR indicated that it viewed the "situation" in Oaxaca as fundamentally deriving from a long legacy of racial discrimination, social exclusion, and economic inequality suffered by the state's indigenous populations. It said further that it had collected:

> denunciations of violent deaths, extrajudicial executions, torture, police brutality, and disproportionate use of force, mass arrests, cases of individuals being held in solitary confinement and incommunicado, the use of snipers and tear gas, assaults on journalists, and public calls for attacks against human rights defenders and social leaders. Reports were also received about police who were held by demonstrators and beaten and injured; attacks using incendiary bombs or Molotov cocktails; and the destruction and burning of the judiciary headquarters and other buildings. According to the information received, public incitements to violence and attacks against the communications media also took place (IACHR 2007).

IACHR made a point of spotlighting the alleged disappearances of two Oaxacan men, Edmundo Reyes and Raymundo Rivera, believed to be held incommunicado by Oaxacan authorities because of their antigovernment political activities. However, the state government has repeatedly claimed it has no record of the men's whereabouts and that they are not in the penitentiary system. When the rebel Popular Revolutionary Army (Ejército Popular Revolucionario) took credit for bombing parts of a natural gas pipeline in Querétaro and Guanajuato in July, one of its principal demands was to know the whereabouts of Rivera and Reyes. IACHR President

---

6 Ruiz Ortiz, whose term runs till 2010, successfully dodged attempts aimed at forcing him out of office and also escaped efforts to federalize the state at the height of the conflict. Considered authoritarian by his detractors, Ruiz nevertheless enjoys the solid support of national leaders in the Institutional Revolutionary Party (PRI). He was able to bolster his support after the PRI won an absolute majority in the Oaxaca legislature in the August 2007 elections.

Meléndez also visited a hospital where a man who allegedly had been beaten by police was being treated in intensive care. In an apparent sop to Meléndez, Ruiz Ortiz ordered the parole of 239 inmates in state prisons who were described in the local press as ethnically "indigenous," a move that Meléndez reportedly welcomed. IACHR emphasized the importance of prosecuting cases against criminal public officials, because impunity only encourages further rights abuses. Likewise, the AI report asserted that "Ensuring that impunity for human rights violations is not allowed to prevail is the best guarantee of preventing future abuses. It would also be a clear demonstration to Mexican society and to the international community that the government of President Felipe Calderón is committed to protecting, ensuring, and fulfilling human rights" (Amnesty International 2007).

Oaxaca's economic situation provides important context here: 73 percent of the state's population lives in extreme poverty (US$1 per day or less); and 80 percent of its 570 municipalities are highly marginalized (with 32 percent very highly marginalized). Seven of the fifteen Mexican municipalities that rank lowest on the human development index are in Oaxaca. Furthermore, in several areas in the state there are problems related to access to water and the privatization of natural resources. In other words, there are violations of economic, social, cultural, and environmental rights in Oaxaca that both generate and are an effect of the violation of civil and political rights. The Oaxacan case provides a clear demonstration that the violation of one or more rights unleashes a multitude of violations to other human rights and to the law; the outcome is an absence of the rule of law.

When a society faces such miserable economic conditions, which themselves can be perceived as violations of basic human rights, it is understandable that radicalized social groups will retaliate by breaking the law. Of course, we must not minimize these violations, and those who commit them must be subject to the law. And that is the key; the official response must be to uphold the law, not to "enforce" it by nonlegal means. The latter approach inherently assumes that some rights must be made more important than others and that the "reason of the state" should be the determining factor in establishing the hierarchy of rights. Yet this suggests a false dilemma. Good public security policy is perfectly compatible with full respect for human rights. As Zepeda argues in this volume, ensuring that compatibility requires a move away from the old punitive model of public security to one that emphasizes community service and the preservation of public safety as the core missions of police agencies. Asserting this view is a paramount task today for researchers, academics, and social activists committed to human rights and the rule of law.[7]

Current Mexican public security policy fails utterly to achieve these goals because of the inefficiency and injustice in Mexico's criminal justice system, as Zepeda's chapter also illustrates. Here, however, I would like to focus on two separate issues. The first is the use of security forces for tasks other than those for which they were created, a problem well documented by Moloeznik in his discussion of the military in this volume. The second is the issue of the sociocultural construction of criminality. To illustrate, I draw on research conducted by Servicios y Asesorías para la Paz (SERAPAZ) in conjunction with the Instituto Tecnológico y de Estudios Superiores del Occidente (ITESO).

THE USE OF POLICE FORCES TO CONTAIN SOCIAL MOVEMENTS

Various human rights and legal defense groups throughout Mexico have documented police actions to inhibit or suppress social movements, especially in southern Mexico. In many cases, the violent repression of these movements by police results in the commission of serious human rights violations. Therefore, conflicts that should be resolved by political means and negotiation—or even through strategies of conflict prevention—wind up being resolved through state violence, with police forces as the direct perpetrators of human rights violations. Like an improperly used tool, police channel the incompetence—or, in the worst cases, the malevolence—of the politicians directing them. Below, I discuss the manner in which social conflict in Mexico generally, and in Jalisco specifically, provides a backdrop for human rights violations and political violence.

Social Conflict in Mexico

SERAPAZ, an nongovernmental organization (NGO) sponsored by Bishop Emeritus Samuel Ruiz García, emerged from the extinct National Intermediation Commission, which mediated between the Mexican federal government and the Zapatista National

7 Academic institutions in Mexico that have adopted this view are the member universities of the Jesuit University System, ITAM, the UNESCO School of Human Rights at UNAM, and the Autonomous University of Aguascalientes.

Liberation Army (Ejército Zapatista de Liberación Nacional, or EZLN) at the start of the EZLN conflict in 1994. Since then, SERAPAZ has been monitoring social conflicts, and in 2006 it conducted the first major study of social conflict by an NGO in Mexico.[8] SERAPAZ's study used a theoretical framework based on definitions of social conflict developed by Lorenzo Cardoso, who documented the number and types of social problems in Mexico. The results are surprising and sometimes worrisome. Looking at reports from various national media outlets from January to October 2006, SERAPAZ identified more than 590 conflicts. In 478 of these, public servants—particularly state-level officials in the executive branch—were the antagonists or instigators in the conflict. The groups that lodged the greatest number of complaints against authorities were peasant farmers and agricultural communities in Chiapas, Guerrero, Mexico State, and Oaxaca. A large number of complaints were also registered in the Federal District (Mexico City).

A significant element in these conflicts is the type of complaint filed. Most numerous were complaints related to the preservation of natural resources and patrimony, at 46.2 percent. Next, at 20.3 percent, were claims related to the need for and pursuit of personal security. This was followed by claims regarding opportunities for development (7.7 percent). Other causes given were: need for recognition (6.6 percent), improving political positions (5.2 percent), the attainment of political power (4.4 percent), the need for social inclusion (3.8 percent), representation (3.7 percent), and prestige (0.3 percent) (see table 8.1).

According to the SERAPAZ research, in 51 percent of cases there is a rights violation.[9] That is, there is a violation of human rights in half of the conflicts in Mexico. The strategies that popular groups most often employ in support of social causes are, in order of significance, street mobilizations, street blockages, public denouncement, street rallies, occupations of public buildings, strikes, and lawsuits. In some cases there was physical confrontation (thirty cases), and in a few cases weapons were used. It is noteworthy that citizens seldom use established channels for conflict

---

8 To my knowledge, there are no previous works on the number and types of conflicts in Mexico. What is available is research on cases of political violence, as well as the limited amount of information the government makes public. It is important to remember that freedom of the press and freedom of information are very new in Mexico, no more than ten years old.

9 Twenty-eight percent arise due to noncompliance with an agreement or pact, and 1.2 percent from noncompliance with international treaties to which Mexico is a signatory.

resolution (public denouncement and lawsuits). Two possible reasons for this are the inefficiency of the criminal justice system and a political culture in Mexico that does not lend itself to the peaceful resolution of conflicts.

TABLE 8.1 Sources of Social Conflict Identified by SERAPAZ (N = 590 incidents)

Source of Conflict	Percentage
Natural resources and personal assets	46.2
Personal security	20.3
Development	7.7
Recognition	6.6
Political positions	5.2
Political power	4.4
Social inclusion	3.8
Representation	3.7
Prestige	0.3

When SERAPAZ looked at the rates of intervention in conflicts that had arisen, it found that some type of action to resolve the problem had occurred in only 47 percent of the conflicts. In 19 percent of the cases there had been no response at all. (In 33 percent there was insufficient information to determine whether an intervention had taken place.) SERAPAZ divided the 47 percent of conflicts where there was some action aimed at resolution into two overarching groups. The first group involved voluntary intervention in the transformation of the conflict, including strategies such as negotiation, mediation, consensus building, and indigenous customary law (*usos y costumbres*). Of the cases involving voluntary intervention, 101 had been resolved through negotiation between the parties, 28 via mediation, 5 through consensus building, and one through customary law.

The second group includes imposed interventions, such as actions by administrative authorities, legal proceedings, arbitration, and repression. Of this category of interventions, 51 cases were channeled through some administrative authority, 35 cases were resolved through repression, 27 cases were resolved and/or stopped by legal proceedings, and 15 were ended through arbitration.

As to the "quality" and seriousness of these conflicts, SERAPAZ selected several paradigmatic conflicts that evidence the level of social conflict in Mexico. Among the cases selected were:

- Government repression against journalists: Demonstrations and protests followed the arrest of journalist Lydia Cacho after she reported on sexual child abuse and sales of child pornography among wealthy industrialists with ties to government officials in Puebla State.
- Civic demonstrations against crime: There have been numerous social mobilizations to protest the recent crime wave in Mexico, including protests against both drug cartel–related violence and against the government's strategy to combat the cartels. For example, demonstrators (reportedly organized by the cartels) took to the streets in Nuevo León to protest the presence of thousands of military troops the federal government had sent to the region to fight drug-related crime.
- Labor demonstrations: Mine workers staged a series of demonstrations after a February 2006 accident in the Pasta de Conchos mine in Coahuila killed 165 miners. The mine was plagued by unsafe working conditions, including substandard structural supports, poor ventilation, lack of monitoring equipment, and lack of emergency exits and alarms. The Coahuila state attorney general's office dropped wrongful death charges against five mine managers after the company issued US$1 million in reparations and paid the equivalent of thirteen months of salary for each miner killed (plus US$70,000 in reparations). Many miners and victims' families continued to protest, however, due to the company's failure to exhume most of the bodies and allegations that government officials had accepted bribes to drop the criminal charges.
- Land disputes: In May 2006, Mexico State police blocked flower vendors from a selling at the Texcoco market, stirring protests by supporters in nearby San Salvador Atenco and provoking a harsh government crackdown. Nearly 2,700 federal, state, and municipal police were called in to put down public protests over community land rights. The altercation left several community members dead, and there were numerous complaints of rape, illegal detentions, and other types of physical violence. In February 2009, by a vote of eight to three, Mexico's Supreme Court acknowledged that grave human rights abuses had occurred, but it absolved Mexico State Governor Enrique Peña Nieto and

> former federal public security secretary Eduardo Medina Mora (currently federal attorney general) of any responsibility, and also exonerated several other federal and state police commanders who planned the operation.[10]

SERAPAZ identified additional grave social conflicts, including protests over natural resource issues (such as demonstrations organized around the Fourth World Water Forum in 2007); demonstrations over human rights violations against Mexican migrants to the United States; protests over the controversial results of the 2006 Mexican presidential election; public outrage over government favoritism accorded to private-sector corporations (as through the Federal Telecommunications Law and the Federal Radio and Television Law); and demonstrations against government repression of political protests (as in the case of Oaxaca, discussed below).

As these examples evidence, there is reason for concern not only regarding the number of social conflicts in Mexico and the means used to resolve them, but also regarding the extraordinary variety and complexity of human rights violations and the structural violence embedded in these conflicts. These include the repression of free speech, corruption, violence against women, sexual child abuse, drug trafficking, human trafficking, and forced migration and exile, among others. SERAPAZ's final conclusions are categorical:

> The strengthening of the drug trafficking social subsystem, as well as crimes against children and women in our country, have increased social conflict due to the authorities' impunity, corruption, and complicity, which lead to a society without defenses and undermine our institutions. The authorities' terrible actions in their intervention in the Texcoco and San Salvador Atenco conflicts, on May 3 and 4 of this year, caused the conflict to escalate and not resolve itself. On the contrary, after five months it is evident that serious violations were committed by the municipal, state, and federal governments against the inhabitants and others who were present there (SERAPAZ 2006, 150).

10 For critics, the exoneration of Peña Nieto, Medina Mora, and other public security officials signaled that no public official would be held accountable for the numerous human rights violations that even Governor Peña Nieto has admitted took place. In contrast, six members of the San Salvador Atenco Peoples' Front in Defense of Land (FPDT) were subsequently captured and sentenced to prison terms of 112 years or more. See Aranda 2009; Torres Pastrana 2009; *La Jornada* 2009.

The Instituto Tecnológico y de Estudios Superiores de Occidente, sponsored by SERAPAZ, conducted a similar monitoring of social conflict in Jalisco for March 2007. Among the very interesting results are the following: In just this one month, there were nine conflicts in the state; four were related to demands for infrastructure and services, one involved problems in the rural sector, and two included demands against discrimination or cultural identity issues (ITESO-SERAPAZ 2007). The strategies of confrontation in Jalisco differ from the nationwide pattern, since the main social action is public denouncement. In the ITESO sample, denouncements were made to the authorities and the media in four of the conflicts, and a strategy of marches and rallies was pursued in three cases. The remaining two cases recurred to lawsuits and blockages of public spaces.

There is another data series that merits our attention. There are human rights violations in a third of the cases examined by ITESO. As to the intervention strategies in the conflicts, there was mediation in three, negotiation in three, no action in two, and imposition by an administrative authority in the final case. Agreement was reached between parties in four cases, but there was no agreement in another four. (There was no information on the remaining case.) ITESO also reviewed follow-up on the agreements: the agreed-upon resolution had been partially complied with in five of the conflicts, but there had been no compliance in two cases (ITESO-SERAPAZ 2007).

The SERAPAZ and ITESO studies reveal the high level of conflict that exists, respectively, in Mexico as a whole and in the state of Jalisco, with their associated levels of human rights violations (50 percent at the national level and 33 percent at the state level), the most sensitive issues being the lack of public security, inappropriate use of natural resources, and discrimination. The research reports show that the intervention strategies pursued by the authorities are insufficient, and not all conflicts are resolved via negotiation or mediation, meaning that in these cases no consensus is reached. Moreover, in many cases where agreements are put in place, they are not carried out in full, creating a breeding ground for continued social unrest.

In other words, as long as the political class does not guarantee the validity of rights, social conflicts will erupt. When they do, government may find an imposed solution to be its easiest path or, if a resolution is negotiated or mediated, those in power may simply fail to live up to their end of the bargain. This creates a scenario where the Mexican political class may use police forces for social conflict resolution, not a purpose for which they were created.

Let us now examine the way in which security forces are being employed by the current federal administration and some state governments in Mexico.

Political Violence in Mexico

At the start of the Felipe Calderón administration, the National Network of Human Rights Civic Organizations "All Rights for Everyone" (Red TDT), which links fifty-seven nongovernmental organizations across Mexico, conducted a brief analysis of the utilization and reform of police forces throughout the country. Among the main findings was the increasing militarization of police forces in both southern and northern Mexico, but for different purposes. In the southern states, militarization was directed at repressing and controlling social movements, while in the north the objective was to combat organized crime.

There has been a series of military deployments in indigenous communities in Mexico's southern states to curtail social conflict and insurgency. This militarization began in 1994, when troops were sent to deal with the Zapatista uprising, but it has now extended to other indigenous regions. In March 2007, at a meeting of the National Indigenous Congress in Tuxpan, Jalisco, attendees confirmed that militarization is a serious problem facing indigenous villages, especially those communities that have chosen to fight for their rights. The newspaper *La Jornada Jalisco* reported on March 13, 2007, that indigenous people had accused the military forces in their communities of provoking an array of problems, including a climate of fear, searches and theft of their belongings, and even cases of rape. Perhaps the most harmful long-term effect of the military's interventions in indigenous communities is the rupture of the social fabric and the appearance of "new" problems that these communities do not know how to counter, such as alcoholism, prostitution, and divisiveness within the community.

In addition to these direct military influences, there are other, indirect consequences, such as the appearance of paramilitary groups—local inhabitants who are trained and armed, sometimes by the military, for the purpose of carrying out counterinsurgency and low-intensity warfare. The "Fray Bartolomé de las Casas" Human Rights Center in Chiapas has been documenting militarization and the resurgence of paramilitary groups in the region. Concurrent with militarization, according to NGOs in the Red TDT, there have been cases of repression and harassment on the part of the police in several states. The Red TDT documented murders in Chiapas,

Guerrero, and Veracruz; "disappearances" in Chiapas and Oaxaca; and several cases of violence against journalists in Oaxaca, Guerrero, and Tabasco.

Meanwhile, military and police forces in northern Mexico and in Guerrero and Chiapas have focused most of their efforts against drug traffickers and organized crime syndicates. Critics view the militarization of the drug war in Mexico as a political ploy more than an effective action against drug trafficking.[11] At the outset of the Calderón administration, there were numerous proposals aimed at enhancing police forces, not only improving their training, numbers, and weaponry, but also increasing their authority and effectively creating a new kind of police force.

This effort was apparent in Jalisco where, in late 2006, then governor Gerardo Octavio Solís presented an initiative to create an undercover police.[12] The central point of his reform proposal was the formation of a secret police that could infiltrate criminal organizations in order to provide the information or evidence that the appropriate authorities needed to perform their crime-fighting mission. It should be noted that the crimes to be pursued were of local jurisdiction. For instance, drug trafficking would not be included, because it is under federal jurisdiction. Another element in Solís's reform proposal was the creation of a witness protection program for persons who provided evidence that would allow for the prosecution of a crime. The witness's identity would be kept secret, and the witness would be allowed to testify via videoconference or other electronic means.

Solís's initiatives met with a great deal of opposition because of the low efficacy and high corruption that characterized the Jalisco police. However, a more fundamental objection involved the ethical and legal dilemmas that undercover policemen would face: What will they do when they have to commit a crime? Do they report the fact at that moment? Do they participate in the criminal event? Do they commit the crime if it is minor and denounce it when it is more serious? This proposal stood on very murky ground and would have legitimized law breaking by agents of the government, raising a whole other set of legal and ethical questions: Is it ethical to fight a violation of the law with another violation? Would undercover policemen be legally exempt? Would they have to carry false government-issued documents so they

---

11 An element that stands out in this regard and that Moloeznik discusses in his chapter in this volume is the high level of desertion in the Mexican army and the federal preventive police.

12 Solís went on to direct the consultants in the Interior Ministry when it was headed by former Jalisco governor Francisco Ramírez Acuña.

would not be identified as members of the police? What would happen in these cases with regard to the laws guaranteeing transparency and public access to information? In the end, the proposal did not win approval.

For the Red TDT, initiatives like this one seriously undermine the protection of human rights. In all of the cases noted above—the shame of Atenco, the repression of the Popular Assembly of the Peoples of Oaxaca, and the low-intensity war in Chiapas—social protest was criminalized and police were used to contain social discontent in a way that contributed to the violation of human rights. This situation is not new, nor are the administrations of the National Action Party (PAN) immune to the problem. When Vicente Fox assumed the presidency in 2000, Mexico had already received a series of international recommendations over human rights violations. For example, the United Nations Human Rights Commission had outlined four points of concern and made thirteen recommendations to the Mexican government regarding torture. Further, the special rapporteur on extrajudicial, summary, or arbitrary executions, Mrs. Asma Jahangir, had asked Mexico to take urgent and preventive measures aimed at protecting the lives and safety of civilians who are victims of police, the armed forces, paramilitary groups, and opposition armed groups. IACHR had made twelve recommendations to guarantee the right to justice and three more recommendations regarding freedom of speech violations (Rocha 2001).

The last finding of the member groups of the Red TDT pertain to types of mobilizations and demands around which people and communities in Mexico are organizing. In southern states, demands focus on issues involving natural resources, indigenous community rights, women's rights, gender and reproductive rights, public security, and abuses by the national petroleum company, Pemex. Red TDT member groups found that social organization in this region tends to be strong. In Mexico's central states there are also numerous organizations that appear to have a solid presence. The demands that galvanize groups in central Mexico regard gender rights, women's rights, natural resource issues, and "La Otra Campaña."[13] Natural resources are the core issue in the western states, but organization in this region is poor. In northern Mexico demands focus on natural resources, migration, public security, and women's rights. As in western Mexico, social mobilization here is low and infrequent.

---

13 In "La Otra Campaña" (The Other Campaign), members of the EZLN traveled by caravan around Mexico, networking as they went with leftist organizations and civil society throughout the country.

Though the level of social mobilization varies by region, it is fairly continuous, and several federal, state, and local police forces have been called upon to contain activists' actions. In the process, there have been violations of free speech and association, torture, and other cruel and degrading treatment—and, ultimately, a failure to achieve peaceful resolution of conflicts and to address social problems.

The practice of torture deserves special mention here. According to Human Rights Watch (2006), the states where torture is most persistently employed are Jalisco, Chihuahua, and Guerrero. In Jalisco, in particular, the Justice Center for Peace and Development (CEPAD) affirms that torture increased 1000 percent from 2000 to 2006, during the term of Governor Francisco Ramírez Acuña (CEPAD 2007). In its evaluation of this six-year period, the "Miguel Agustín Pro Juárez" Human Rights Center (PRODH) pointed to a "hard-line" trend of increasing sentences and charging minors as adults (Centro de Derechos Humanos "Miguel Agustín Por Juárez" 2006). Both the Red TDT (2006) and Human Rights Watch (2006) agree that the situation in Mexican jails is very serious; they highlight in particular the excessive use of preventive incarceration, which creates an environment conducive to torture and abuse. Given the use of repressive measures to curtail social protests, many of the alleged "criminals" awaiting trial and sentencing in Mexican prisons are actually social advocates and members of grassroots organizations.

Under the current situation in Mexico, it is clear that the strategies employed in the name of protecting public security are not compatible with the protection of human rights. A crucial step toward reestablishing compatibility between public security tasks and respect for human rights would be to eliminate the impunity now enjoyed by both the perpetrators of human rights violations and those who direct them. Recent reforms to the criminal justice system and public security tasks represent important advances in this direction, strengthening protections for the accused, reducing the use of pretrial detention, and providing access to effective legal defense for everyone, not just the privileged few who already enjoy the benefit of good counsel.

THE SOCIOCULTURAL CONSTRUCTION OF CRIMINALITY IN MEXICO

Because of the many flaws and lacunas in Mexico's current criminal and public security system, discretionary elements loom large in the prosecution of crime, paving the way to a series of unwritten though effective policies. One of these unwritten policies is the sociocultural construction of criminality, which I define as the stigmatization and persecution of certain sectors, groups, and social practices as alleged or potential criminals. That is, in the social imagination, specific groups are identified as breakers of socially and morally accepted customs and, hence, as inherently evil.

These "evil ones" can be identified by specific characteristics: they dress a certain way and live in very well-defined areas. They even have a particular phenotype, giving rise to the "crime" of having a certain physical appearance, the "wrong look" (*portación de rostro*). These social groups are denounced a priori and they are harassed on a daily basis. Unfortunately, the media have confirmed and disseminated this assignation of the imagination of evil. This yellow journalism is an indisputable example of the social construction that proposes these imaginariums and makes them effective in the construction of social relationships.

The social groups that have been portrayed as evil or having a proclivity to crime include homosexuals, indigenous people, youths, and the urban poor, among others. ITESO has reviewed the phenomenon of the criminalization of young people and found several flagrant violations of youths' rights in Jalisco.

The first case that brought public attention to this problem occurred in Tlajomulco, a suburb of Guadalajara, on May 4, 2002. Young people were holding a rave, with dancing and loud music; the event's organizers had all the appropriate permits for the party. Around midnight, however, more than one hundred agents from various law enforcement agencies broke in, without any judicial order, and forced the 1,500 attending youths to lie face down on the floor. Anyone who tried to talk, move, or resist met with degrading and cruel treatment, ranging from blows and insults to being threatened by police at gunpoint. The reason the police gave for the operation was that they were searching for drugs. In the end, only twenty-five people were arrested, and twenty of these were later released without charges being filed. Five were booked, three were prosecuted, but none was found guilty. In effect, these youths were "criminalized" for holding a wild party.

The second case occurred on May 28, 2004, when a march was held in downtown Guadalajara to protest the III Summit of Latin America, the Caribbean, and the European Union (LACEU). At the end of the march, the demonstrators and security forces clashed. No one was arrested, but later a wave of arbitrary detentions took place downtown that yielded seventy-three illegal detentions, fifty-five cases of cruel and degrading treatment, nineteen people tortured, and documented cases of sexual harassment of women, according to the Special Report from the National

Human Rights Commission (Espeleta 2007). In the Mexico section of Amnesty International's 2006 report, under the heading of "arbitrary detention, torture, and mistreatment," there are comments on twelve cases in which people participating in the Guadalajara march were prosecuted based on confessions extracted under torture. Further, the Amnesty International report makes special note of the authorities' refusal to investigate the accusations of torture. Human Rights Watch, in its Mexico report (2006), also presents the case of the Guadalajara march as a situation of great concern.

The common denominator in both of these cases of human rights violations in Jalisco is that most victims were youths, since that was the criterion used for the arrests. Violations of the rights of this age group are now a central issue in public debate, and they are present as a backdrop in several recent incidents:

- The first of these incidents involves measures taken by the Mexican Soccer Federation and police forces in several cities against soccer teams' fan clubs, sometimes restricting their access stadiums, subjecting them to often-demeaning searches at building entrances, prohibiting sales of alcohol only in stadium sections frequented by the clubs, and using public and private security forces to keep those same sections "under siege." In fact, in some stadiums there is even a mobile unit from the public prosecutor's office in place.
- The second example is the trend toward privatizing higher education, which reinforces the elite identity present among student groups and denies access to this type of education to broad segments of the youth population. Policy makers consider many arguments when implementing educational policies, but they rarely take into account the opinion of the youths who will be affected.
- The third situation is the systematic persecution and curbside extortion of youths in the Guadalajara metropolitan area, especially young people who are poor or members of an "alternative" culture.[14] The latest incident of this type was the severe beating given to two youths from the Street Cultural House, a space for youths' citizen formation, in June 2007. Judicial policemen allegedly assaulted the youths over some neighborhood problem. Their brutality was so excessive that one of the young people suffered skull fractures. Again we see a space occupied by young people subjected to rights violations. This is echoed

14 These subcultures include anarko-punks, alter-globalizationists, and Goths, among others.

in recent legislative proposals in Jalisco that would impose stiffer penalties on "taggers," whose graffiti a local legislator compared to "dogs marking their territory."

- Other tendencies that follow along these same lines are the repressive policies concerning the sexuality of young people, influenced by the Catholic Church's conservative moral strictures and uninformed by scientific information; and crime-fighting strategies in the "Clean Mexico" initiative that propose searching backpacks and doing drug tests on elementary and middle school students. Once more we find the victims treated as if they were criminals.

Other data that shed light on the situation of youths in Jalisco are UNICEF's Indicators for Children's Rights in 2005 and 2006, which measure Mexico's performance on basic human rights (to survival; to develop to the fullest; to protection from harmful influences, abuse and exploitation; and to participate fully in family, cultural, and social life) at each life stage of a child or adolescent. The measures are based on a scale of 0 to 10, with the highest score assigned when a right is fully exercised (*Gran Alianza por Jalisco* 2007).

The scores for Jalisco, where children and adolescents form 38 percent of the state's population, reveal important deficits in terms of the UNICEF Convention on the Rights of the Child, especially with regard to adolescents (see table 8.2).

TABLE **8.2** **Rankings on "Protection of Children's Rights" in Mexico and Jalisco (0–10 scale)**

Age	National Average	Jalisco	Jalisco's Ranking among Mexico's 32 States
0–5 years	5.71	6.41	15
6–12 years	6.53	5.91	23
12–17 years	5.53	5.05	25

These varied incidents all share a common thread: the invisibility of the validity of youths' human rights. Young people in Jalisco, and also in Mexico more generally, are often presumed to be criminals, violent, lazy, lowlifes, and sexually deviant. They are presumed to be prone to behaving without concern for the law or social mores and must, therefore, be "kept in line." Some social sectors perceive that youths have lost traditional values, live only for the moment, do not prepare themselves sufficiently for the future, do not read, and are overly materialistic. Others see Mexico's youth as a prime market, to be saturated with advertising about fashion and personal appearance, high-tech gadgetry, and music—all aimed at transforming young people into natural consumers. Still others see them as a transition group to be molded for incorporation into the globalized world of work and marketplace, shaping them, as Brazilian educator Paulo Freire (1988) remarked, for productivity and globalization. They are the new reserve army for the capitalist system. According to this view, those who do not fit the mold are a threat to the social order. Hence they are labeled as criminals, gang members, and thugs in another example of the social construction of criminality, which creates the stereotypes of social "goodness" and "evil" upon which the policies base their actions.

There are other stigmatized groups in Jalisco, such as the Indigenous Migrant Support Team (Equipo de Apoyo al Migrante Indígena, or EAMI), which aids indigenous people in the Guadalajara metropolitan area, and the Colectivo Ollín, which supports the rights of advocates of sexual diversity and sexual and reproductive rights. Both groups have been targeted by the police; police abuses against them have included extortion and demands for sexual favors.

However, as the following cases illustrate, one social group has been targeted for abuse even more than these others: homosexuals. The first notable case occurred when a transvestite prostitute in the Plaza del Sol shopping district was shot, for no apparent reason, by individuals in a pickup truck. The second case was one of harassment—death threats and destruction of property—directed against workers from the Human Rights Commission of Jalisco (CEDHJ) and members of the nongovernmental organization CAMPO, A.C. because of their advocacy for sexual and reproductive rights. In the third case, in 2007, state authorities denied custody rights to a transsexual parent, asserting that the parent constituted a negative influence on his/her adopted child. The child, a girl, had been cared for by the transsexual parent for eight years, after being abandoned by her drug-addicted biological mother. The transsexual had cared for and provided for the daughter, and the only reason for terminating legal custody was that he/she was perceived to have a "deviant" sexual orientation.

The media contribute to the underlying sociocultural constructs that determine who and what is deviant. For Tina Rosenberg (2004), the media coverage of public security issues has encouraged three misperceptions among Mexican society. First, the media promote a highly erroneous perception about crime levels. In several studies Rosenberg found that people who watch television news are very frightened, and they view public security as being worse than it is perceived by people who do not depend on televised news for their information. The University of Guadalajara conducted a survey in 2006 on media consumption and found that 85.4 percent of city residents watch television newscasts (Universidad de Guadalajara 2006). Of the people who watch television, 26.1 percent cite news programs as their favorite broadcast type, putting this programming on par with the highly popular soap operas. If Rosenberg's correlation between TV news viewing and feelings of public insecurity holds true, we would expect to find a widespread sense that public security in Guadalajara is low. This is confirmed by results from a survey conducted by the Citizens' Institute for Study of Insecurity (ICESI) in 2006; even though crime indicators had fallen in Guadalajara in 2005, 53 percent of the Guadalajara residents surveyed by ICESI said they felt unsafe in their city.

The media's second effect on public opinion is that they increase popular support for "firm-handed" policies. The media often link information about government plans to involve the military or police with the presence of "evil" or "deviant" people in society, rarely offsetting this biased coverage with attention to deeper, structural issues in need of a government response. Hence it is not surprising that consumers of television news support enhanced punishment for juvenile criminals, advocate longer prison sentences and the death penalty, and countenance inhumane prison conditions.

The third effect that Rosenberg identified is the media's promotion of racism. Rosenberg described countless incidents in which more coverage was given to cases in which the victim was white and the alleged offender was a minority than to cases where the actors' ethnic or racial attributes were reversed. This feedback loop of the reinforcement of stereotypes contributes to building the "sociocultural criminality construction." This plays out in Mexico in the severe and systemic repression of indigenous people who dare give voice to their demands, and these are the same individuals who are the least likely to enjoy legal protections in the face of militarized justice and police repression.

What we have then, in the face of this legal and institutional vacuum, is a de facto public security policy that socioculturally builds criminality and pursues persons and social groups, not for committing crimes, but for having belonged to certain social groups or having realized certain social practices. This presents an inherent contradiction or dilemma for Mexican police, moreover, because a large fraction of them come from these very same groups or social strata, giving rise to the "cacique" phenomenon (Freire 1988)—a reference to the bosses in farming communities who mistreated and assaulted their own brethren. It is clear that the unwritten public security policy consisting of the sociocultural construction of criminality is incompatible with respect for human rights, especially rights linked to tolerance, difference, and diversity.

CITIZEN ALTERNATIVES

The de facto incompatibility between respecting human rights and maintaining public security remains an urgent challenge for Mexico, but it need not continue unresolved. Through discussion, debate, and reflection we can develop guidelines to reform police forces in ways that enable them to achieve public security for everyone while also respecting everyone's human rights. We should also look to the experiences of other countries, exchanging best practices and establishing agreements for collaboration.

Still, though observing other nations' experiences in this area is important, Mexico must develop an approach to human rights that responds to the particulars of its regions and its people, especially given its notable social and territorial diversity. For example, the public security problem in Guadalajara, which has a population of 4.5 million in an eminently urban area, is not the same as that of Techaluta, a rural municipality seventy kilometers away, with a population of only three thousand inhabitants. Thus, rather than developing broad national policing models, Mexico would do better to address local experiences and generate changes from that basis.

Nongovernmental organizations and research institutes have identified four core principles that should guide public security policies: (1) prioritized attention to the citizen, (2) absolute respect for the law, (3) absolute respect for human rights, and (4) transparent policies and actions by police agencies (CDHDF et al. 2004). An additional and equally crucial component for police reform—consistent with the goal of protecting both public security and human rights—is establishing accountability mechanisms. That is, while the use of discretionary power is an integral component in policing, police decisions and actions must be subject to criteria that are clearly defined in advance and to subsequent appraisal after the fact. The guiding criteria must emphasize not only police effectiveness and efficiency but also the proper treatment of crime victims and suspects. Recent efforts to strengthen protections for individuals accused of a crime (including access to a strong public defense) constitute an important step in this direction. In addition, individual citizens and civil society as a whole must play a role in the development of accountability mechanisms, including as citizen review boards and watchdog groups.

Another thread in police reform may be to encourage experimentation with alternative models of justice—especially the rich historical tradition of alternative justice mechanisms that exist in Mexico's indigenous communities. Over the last decade, for example, sixty-two communities in six municipalities in Guerrero[15] have developed their own community police and alternative sentencing mechanisms (such as compensation for material damages) through the Community System for Security, the Administration of Justice, and Reeducation (Sistema Comunitario de Seguridad, Impartición de Justicia y Reeducación) (CDHDF et al. 2004). This system, which has been endorsed by the "Tlachinollan" Mountain Human Rights Center, has thus far reduced the crime rate by 95 percent (Centro de Derechos Humanos de la Montaña "Tlachinollan" 2005), providing a real alternative to reliance on municipal police and local prosecutors.

Another example is the indigenous judges in Chiapas, who promote conflict resolution in Tzeltal communities and have won the endorsement of the Indigenous Rights Center (Centro de Derechos Indígenas, CEDIAC) in Bachajón, Chiapas. According to Arriaga (2002), the system of Tzeltal judges relies on civilians designated to serve as the *jmeltsa'anwanej* (central arbiter or judge) and the *jcoltaywanej* (advocate of indigenous peoples' rights). These judges follow well-defined criteria for regulating social behavior in harmony with local culture and custom. Individuals who deviate from local norms are subject to a process of reconciliation that includes direct encounters between the involved parties and draws on the guidance of civic and community leaders. The fundamental elements of this system are the acceptance of responsibility, forgiveness, counseling in an environment of harmony, and reconciliation. In some cases, individuals are required to pay restitution of material damages or are sanctioned in other ways defined in Tzeltal tradition (Arriaga 2002, 1).

The common denominators in these two examples of alternative justice mechanisms are that both derive from organized grassroots efforts, draw on native customary

15 The municipalities are San Luis Acatlán, Malinaltepec, Marquelia, Metaltonoc, Copanotoyac, and Tlapa de Comonfort.

law (*usos y costumbres*), and are efficient. Such practices offer the hope that alternative forms of justice can play an important role in Mexico's approaches to justice sector reform over the longer term, at least in certain local contexts.

CONCLUSIONS

This chapter documents how the alleged incompatibility—the false dichotomy—of preserving public security and respect for human rights is based on an erroneous assumption that is tied to the problems of the police forces and has no theoretical or empirical support. Mexico can no longer use the police to contain social discontent or create socioculturally based profiles of criminality. The sociocultural construction of criminality, which extends beyond police forces to permeate all of society, leads to police inefficiency and corruption and to violations of human rights.

A stronger citizen presence is needed in the debate and also in the ongoing oversight of public security policies. Citizens can also promote and support promising alternative justice mechanisms. A key element in this regard is to build alternatives at a local level, models that reflect local experiences, are regionally appropriate, and respond to each community's cultural practices.

REFERENCES

Amnesty International. 2006. *2006 Annual Report on Human Rights Worldwide.* Madrid.

———. 2007. "Oaxaca: Clamour for Justice," Mexico Report, August 1. http://www.amnesty.ie/amnesty/upload/images/amnesty_ie/campaigns/mexico/Mexico%20-%20Oaxaca%20Clamour%20for%20Justice.pdf. Accessed August 4, 2007.

Aranda, Jesús. 2009. "SCJN exonera a Peña Nieto y Medina de abusos en Atenco," *La Jornada,* February 12.

Arriaga, Luis. 2002. "El sistema jurídico tzeltal." Manuscript.

CDHDF (Comisión de Derechos Humanos del Distrito Federal), Insyde, PRODH, Fundar, Red TDT. 2004. *Seguridad pública, prevención del delito y derechos humanos: Construyendo alternativas desde la sociedad civil y los organismos públicos de derechos humanos.* Mexico: CDHDF.

Centro de Derechos Humanos de la Montaña "Tlachinollan." 2005. *Migrar o morir: El dilema de los jornaleros agrícolas de la montaña de Guerrero.* Mexico.

Centro de Derechos Humanos "Miguel Agustín Pro Juárez." 2006. *Derechos incumplidos, violaciones legalizadas: Los derechos humanos en el sexenio 2000–2006.* Mexico: PRODH.

CEPAD (Centro de Justicia par la Paz y el Desarrollo). 2007. *Informe sobre la situación de los derechos humanos en Jalisco 2006.* Guadalajara: CEPAD.

CNDH (Comisión Nacional de los Derechos Humanos). 2007. "CNDH Special Report on Events in Oaxaca City between 2 June 2006 and 31 January 2007." http://www.cndh.org.mx.

Espeleta, Mariana. 2007. *Derechos civiles y políticos de los jóvenes de Jalisco en el sexenio 2000–2006.* Guadalajara: CEPAD.

Freire, Paulo. 1988. *Pedagogía del oprimido.* Mexico: Siglo Veintiuno.

Gallardo, Helio. 2000. *Política y transformación social: Discusión sobre derechos humanos.* Quito, Ecuador: Tierra Nueva.

Gran Alianza por Jalisco. 2007. "Propuesta de la Mesa Temática de Derechos Humanos de la Gran Alianza por Jalisco." Unpublished.

Herrera, Joaquín. 2000. *Hacia una visión compleja de los derechos humanos: En el vuelo de anteo.* Bilbao, Spain: Desclée de Brouwer.

Human Rights Watch. 2006. *El cambio inconcluso: Avances y desaciertos en derechos humanos durante el gobierno de Fox.* New York: Human Rights Watch.

IACHR (Inter-American Commission on Human Rights). 2007. "IACHR President Urges Investigation into Acts of Violence in Oaxaca." Press Release No. 45/07. http://www.cidh.org/Comunicados/English/2007/45.07eng.htm. Accessed April 1, 2009.

ICESI (Instituto Ciudadano de Estudios sobre la Inseguridad). 2007. "Cuarta encuesta sobre seguridad 2006." www.icesi.org.mx/documentos/encuestas/encuestasNacionales/ensi4_urbana_2005.pdf.

ITESO-SERAPAZ. 2007. "Informe de la conflictividad social en Jalisco, Michoacán y San Luis Potosí." Unpublished. Tlaquepaque, Mexico.

La Jornada. 2009. "Suprema impunidad," February 13.

Red TDT. 2006. *Agenda de la Red Nacional de Organismos Civiles de Derechos Humanos "Todos los derechos para todas y todos."* Mexico: Red TDT.

Reséndiz, Francisco. 2006. "Denuncia APPO captura de tres activistas," *El Universal,* December 7.

Rocha, Jorge. 2001. "¿Una moneda de dos caras? Los derechos humanos y el nuevo gobierno." In *Fox a un año de la alternancia.* Tlaquepaque, Mexico: ITESO.

Rosenberg, Tina. 2004. "Si sangra, encabeza las noticias: Los costos del sensacionalismo." In *Violencia y medios.* Mexico: Incide-CIDE.

Ross, John. 2007. "Who Killed Brad Will?" *San Diego Citybeat*, August 8.

SERAPAZ (Servicios y Asesorías para la Paz). 2006. "Informe de la conflictividad social en México." Unpublished. Mexico.

Torres Pastrana, Sandra. 2009. "Represión en Atenco, necesario precedente para decidir voto ciudadano," *CIMAC Noticias*, February 17.

Universidad de Guadalajara. 2006. "Encuesta estatal sobre medios y audiencias en Jalisco 2006." Guadalajara: Universidad de Guadalajara.

Future Directions for Police and Public Security in Mexico

David A. Shirk

The authors assembled in this volume provide insights into some of Mexico's most critical contemporary public security challenges, with special attention to the multiple dysfunctions of the country's police agencies. This concluding chapter lays out some final observations on Mexico's overall public security situation, with a view to the long-term prospects for achieving the rule of law. The volume's authors offer several practical recommendations, which are summarized here along with consideration to the major changes that are to be introduced to Mexico's justice system over the next decade. This concluding chapter also points to the vital role that the United States can play in helping to improve Mexico's public security situation, as well as the important benefits that could result from doing so.

REFLECTING ON MEXICAN PUBLIC SECURITY

As this monograph came to press in early 2009, Mexico's situation had deteriorated to the point that some U.S. analysts viewed Mexico as one of the two countries worldwide—along with Pakistan—most likely to suffer a sudden collapse into a failed state.[1] Even amid the problems of elevated drug violence and rampant corruption that Mexico currently faces, the prospect of total state failure appears to be greatly exaggerated. Despite a potentially serious legitimacy crisis in Mexico's 2006 presidential succession, the country's basic governance institutions remain highly functional. Indeed, in the first three years of his term, the government of President

1 Specifically, the report asserted, "In terms of worst-case scenarios for the Joint Force and indeed the world, two large and important states bear consideration for a rapid and sudden collapse: Pakistan and Mexico.... The Mexican possibility may seem less likely, but the government, its politicians, police, and judicial infrastructure are all under sustained assault and pressure by criminal gangs and drug cartels. How that internal conflict turns out over the next several years will have a major impact on the stability of the Mexican state. Any descent by Mexico into chaos would demand an American response based on the serious implications for homeland security alone" (United States Joint Forces Command 2008).

Felipe Calderón sustained consistently high approval ratings. Further, Calderón's government achieved several significant reforms—fiscal, energy, education, and justice reforms—that proved elusive for his predecessor, Vicente Fox. Meanwhile, in 2009, despite the still unresolved 1994 Chiapas rebellion and isolated attacks by other insurgent groups, the central government maintained a solid monopoly of territorial control throughout the country. Moreover, despite fears of "Colombianization," Mexico's drug-related violence—even in heavily saturated states like Chihuahua, Sinaloa, and Baja California—remains well below the levels seen in Colombia in the 1990s and 2000s.[2]

Still, there is no doubt that high-profile violence and criminal impunity, the ineffectiveness and corruption of the state's security apparatus, and a dire lack of access to justice all present severe challenges for Mexico. Indeed, Mexico's overall picture is one in which the combination of elevated levels of violent crime and ineffective law enforcement contributes to severe "public insecurity," with negative implications for Mexico's domestic political and economic situation. In recent years, organized crime groups have targeted numerous government personnel at the federal, state, and local levels for assassination and kidnapping, including public officials who are not strictly linked to public security matters. There is also some concern that Mexico's public security situation has become a detriment to Mexico's economy, particularly the tourism industry.[3]

As noted throughout this monograph, domestic law enforcement capabilities are so ineffective that they have been largely stripped of key functions, and public officials have increasingly turned to the military as a last resort to provide for basic order. As observed by Zepeda, the core functions of Mexican law enforcement have been gradually transferred away from local preventive police forces and concentrated in state and federal judicial police agencies. Local police officers, who represent the vast majority of Mexican police, are not authorized to receive crime reports from citizens,

---

2 Due to a combination of cartel, insurgent, and political violence, homicide rates in Colombia spiked dramatically during the 1990s and remained very high in the 2000s. According to SIGOB (n.d.), Colombia's homicide rate ranged between 57 and 79 per 100,000 inhabitants from 1990 through 2000. According to the BBC (1999), Colombia's 1999 rate of 59 per 100,000 meant that there was an average of three murders every hour.

3 It is not clear to what extent cartel violence has had an effect on the Mexican business climate or Mexico's US$13.3 billion tourism industry. In 2008, international visits actually increased by nearly 6 percent, according to Carlos Behnsen (2009), head of the Mexico Tourism Board.

are not equipped to conduct criminal investigations, and are not properly prepared to preserve crime scenes and evidence. Moreover, most Mexican police officers lead lives that are terribly impoverished and characterized by victimization, low self-image, and constant disparagement by citizens.

Meanwhile, as Moloeznik asserts, the expansion of the military's mandate correlates with the public's negative evaluations of the competence and reliability of civilian police agencies. As Moloeznik notes, the meager results offered by domestic police pave the way for the "militarization of public security." Among public sector institutions, the military has enjoyed the highest approval ratings in all of Mexico.[4] Unfortunately, the military is a very blunt instrument, lacking the proper mandate and training for domestic law enforcement, and its involvement has already contributed to significant allegations of human rights abuses. Moreover, the ongoing commitment of troops raises critical questions about whether the military is in truth immune to the kind of corruption found in Mexican police agencies, whether its integrity can be sustained over an extended period, and when its domestic law enforcement mandate will finally end. Indeed, once the military genie is released, putting it back into the bottle may prove difficult.

As Moloeznik points out, there have been disturbingly high levels of defection by Mexican military personnel, many of whom appear to have developed ties to organized crime. In fact, in recent years organized crime groups have brazenly taunted and recruited military personnel to join their ranks, with promises of higher pay, better food, and a more glamorous lifestyle. All of these trends raise serious concerns for democratic governance in Mexico, as ordinary citizens legitimately fear for their basic safety, lose confidence in public officials and institutions, and show a worrying willingness to trade civil liberties for security.[5]

---

4 In polling conducted by Parametría (2006), the military ranked first in public approval among all public sector institutions and second to the Catholic Church among major institutions in Mexico.

5 In January 2009, the National Human Rights Commission (CNDH) reported that complaints of human rights abuses at the hands of the military had nearly doubled from 2007 to 2008, with 631 complaints against the military by mid-December 2008 (*Reforma* 2008). Meanwhile, Mexican support for the use of the harsher penalties—including the death penalty—appeared to grow along with the public's concerns about heightened insecurity. Indeed, in a national poll published by the polling agency Consulta Mitofsky in December 2008, a vast majority of respondents (94.8 percent) approved of increasing penalties for violent crimes. A smaller number, though still a strong majority (74.8 percent),

Many casual observers, and even some crime experts and high-ranking public officials, view Mexico's current public insecurity crisis as the result of a "culture of lawlessness."[6] Yet, as the authors in this monograph make clear, Mexico's criminal justice system is undermined by serious systemic problems related to institutional function, incentive structures, and human capital formation. Mexico's public security agencies are ill equipped, police lack professional training and preparation, their mandates are incongruent with the challenges they face, and there are inadequate mechanisms to ensure effective public oversight of police conduct. These institutional weaknesses in the public security apparatus suggest that Mexicans are not inherently lawless—at least no more so than people in the United States or elsewhere. Rather, in the absence of effective law enforcement, criminal impunity reigns.

In addition to the institutional factors noted above, Mexico's rule-of-law challenges are also fundamentally tied to Mexico's recent economic situation and the process of democratic consolidation. The volatile economic conditions and political transformation that Mexico has experienced over the last thirty years have coincided with elevated levels of crime and violence. In effect, Mexicans have been subjected to two very different forms of uncertainty that have compromised the rule of law. Major currency fluctuations and economic difficulties beginning in the 1970s appeared to increase certain forms of criminality in Mexico, notably robbery. For some Mexicans lacking opportunity, crime seems to have been an alternative means of economic survival in difficult times. More recently, in some Mexican communities—notably along the U.S.-Mexican border—there is danger that a vicious circle is developing, in that criminal activity harms the economic outlook by discouraging tourism and driving away foreign direct investment. Recent reports suggest that low-level hired gunmen working for the cartels pull "jobs" for as little as US$300 per hit (Díaz 2009).

Until recently there was some cause for expectation that Mexico was headed toward a more prosperous economic situation, as measures of poverty appeared to decline, the middle class appeared to experience modest growth, and in 2008 per

---

approved of applying the death penalty for certain crimes, particularly rape, homicide, and kidnapping (*Consulta Mitofsky* 2008).

6 Indeed, during the July 2007 conference in Guadalajara that convened the scholars featured in this monograph, State Secretary for Public Security Carlos Nájera expressed precisely that perspective.

capita GDP rose above US$10,000 for the first time.[7] Moreover, some Mexican economists and officials expressed their confidence that Mexico's economy was effectively becoming "delinked" or "decoupled" from the U.S. economy, and would therefore not be entirely dependent on U.S. economic fortunes (or necessarily subject to its misfortunes).[8] However, the downturn in the U.S. and global economies in 2008 had substantial impacts in Mexico. In October 2008, Mexico began to experience the worst decline in the value of the peso since 1994, leading to a 45 percent drop relative to the dollar by February 2009. Since some forms of common crime (notably robbery) appear to be related to Mexico's economic difficulties over the last three decades, the severe downturn of the global economy could spell further increases in crime in Mexico in the coming years.

The rule of law in Mexico has also been significantly affected by macro-level political changes in recent decades. As single-party rule gradually gave way to an increasing political pluralism in the 1990s, this introduced a host of new and different governance challenges. As Flores contends, democratization disrupted a once stable and predictable system of official corruption that operated at disturbingly high levels. In February 2009, allegations by former drug kingpin Miguel Ángel Félix Gallardo appeared to corroborate Flores's analysis. Félix Gallardo produced a 32-page handwritten prison manifesto asserting that high-level officials from the Office of the Federal Attorney General (PGR) under the Salinas administration distributed the *"plazas"* to Mexico's major drug traffickers in the 1980s (Castillo García 2009). Over the 1990s the gradual decline of the Institutional Revolutionary Party (PRI)

7 As pointed out by the Mexico City–based business news service *Mexico Watch* (2008), there is some debate about when Mexican GDP per capita reached the above-mentioned milestone. In August 2008, the Mexican statistical agency, INEGI, announced second-quarter GDP figures that showed gross domestic output reaching 114,891 pesos per capita, placing nominal GDP per capita at greater than US$10,000 for the first time using present, end-of-quarter, and average second-quarter exchange rates. However, using purchasing power calculations, the World Bank actually put Mexican GDP per capita at $10,040 in 2003 and at $12,580 by 2007.

8 Writing in 2007, prior to the deep economic retrenchment of the following year, Morgan Stanley analyst Luis Arcentales observed that Mexican exports to trading partners other than the United States were on the rise to such an extent that it might help to abate the effects in Mexico of a U.S. economic downturn. While cautious about the extent of de-linking, Arcentales observed that "the dynamism of Mexican non-U.S.-bound exports is helping to soften the hit on Mexican economic activity from sharply lower U.S. import demand." http://www.morganstanley.com/views/gef/archive/2007/20071024-Wed.html#anchor5715.

dramatically shifted the political landscape and complicated the context for Mexican organized crime. By 2000 there was newfound political will at the federal level and in several states to combat drug trafficking. After several significant blows against the major drug traffickers, these organizations began to splinter and battle each other for turf in a more uncertain political context, where politicians could not be as easily co-opted as part of a grand bargain with Mexico City.

To be sure, official corruption by the cartels persists. A January 2009 *Reforma* newspaper investigation found that 759 police were arrested in sixteen Mexican states in 2008 (most of them with ties to drug trafficking). Moreover, corruption continues to be a problem at all levels of government, with major indictments accomplished through Operation Cleanup (Operación Limpieza) in the last months of 2008 against some of the highest-ranking officials in Mexican law enforcement, such as Mariano Herrán Salvatti (Mexico's drug czar in the 1990s, charged with embezzlement during a recent five-month stint in the Chiapas state government); Noé Ramírez Mandujano (former chief of the PGR's SIEDO unit, charged with investigating organized crime); and two former directors of Interpol Mexico, Rodolfo de la Guardia García and Ricardo Gutiérrez Vargas. In May 2009, in the most spectacular anti-corruption initiative in Mexico in recent memory, federal authorities detained ten mayors and other local officials in the state of Michoacán, the home state of President Felipe Calderón and a longtime locale for the production and transit of drugs (De la Luz González and Gómez 2009). Such advances present a stark contrast to the old "hierarchical" model described by Flores, where organized crime was pervasive and virtually unstoppable, and corrupt public officials were protected at all levels by a lack of checks and balances. Seemingly, as Flores suggests, democracy has introduced greater uncertainty and instability for organized crime, since the political pluralism and alternation of elites in power has resulted in sincere efforts by public officials to introduce transparency, accountability, and good governance. At the same time, it is also possible that the seemingly honest intentions of some public officials also serve—unwittingly or otherwise—the interests of competing drug-trafficking organizations battling for market share. A blow against one cartel may simply benefit another. Hence it is difficult to determine whether these incremental gains against organized crime will bear fruit.

What is clear is that an overhaul of the entire justice sector is severely needed to support the consolidation of democratic governance in Mexico. This reform must

TABLE 9.1 Key Policy Recommendations

The findings of the authors in this volume point to a number of useful policy prescriptions that should be taken into consideration as Mexico moves forward with other efforts to reform its criminal justice system.

POLICE PROFESSIONALIZATION

- Police professionalization requires not only greater education and training for officers (well beyond the average four months of academy training), but also higher standards for recruitment, more generous compensation and benefits, and stronger civil service protections.
- Police professionalization requires a wholesale transformation in the internal organization of the corps in order to reduce systemic corruption, but also changing the day-to-day realities and working conditions of Mexican police officers in order to establish a viable career in public service.
- Police professionalization requires the institutionalization of good governance practices, including measures to ensure continuity within police agencies across governmental administrations.
- In steering law enforcement agencies toward community-oriented policing, civic groups and communities can and should play a central role in monitoring and engaging police agencies to ensure transparency and accountability in law enforcement. In particular, citizen oversight councils for police require greater institutionalization, financial support, and access to information.

THE PERILS OF MILITARIZATION

- At present, policy makers evidently may have little choice but to continue the deployment of the military for domestic policing activities in order to address organized crime and transnational security challenges, but this strategy must be a short-term option with a constant eye toward the long-term improvements in the domestic public security apparatus.
- Careful monitoring of the military is needed to prevent the pernicious effects of corruption and increased human rights violations.

Table 9.1 Key Policy Recommendations (*Continued*)

- Measures are needed to ensure effective civilian-military collaboration because military personnel are not trained or authorized to conduct the kind of investigative police work that is necessary to aggressively prosecute crime in Mexico.

JUSTICE REFORM AS A LONG TERM STRATEGY

- An efficient, transparent, and fair criminal justice process, while urgently needed, will require large and sustained investments—in training and education—over the span of the next decade.
- The development of a strong legal profession—particularly the development of adequately supported public defenders—will be a critical check on law enforcement; the best quality control for police is a strong public defender's office.

OTHER CONSIDERATIONS

- In structuring agency and institutional relationships in law enforcement, centralization of power involves serious risks and hazards, including high-level complicity with organized crime.
- Crime-fighting efforts must take care to avoid stigmatizing and targeting certain social groups considered "deviant," such as young people, soccer hooligans, and gays and lesbians.

be broadly based, with an emphasis not only on achieving basic security but also on the more elusive goal of promoting the "rule of law." This concept—the rule of law—includes the provision of public order (effective enforcement of the law in society), a degree of accountability on the part of public officials (government bound by law), and a level of access to justice (fair and efficient treatment under the law), elements that are severely lacking in Mexico. Mexico's current rule-of-law crisis provides a unique opportunity to bolster the rule of law, given that there is presently widespread support for major reforms to Mexico's justice sector.

As the authors in this volume illustrate, police reform must be a major component of any such reform effort. An increase in the number of Mexican police officers has not translated into either corresponding drops in crime rates or a decrease in the public's perception of the crime rate; hence the focus must be on improving the quality of police and policing. Moreover, it is important to understand that Mexico's police and police agencies historically performed "order maintenance" functions, and were not tasked with promoting the rule of law in a context of democratic governance. Even in this basic sense, Mexican police agencies are in dire need of greater resources, modernization, professionalization, and technical training. Yet, taking into consideration their broader functions in contributing to the rule of law, Mexican police agencies must also be made more accountable to public scrutiny and better equipped to protect the rights of victims, suspects, and convicted criminals. The authors in this volume offer numerous valuable policy recommendations for improving policing and public security, most of which emphasize the urgency and complexity of professionalization.

There are three major considerations for moving forward. First, the authors in this monograph offer several important lessons and recommendations regarding police and policing, which are outlined briefly below (see table 9.1). Second, the sweeping changes introduced by recent Mexican justice sector reforms will also have major implications for law enforcement, and they must be taken into consideration in the context of our discussion of police reform. Finally, given the impact of transnational organized crime on Mexico's domestic security situation, there are inevitable international considerations, particularly with respect to the possible role of the United States in helping to address these challenges.

RETHINKING MEXICAN POLICING

There are two major considerations regarding the reform of Mexican policing. The first is that police reform is essential for sustained democratic governability in Mexico. As Zepeda points out, the transition to democratic governance has changed the role and expectations for Mexico's law enforcement institutions. The "face of the state," as Zepeda describes it, must become friendlier and better suited to the needs and expectations of the citizenry. No longer an instrument of repression or political control, police must now play a role as civil servants and protectors of the public. This transformation will require a major overhaul of police institutions in Mexico, with an emphasis on public service, professionalism, and community policing.

Yet, as the authors in this volume make clear, contemporary Mexican policing suffers from a lack of professionalism in large part because of the institutional incentives and conditions under which police operate. Azaola and Suárez offer useful, if disturbing, insights into the daily working conditions of police. Police lack proper equipment and training, they are burdened with long hours and stressful conditions, and they are integrated into an organizational climate where there are few rewards for virtue and many opportunities for vice. Their work suggests that police are a product of their organizational context.

In theory, the transformation of Mexican policing and public security ought to be facilitated by the pressures and expectations resulting from democratic governance. That is, given greater political pluralism and more democratic processes, over time citizens should be able to hold their elected leaders accountable more effectively at the ballot box. However, the ban on consecutive reelection in Mexico creates a serious obstacle, both for policy makers and for the public.[9] The ban on reelection means that mayors and governors are restricted to a single three- or six-year term, respectively, which seriously limits policy continuity. The ban on reelection also deprives citizens of the opportunity to reward success, since there is no direct electoral connection between elected officials and their constituents. If officials in a given administration fail to make improvements in public security, it is not those officials that necessarily pay the price. Rather, citizens must vote another party into office and hope that this results in the change that they desire. Sabet's research on local policing in Chihuahua underscores the gains that can be made when effective policies are transferred from one administration to the next, but it also illustrates that—in a context of no reelection—such continuity is highly dependent on informal serendipity. Thus one major recommendation for improving Mexican policing is to develop more effective formal institutional mechanisms to promote continuity across administrations. Reelection offers only one solution, and it is arguably not the most viable in the near term.

---

9 Concerns about reelection date back to the 1910 Revolution, when Mexicans rose up in opposition to the perpetual presidency of General Porfirio Díaz. Yet these concerns are also reinforced by a widespread distrust of politicians today. For most Mexicans, the ban on reelection provides a comforting guarantee that the "rascals" will be booted out of office at the end of every term.

Another option is the development of civic organizations and citizen oversight committees, which can play a positive role in promoting better practices and greater policy continuity. In recent years there has been a proliferation of civic organizations that serve as watchdogs for police and public officials, including groups like Mexico United Against Crime (México Unido Contra la Delincuencia) and the Citizens' Institute for the Study of Insecurity (Instituto Ciudadano de Estudios Sobre la Inseguridad, ICESI). In addition, the establishment of citizen oversight committees offers a formal channel by which the public can monitor and promote greater accountability for police agencies. At present, most citizen oversight committees in Mexico are appointed by the sitting mayor or governor, have very limited formal authority, and in many cases lack the time, information, or professional qualifications to serve as effective watchdogs. Such oversight committees could be strengthened by:

- developing more democratic selection procedures for members of state and local citizen oversight committees;
- extending oversight committee members' terms of office to overlap those of elected officials, such as the use of a four- or five-year term;
- staggering the selection of oversight committee members at different points in time to insulate the committee from abrupt changes and allow for greater institutional memory within the committee; and
- establishing requirements for police agencies to ensure the standardized reporting of crime indicators and basic operational information (as, for example, the size of the police force, salary ranges, and so on).

The above reforms are particularly attractive because they would help to introduce greater transparency and accountability without significantly greater cost. Additional efforts to strengthen citizen oversight committees might also be worth considering, such as the approval by a majority of citizen oversight committee members for the appointment, demotion, or dismissal of command-level personnel. However, since most citizen oversight committees require members to volunteer their time, increasing their obligations for very detailed evaluations of police operations could prove excessively burdensome and counterproductive.

A second important consideration with regard to Mexican policing has to do with the structuring of Mexican police agencies and their function within the overall criminal justice system. The different components of the Mexican criminal justice system have not traditionally been integrated; that is, historically the provision of "public security" in Mexico has been treated as separate and distinct from the legal processes and institutions involved in "the administration of justice." This separation of functions has meant that, until recently, most Mexican police have had a very different role than that played by their counterparts in the United States, where local police are entrusted with investigative powers to collect evidence that can be used in trial. Thanks to recent justice sector reforms, Mexican police agencies will begin to have a larger role in criminal investigations, and they will need to develop the capacity to play this critical support role in the administration of justice.

At the same time, the restructuring of Mexican police agencies will necessarily involve a certain degree of decentralization and policy innovation at the state and local levels. During the period of PRI rule, power was effectively centralized by virtue of the ruling party's monopoly in all branches and levels of government in Mexico's federal system. State and local governments had extremely limited resources and operational capacity, and were heavily dependent on the federal government. Beginning in the 1980s and 1990s, Mexico began to experience a greater degree of decentralization, in the form of greater power sharing and a more equitable distribution of resources among the federal, state, and local (municipal) levels of government. Along the way, decentralization has allowed for local experimentation in the policies and practices used by police agencies. However, faced with the complex challenge of confronting organized crime and severe public security threats, some national authorities have advocated for the centralization of Mexico's public security apparatus, including the possible creation of a national police.

While these recommendations focus on increasing the effectiveness and accountability of police, it should be noted that there are limits to police reform with regard to both the speed with which it can be accomplished and the ultimate effectiveness of police in society. Police reform efforts should not be expected to yield immediate results, and simply throwing money at the problem—for example, by paying police higher salaries—is not sufficient. The kind of police reform required in Mexico will involve a prolonged process, in which police must be properly trained, their agencies and units must be adequately equipped, their compensation and benefits must be increased, civil service protections must be developed, effective oversight mechanisms must be created, and more positive community relations must be developed.

Moreover, even after major advances have been made in achieving these objectives, the overall effectiveness of police may be limited. In the 1990s, police expert David Bayley (1994) emphasized that the conventional wisdom about police—that police can have an impact in reducing crime—has not been well supported empirically. Indeed, his comparative studies of policing suggest that there is little correlation between crime rates and a number of different aspects of policing: the size of a police force, the intensity of patrolling, the efficiency of crime clearance rates, or the rate of incarceration.[10] Moreover, most police work around the world is very routine—which is to say, largely boring and trivial—with about two-thirds of police time spent on patrol and the remainder taken up attending to investigation, traffic management and moving violations, operational support, and administrative details. According to Bayley, only a small fraction of their activities attend to problems of major or violent crime, while the rest involves responding to things "that-ought-not-to-be-happening-and-about-which-someone-had-better-do-something-now." Furthermore, Bayley's work suggested that police are ultimately not particularly effective in "solving" crimes. Even in developed countries with highly professional police forces, police tend to be very ineffective in solving crimes, with clearance rates of 45 percent in Canada, 35 percent in Great Britain, 30 percent in Australia, and 22 percent in the United States (Bayley 1994: 20–21).

Over the 1990s, however, as crime rates fell significantly in the United States, a different perspective on policing began to emerge. A pervasive view began to develop among criminologists that even the relatively minor contributions made by police are important in reducing crime. This new school of policing derived from "broken windows" theory, which posits that minor crimes communicate the idea that no one cares and thereby contribute to larger offenses. This school of thought suggests that police can have a significant impact in reducing crime through effective community policing and rigorous law enforcement for even minor infractions. One problem with the broken windows approach is that it primarily focuses on taking criminal offenders off the streets, with little attention to subsequent consequences. Short-term incarceration for petty crime may unnecessarily stigmatize minor offenders, build undesirable networks among criminal offenders in prison, reduce opportunities for

10 Hence it may be that police are to crime what doctors are to a traffic accident; while they can help to address the problem after the fact, they have little effectiveness in prevention.

later social integration (such as employment and property rental), and ultimately contribute to higher rates of recidivism for that offender.

In short, expectations for contemporary efforts to promote police reform in Mexico must be tempered against the reality that results will not come quickly and may not achieve what is so sorely needed: an overall reduction in crime and violence in Mexico. This is not to say that police reform is futile. Indeed, given rampant problems of corruption and ineptitude, reform remains an urgent priority if only to protect the public *from* the police. In other words, one of the main goals of police reform initiatives in Mexico should be to make law enforcement agencies more benign and less of a detriment in society. Once that feat is accomplished, any gains in reducing crime and violence would be a welcome and added benefit.

Finally, some of the most important influences on the function and effectiveness of police will be the changing expectations that result from larger reforms to Mexico's criminal justice system. In March 2008 the Mexican Congress and the administration of President Felipe Calderón approved a major package of constitutional and legal reforms that will dramatically transform the functioning of the Mexican judicial sector over the next decade. These reforms will implement an eight-year transition from Mexico's long-standing inquisitorial system of criminal justice to a more rights-based accusatorial model, similar to the one that has developed in the United States over the last forty years. Advocates of judicial reform hope that these changes will ultimately make the Mexican criminal justice system more effective, efficient, and just. The implications for police are enormous, since the reforms will introduce new investigative capabilities as well as new expectations for the role that police will play in the administration of justice in Mexico. The implications of Mexico's justice sector reforms are considered in more detail below.

JUSTICE SECTOR REFORM

There are five main elements of Mexico's new justice sector reforms. First, the reforms clearly establish the bases for an accusatorial system, in which prosecutors and the accused present their cases in a public, oral trial before a neutral judge. The reforms specifically assert the presumption of innocence, the right to a quality defense provided by the government, and the physical presence of a judge during trial proceedings (since many cases are presently handled by clerks).

Second, the reforms specifically seek to limit the use of preventive detention, or "pretrial" detention. Currently, because of case backlogs and inefficiencies, an estimated 40 percent of Mexico's prison population has not been sentenced and is awaiting a final verdict. Many suspects are detained even when charged with relatively minor offenses, such as shoplifting or causing an automobile accident. Moreover, pretrial detainees are frequently mixed with the general prison population and in many instances do not receive a sentence for years. Under the new reforms, pretrial detention would apply only in cases of violent or serious crimes, would require separate prison facilities, and would be limited to up to two years without a sentence.

Third, the new reforms introduce a number of important changes for Mexican police agencies. Specifically, the reforms strengthen the formal investigative capacity of police to gather evidence and investigate criminal activity, in collaboration with the public prosecutor, or *ministerio público*. This is significant because, until recently, as many as 75 percent of Mexico's more than 400,000 police lacked investigative capacity and were deployed primarily for patrol and crime prevention. Under the reforms, police are also now subject to special labor provisions which give administrators greater discretion to dismiss law enforcement personnel.

Fourth, the reforms introduce new provisions to help crime victims. Under the present system, rape cases frequently require the use of a *carreo*, a face-to-face confrontation between the victim and the accused. However, the new reforms include privacy protections to conceal the identity of the victim and allow for reparations for harms resulting from the crime. Importantly, the reforms also establish a right for the victim to challenge actions or inaction by the judge or prosecutor in a criminal case.

Finally, the new reforms also target organized crime, defined in accordance with the United Nations Convention against Transnational Organized Crime, signed in Palermo, Italy, in 2000. That convention broadly defines an organized crime syndicate as "a structured group of three or more persons, existing for a period of time and acting in concert with the aim of committing one or more serious crimes or offences [with a maximum sentence of four or more years in prison] … in order to obtain, directly or indirectly, a financial or other material benefit." In cases involving organized crime, the Mexican Constitution has now been amended to allow for the holding of suspects under *arraigo*, arrest without formal criminal charges, for up to forty days (with possible extension up to eighty days). Under the reforms, prisoners may also be sequestered, held in solitary confinement, and placed under special house arrest. Furthermore, in order to facilitate extradition, the reforms also allow for the suspension of judicial proceedings in criminal cases.

In short, the scale of change that these reforms will bring is enormous. Courtrooms will need to be remodeled, lawyers will need to be retrained, and existing legal codes and norms will need to be radically overhauled. Mexico's thirty-two state governments have been given up to eight years to fully implement the reform. Several states—notably Chihuahua, Oaxaca, and Nuevo León—had already adopted elements of the reform prior to 2008, providing important precedents to inform the federal-level reforms. In a relatively short period, those states have seen significant increases in judicial sector efficiency, which provide cause for optimism as the reforms are implemented elsewhere.

Proponents of Mexico's justice sector reforms point to successful transitions from inquisitorial to accusatory systems elsewhere in Latin America, notably Chile. The use of oral procedures reduces paperwork, increases efficiency, and helps to eliminate case backlogs. The emphasis on rights—for both the victim and the accused—strengthens the rule of law by promoting not only "law and order" but also governmental accountability and equal access to justice. Yet Mexico's reforms have also faced serious criticism, both from traditionalists and from advocates of more substantial reform. Adherents to Mexico's traditional inquisitorial system have expressed concerns that the reform constitutes an ill-conceived, costly, and potentially dangerous attempt to copy the Anglo-Saxon model of justice, without consideration of the intricacies and nuances of the civil law tradition. In other countries where similar reforms have been implemented, such as Honduras, inadequate professional capacity in supporting areas (such as police investigation) has undermined effective administration of justice. Critics worry, therefore, that the reforms may be trying to do too much with too few resources and too little preparation.

Meanwhile, others worry that the reforms have not gone far enough to protect the rights of the accused, having introduced measures—such as the holding of organized crime suspects without charge—that they feel may actually undermine fundamental rights and due process of law. To be sure, protecting the legal rights of crime suspects is often unsavory to the public, but it helps to ensure that the government is itself bound by the law and that all citizens have access to justice. In Chile and elsewhere, concerns about pretrial release and the risk of flight by the accused have led to backsliding on reforms that provided important protections for the presumption of innocence. Hence there is some concern that Mexican authorities may give in to practical and public pressures that will undermine the rights-based aspects of the reforms.

In May 2009, Mexico's Federal Attorney General Law (Ley Orgánica de la Procuradoría General de la República) and Federal Police Law (Ley de la Policía Federal) passed both chambers of Congress, giving more investigative powers to the Public Security Ministry (SSP) through the creation of the Federal Police and effectively dissolving the Federal Agency of Investigations (AFI) of the federal Attorney General's Office's (PGR), to be replaced by the Federal Ministerial Police.[11] The Federal Attorney General Law gives the PGR an investigative police force that can now respond to the new challenges posed by organized crime in Mexico, a function that the AFI carried out until early June, when the law went into effect.[12] The AFI came under fire in 2005 as the object of widespread allegations of corruption, and in December of that year the PGR announced that nearly one-fifth of the agency's officers were under investigation for suspected involvement in organized crime. Agents of the AFI took to the streets in April 2009 to demand that the PGR and Congress not allow the agency to disappear. Nonetheless, the measure was approved by Congress, and President Calderón signed it into law on May 29 (*El Economista* 2005; *El Financiero* 2009; Méndez 2009; Ramos and de la Luz 2009).

Under these reforms, agents of the Attorney General's new police force will have greater powers to investigate crimes but will also be subjected to more rigorous compatibility tests. The Federal Ministerial Police will be led by Nicandra Castro Escarpulli, who in the past worked as head of the kidnapping department under the Assistant Attorney General for Special Investigation of Organized Crime (Subprocurador de Investigación Especializada de Delincuencia Organizada, SIEDO). From the date the new law went into effect, the PGR had thirty days to purge its rosters of undesirable personnel. Former AFI agents who can pass toxicology, medical, psychological, and background checks will be given priority in the new agency. For its part, the Federal

11 For this discussion of Mexico's new police reforms, we are indebted to TBI Research Associate Cory Molzahn, who authored the original discussion for our Justice in Mexico Monthly News report in May 2009.

12 The AFI was created by presidential decree in 2001 to bolster the investigative capacity of the Federal Attorney General's Office (PGR). At that time, the AFI replaced the corruption-plagued Federal Judicial Police in order to bring about a more professional, scientific, and comprehensive investigative process that would take aim at the operational foundations of organized crime—similar to the stated goals of the new Federal Ministerial Police.

Police Law effectively bestows investigative powers upon what was previously the Federal Preventive Police (PFP), which carried out a strictly preventive function. The agency will remain within the Public Security Ministry (SSP), and upon approval of the reform SSP director Genaro García Luna initiated a twelve-week course in the Iztapalapa Central Command for the agency's first aspiring investigative police. Under the new law, Federal Police officers will be able to collaborate with the PGR on its investigations. However, the law is clear in stating that in such cases, the Federal Police will act under the supervision of the PGR.

Of significant concern to advocates of civil liberties, the Federal Police's new investigative powers include the ability to seek judicial orders to monitor telephone, satellite, and Internet communications in the investigations of organized crime activity. Under the law, the exercise of such functions must again be performed under the supervision of the PGR. Other dedicated responsibilities of the Federal Police will now include securing crime scenes, executing arrest orders, and processing evidence, all formerly functions of the AFI. Federal Police agents will also have authorization to operate undercover to infiltrate criminal organizations. The changes come as part of broad justice reforms passed by Congress in 2008. In his proposals for that justice reform initiative, President Calderón had envisioned a total unification of the nation's federal police, an idea that was generally not received well in Congress. The May 2009 police reforms therefore constituted a compromise by maintaining an investigative unit within the Federal Ministerial Police.

Ultimately, whether Mexico's justice sector reforms are successful depends largely on how they are implemented, and by whom. Mexico now needs to invest in training and supporting the lawyers and practitioners who will operate this new legal framework, working to ensure that justice is swift, predictable, and fair. For comparative perspective, it is worth noting that in the United States several key reforms to professionalize the administration of justice and promote a rights-based criminal justice system only took effect in the postwar era. In the 1960s and 1970s the United States established crucial provisions to ensure due process for criminal defendants (*Miranda v. Arizona,* 1966), access to a publicly funded legal defense (*Gideon v. Wainwright,* 1963), and other standards and practices to promote "professional" policing. In effect, due process rights for the accused helped raise the bar for police and prosecutors, promoting the professionalization of the U.S. criminal justice system.

Moreover, it took at least a generation and major, targeted investments to truly professionalize the U.S. law enforcement and judicial sectors. The Safe Streets Act of 1968 mandated the creation of the Law Enforcement Assistance Administration (LEAA), which helped fund criminal justice education programs. LEAA also supported justice sector research through the National Institute of Law Enforcement and Criminal Justice, the precursor to the National Institute of Justice. In order to be successful, Mexico will likely need to make similar investments alongside the reforms it already has planned over the next decade. In 2008, a special fund—the Subsidy for Municipal Public Security (Subsidio para la Seguridad Pública Municipal, SUBSEMUN)—was created by the federal government (under budget line #36) to supplement local expenditures on police professionalization, equipment, and infrastructure. SUBSEMUN is administered by the Ministry of Public Security (Secretaría de Seguridad Pública, SSP), and provides substantial new resources targeted toward the improvement of local public security agencies.[13]

Meanwhile, efforts to promote greater professionalism among lawyers, who will be primarily responsible for "quality control" in the Mexican criminal justice system, will be of special importance. Although Mexico has recently adopted a new code of ethics, Mexican lawyers are not presently required to receive postgraduate studies, take a bar exam, maintain good standing in a professional bar association, or seek continuing education in order to practice law. All of these are elements of legal professionalism that developed gradually and in a somewhat ad hoc manner in the United States, and mostly in the postwar era.

Again, it is important to keep in mind that reform will be an incremental process. Mexico is working to make major progress in a relatively short period, attempting to overhaul three hundred years of independent legal tradition (and three hundred years of Spanish colonial legal tradition) in less than a decade. Arguably, Mexico can look to and learn from both the positive and negative experiences of other Latin American countries that have adopted legal reforms in recent years (including Chile, Colombia, Costa Rica, El Salvador, Honduras, and Venezuela). In the end, the success of these efforts will rest on the shoulders of a new generation of legal practitioners and citi-

13 At the outset of 2008, SUBSEMUN allocated over Mex$3.5 billion, or US$329 million, to 150 local governments. In 2009 the total funding for SUBSEMUN was expanded to an additional fifty-six local governments, and the total budget line increased to Mex$4.1 billion, though due to a severe devaluation of the peso this allocation amounted to only US$290 million (Presidencia n.d.; Ortiz 2009). (Currency conversions are based on the dates upon which funding was announced—January 31, 2008, and January 31, 2008—and calculated using Oanda.com.)

zens, who will be both the stewards and the beneficiaries of Mexico's new judicial reforms.

U.S.–MEXICO COLLABORATION

Because Mexico is a neighbor, a vital trading partner, a major supplier of oil and other energy needs, and the primary source of U.S. immigration (both authorized and undocumented), what happens in Mexico has an enormous impact on everyday life in the United States. The United States has a special interest in the resolution of Mexico's recent rule-of-law challenges, particularly in light of the possible threats to U.S. interests in Mexico and the cross-border "spillover" of crime, violence, and corruption. With regard to U.S. interests in Mexico, U.S. authorities have expressed serious concerns in recent years about the implications of Mexico's public security crisis for U.S. citizens traveling abroad, particularly in light of recent drug violence and rampant kidnappings.[14] Also, while not solely targeting U.S. entities, attacks by domestic insurgent groups on foreign financial institutions[15] and domestic energy pipelines have presented a serious concern in recent years.[16]

Furthermore, with regard to cross-border spillover, U.S. officials have expressed their concerns about the proliferation of Mexican and Central American organized crime networks in the United States (including both drug- and weapons-trafficking organizations); kidnappings and gang-related activity in U.S. border states; and

---

14 U.S. Ambassador Tony Garza issued two State Department warnings for visitors traveling to Mexico and subsequently closed the U.S. Consulate in Nuevo Laredo in what Garza described as a U.S. effort to "punish" Mexico for its failure to control the drug situation (Althaus et al. 2005; *Reuters* 2005).

15 In August 2001, bombs planted by the Revolutionary Armed Forces of the People (FARP) were exploded outside three separate branches of Banamex as Citibank was in the process of purchasing the Mexican-owned bank. In May 2004, bombs planted by a group known as the Comando Jaramillista Morelense 23 de Mayo were detonated outside of three foreign-owned banks. In November 2005, one of two bombs planted at two branches of Spanish-owned Bancomer, a subsidiary of Banco Bilbao Vizcaya Argentaria, exploded in the outskirts of Mexico City; this attack was attributed to a previously unidentified group, named in a letter as the Barbarous Mexico Revolutionary Workers' Commando (Perez 2005).

16 Attacks on natural gas pipelines in central Mexico in July 2007 and on oil pipelines in Gulf coast states in September 2007 were allegedly propagated by the Popular Revolutionary Army (EPR). There is some doubt about whether the EPR was in fact responsible, despite their efforts to claim credit.

FIGURE 9.1 **Lifetime Usage of Illicit Drugs, Percentage of Population by Age Group, 1979–2007**

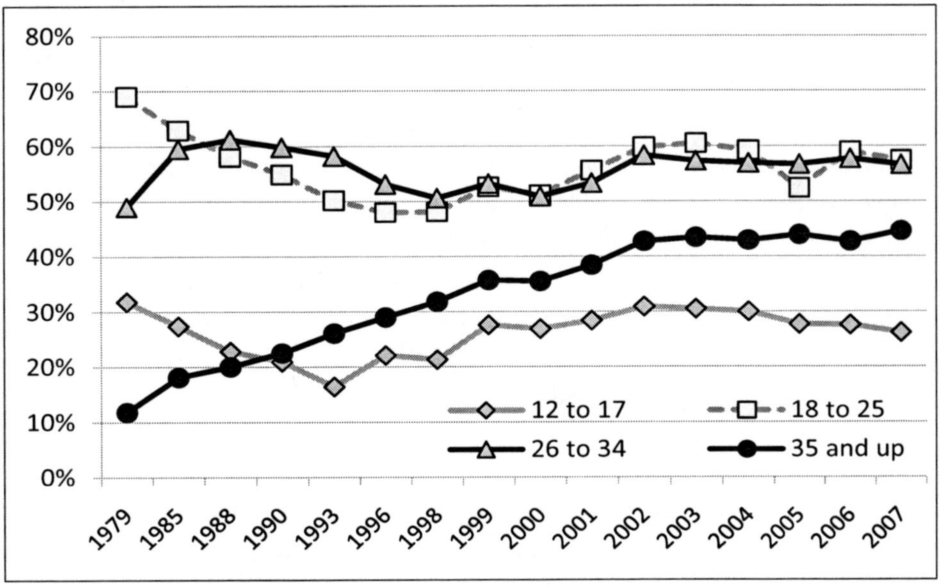

Source: Office of Applied Studies 2008.

impacts of Mexican drug-related violence on U.S. border communities. In 2008 in Ciudad Juárez, adjacent to the U.S. border city of El Paso, drug-related violence resulted in greater pressure on U.S. service providers, who attended to several victims of shootings that occurred on the other side of the border. Treating victims of drug violence potentially places hospital personnel in harm's way, as suggested by the experience of Mexican hospitals where drug hit men have occasionally tracked their victims to medical facilities in order to finish them off (Bustillo 2008).

In addition, another deeply disconcerting problem in recent years has been the reduced integrity of U.S. border security agencies, due in part to agency growing pains and corruption by organized crime. Increased recruitment efforts at the Department of Homeland Security have brought in greater numbers of inexperienced agents, if not also some under-qualified personnel. Moreover, tighter scrutiny at the border has provided criminal organizations with greater incentives to infiltrate or corrupt

U.S. border security agents (Vartabedian, Serrano, and Marosi 2006). In 2004, the Office of Internal Affairs for the U.S. Customs and Immigration Service compiled 2,771 complaints against the agency's employees, including more than 550 involving criminal allegations and more than 100 involving allegations of bribery (Arrillaga 2006). From October 2003 to April 2008, there were numerous cases of alleged corruption identified along the border: 125 in California, 45 in Arizona, 14 in New Mexico, and 157 in Texas (Archibold and Becker 2008). Conducting investigations into law enforcement corruption is a sensitive and often lengthy process, given that ample evidence is needed in order to compile a successful case for prosecution. The emergence of hundreds of cases of alleged Border Patrol corruption over the last few years suggests that the overall problem of official corruption among U.S. border security and law enforcement personnel may be far greater than the number of cases identified thus far. While incidences of corruption were not exclusively the result of penetration by Mexican organized crime, they underscore the potential vulnerability of U.S. law enforcement.

In addition to these concerns about Mexico and its potential effects on U.S. interests, the United States also has an enormous impact on Mexico that must be seriously considered, particularly with regard to U.S. demand for drugs and the role of U.S. suppliers in arming organized crime groups. First, despite relatively minor increases and decreases—and aside from shifts in tastes and preferences—the overall supply of illicit drugs and the level of U.S. consumption have remained relatively constant. According to the 2007 National Survey on Drug Use and Health, 19.9 million U.S. residents twelve years of age or older who were interviewed were current drug users (within the past month), or roughly 8 percent of the population in that age group.[17] Moreover, over the last three decades, the aging of early generations of high-level drug users has gradually produced a majority of people over the age of thirty-five who have some lifetime drug usage (see figure 9.1).

Second, in recent years the Mexican federal government has seen substantial increases in the number and array of weapons seized, with a significant increase in

17 Drugs included marijuana, cocaine, crack cocaine, heroin, hallucinogens, inhalants, and nonmedical use of prescription psychotherapeutic drugs. Marijuana was the most commonly used illicit drug, with 14.4 percent current users. Over 26 percent of high school students had tried marijuana by their senior year, compared to 4 percent for cocaine, 35 percent for cigarettes, and 58 percent for alcohol. Drug use was significantly higher among unemployed persons, of whom 18.3 percent were current illicit drug users (Office of Applied Studies 2008).

the proportion of high-powered weapons (including 9mm pistols; .38 caliber "super" pistols, also known as cop killers; .45 caliber pistols; and AR-15– and AK-47–type assault rifles; grenades; and bazookas).[18] Despite the large number of weapons confiscated in recent years, firearms are heavily restricted in Mexico.[19] Restrictions on the sale and personal possession of firearms in Mexico make arms trafficking the primary source of weapons for Mexican drug cartels and other organized crime syndicates (Lumpe 1997). The legal availability of firearms in the United States—including advanced high-caliber, semi-automatic weapons that are especially sought after by organized crime—creates a readily accessible market for the purchase of weapons that are illegally trafficked into Mexico.[20] Thus, in addition to crime linked to the northbound flow of drugs, Mexico has faced significant challenges due to the southbound flow of weapons in recent years. Indeed, authorities estimate that 90 percent of weapons confiscated in Mexico come from the United States, which effectively serves as a "gray market" for arms traffickers (Serrano 2008). The border plays an important part. An estimated 6,700 dealers,[21] out of some 54,000 nationwide,[22] are located along the U.S.-Mexico border. In 2007, a Bureau of Alcohol, Tobacco, and Firearms (ATF) trace of weapons confiscated in Mexico found that 1,805 of 2,455 weapons (73.5 percent) came from three border states: Arizona, California, and Texas. Moreover, gun shops are weakly regulated, with only 5 percent of all

---

18 From January to June 2008, 7,645 weapons were seized, compared to only 3,801 during the same period the previous year. Particularly disturbing was the increase in the proportion of "long-arm" weapons (*armas largas*), which went from 1,877 (or 49.3 percent) of weapons seized in the first half of 2007 to 4,465 (58.4 percent) of weapons seized in the first half of 2008 (Calderón 2008, 24).

19 In 2007, there were an estimated 4,300 registered firearms in Mexico (Grillo 2007).

20 The vast majority of the 218 million privately owned firearms in the United States are owned by a small percentage of the population, with nearly half of all individual gun owners (48 percent) possessing four or more weapons, and only 20 percent of owners holding 65 percent of all guns (Hepburn et al. 2007).

21 Estimates for the number of gun shops along the border vary, but ATF reports 6,647 federal firearms licensees in the Southwest Border region (Krouse 2008). See also Grayson 2007; Corchado and Connolly 2008; Serrano 2008).

22 Estimates for the total number of gun dealers in the United States vary, but by all accounts they have declined dramatically over the last decade—from 245,000 to 54,000—thanks to tougher enforcement by ATF and tighter gun regulations, such as the Brady Handgun Violence Protection Act of 1993 (Marks 2006). See also Vernick et al. 2006.

gun dealers in the country inspected annually (Marks 2006). There are an estimated 100 U.S. firearms agents and 35 inspectors along the border since the ATF initiated Operation Gunrunner to help stop the southbound flow of guns, and funding for additional agents has been appropriated for 2009.

Amid these shared concerns, U.S.-Mexico collaboration on law enforcement and security matters has experienced fits and starts over the past few decades. At present, the existing institutions for facilitating cross-border collaboration in law enforcement and security are relatively weak and ad hoc. The North American Free Trade Agreement (NAFTA), arguably the most important institutional framework for U.S.-Mexican relations in recent years, has a limited focus on facilitating trade and no provisions to manage North American security relations. Small changes in the current policy framework for managing North American security would go a long way to enhancing cooperation between the three NAFTA countries and lend much-needed support to Mexico to strengthen the weakest link in the North American security chain. For example, after 9/11, Department of Defense strategic operations along the border were centralized into the U.S. Northern Command (NORTHCOM), which operates Joint Task Force North and provides support to civilian authorities on the southwest border and now the northern border as well. NORTHCOM also coordinates on defense issues with the Mexican military, including joint naval exercises and pilot and maintenance training. The Mexican navy has also collaborated regularly with the U.S. Coast Guard on counter-drug operations. The United States could continue to work with Mexican armed forces to deepen collaboration through NORTHCOM and other national defense frameworks, since this helps to strengthen and consolidate long-term bilateral cooperation.

At the same time, the Security and Prosperity Partnership (SPP) establishes a multilateral framework and shared priorities for promoting a secure regional trading relationship in North America. The ongoing dialogue on security matters established through the SPP likely helped strengthen the U.S. commitment to aid Mexico in its war on drugs through the Mérida Initiative. The Mérida Initiative represents an important symbolic gesture, in that it communicates the willingness of the United States to share responsibility for Mexico's war on drugs. However, the overall impact is likely to be slight. Much of the $1.4 billion allocated through the Mérida Initiative over the next three years will actually stay in the United States, with the purchase of helicopters and other equipment from U.S. contractors. The total amount of aid also represents just a fraction—perhaps as little as 4 percent—of Mexico's total expenditures in the war on drugs, and should therefore not be expected to result in huge gains in overall security.

Both the SPP and the Mérida Initiative illustrate the tremendous opportunities and benefits that can arise from cooperation, but also the extent to which such collaboration presently hinges on goodwill and mostly ad hoc initiatives. Institutionalized collaboration on security issues could provide mutual benefits, in the form of a stronger framework for addressing transnational security problems. Such collaboration would require some "out-of-the-box" thinking in both Mexico and the United States, but it could essentially build on existing institutions and agreements to develop a variety of initiatives such as the following:

- A permanent trinational commission for security collaboration through SPP, charged with convening forums for the purpose of identifying regional security priorities and harmonizing policy coordination;
- A permanent binational office for the coordination of the U.S.-Mexico border governors' conference to provide greater consistency, institutional memory, and follow-up on a wide array of policy measures, including security;
- Joint facilities for management of customs and immigration at border points of entry, allowing more effective inspection of northbound *and* southbound flows; and
- Formal integration of Mexican security forces into NATO and other regional security initiatives (including the possible renegotiation of security collaboration to reinstitute a version of the Rio Treaty).

However, international cooperation must go beyond strictly national security problems, to address the longer-term challenges related to the rule of law in Mexico. In this regard, the United States has made some significant efforts over the last decade to expand funding and programs for rule-of-law promotion in Mexico through the U.S. Agency for International Development (USAID). For the most part, following the agency's general approach to rule-of-law promotion used in other countries, USAID's efforts have been narrowly focused on promoting rule-of-law reform through new legislation that increases the efficiency and due process elements of Mexican criminal procedure, as well as the training and preparation of Mexico's prosecutors, public defense attorneys, and judges to begin working under the new regime. Still, increased attention (that is, funding) will be needed to other aspects of the criminal justice system, particularly on the "security" side. Key areas for further aid and training include law enforcement techniques, management of prison facilities, prisoner rehabilitation and prison system management, and the oversight of crime suspects and criminals during pretrial release and parole.

RETHINKING DRUG CONTROL STRATEGIES

These trends ignore the fundamental problem with the current framing of U.S. drug policies. There are effectively two kinds of policy "problems": those that can be definitively solved, and those that cannot be solved definitively but must be managed. Drug consumption is a societal problem that cannot be solved. Yet the framing of drug control efforts as a "war on drugs" creates false analogies that suggest otherwise, and ultimately contributes to the escalation and ultimate militarization of drug control policy, even though the "war" cannot be won per se. As articulated, the main objectives of the war on drugs—reducing the supply and consumption of illicit drugs—have proved unattainable despite consistently increasing law enforcement and military resources over the last thirty years.

This said, there are important questions about drug legalization. For most policy makers, the subject of legalization is considered taboo, as there appears to be too little political support for legal drug use, especially for drugs deemed highly addictive and destructive (such as cocaine, heroin, and methamphetamines). While the General Social Survey (GSS) conducted biannually since 1972 demonstrated an increase in support for marijuana legalization beginning in the 1990s, public approval has never exceeded 35 percent of GSS respondents (National Opinion Research Center n.d.). In Mexico, an April 2009 BGC-Ulises Beltrán poll suggested that support for legalization was slightly higher than in the United States, with 40 percent supporting the legalization of marijuana. Mexicans showed much less support for legalization of other drugs, like cocaine (17 percent), crack cocaine (14 percent), ecstasy (13 percent), methamphetamines (12 percent), and heroin (11 percent).[23] Such indicators appear to limit the prospects for the legalization of drugs in the immediate future.

---

23 The same poll reported that more than two-thirds of respondents perceived drug consumption to be a national problem in Mexico, rather than a regional problem. Forty-six percent supported giving addicts legal access to drugs during rehabilitation, while 49 percent opposed this option (Beltrán 2009).

Still, the possibility of drug legalization has been championed by some economists and has begun to gain political traction in both Mexico and the United States, as well as internationally.[24] In a joint statement to the Latin American Commission on Drugs and Democracy, former presidents Fernando Henrique Cardoso (Brazil), César Gaviria (Colombia), and Ernesto Zedillo (Mexico) expressed their opinion that prohibition and criminalization of consumption has not worked. In their words:

> The war on drugs has failed. And it's high time to replace an ineffective strategy with more humane and efficient drug policies.... Prohibitionist policies based on eradication, interdiction and criminalization of consumption simply haven't worked.... Today, we are further than ever from the goal of eradicating drugs.... The revision of U.S.-inspired drug policies is urgent in light of the rising levels of violence and corruption associated with narcotics.... The first step in the search for alternative solutions is to acknowledge the disastrous consequences of current policies. Next, we must shatter the taboos that inhibit public debate about drugs in our societies.... In this spirit, we propose a paradigm shift in drug policies based on three guiding principles: Reduce the harm caused by drugs, decrease drug consumption through education, and aggressively combat organized crime.... The inauguration of President Barack Obama presents a unique opportunity for Latin America and the U.S. to engage in a substantive dialogue on issues of common concern, such as the reduction of domestic consumption and the control of arms sales, especially across the U.S.-Mexico border.... The time to act is now, and the way forward lies in strengthening partnerships to deal with a global problem that affects us all (Cardoso, Gaviria, and Zedillo 2009).

In August 2009, both Mexico and Argentina took significant steps in this direction. Argentina's Supreme Court ruled that incarceration for marijuana possession was unconstitutional, while Mexico moved to revamp its minor possession laws

24 At a keynote address presented at the Fifth International Conference on Drug Policy Reform in Washington, DC, on November 16, 1991, Nobel Prize–winning economist Milton Friedman argued that, "The war on drugs is a failure because it is a socialist enterprise.... The U.S. government enforces a drug cartel. The major beneficiaries from drug prohibition are the drug lords, who can maintain a cartel that they would be unable to maintain without current government policy" (Trebach and Zeese 1992).

(dating back to 1978) to establish new regulations for minor possession of a wide array of drugs, including marijuana cocaine, heroin, and LSD. This trend toward decriminalization —eliminating jail time and reducing fines associated with personal consumption of illicit drugs— has also been prevalent in different U.S. states in recent years. Decriminalization is deemed to have two main advantages. First, it theoretically allows beleaguered law enforcement agencies to concentrate their time and resources on larger dealers and trafficking operations (though opponents object that it also increases other illegal activities). Second, decriminalization eliminates opportunities for police to harass and extort drug users, and thereby may increase addicts' opportunities to receive treatment for their addiction without legal penalties. In this sense, the decriminalization of drugs is seen by proponents as an important step toward treating drug abuse as more of a public health problem than a public security problem. Unfortunately, though, Mexico's recent legislation does not provide significantly greater support for the treatment of addicts. More worrying, as long as the production and distribution of drugs remains illegal, decriminalization may make law enforcement's job more difficult by expanding the market share of the criminal organizations that purvey and profit from illicit drugs. As a drug control strategy, decriminalization therefore faces critics on both sides: those who view decriminalization as inciting greater illicit drug use, and those who see it as an inadequate substitute for full scale legalization.

Generally speaking, however, there has been little serious attempt to gauge the possible consequences of legalization for the United States, Mexico, or other drug-producing countries. Many pro-legalization activists assume that legalization will be a simple cure-all for drug-related crime and violence, since it would rob organized crime of profits and "decriminalize" thousands of otherwise innocent users and distributors who are currently behind bars. Yet organized crime is highly adaptable and would no doubt venture into other high-profile criminal activities (such as kidnapping or pirated materials). Moreover, as with other controlled substances, like tobacco and alcohol, recreational drug use represents a potentially serious harm to individual users and to society. On the one hand, legalization would likely result in a significant increase in the harms associated with drug use, including traffic fatalities, overdoses, and addiction. On the other hand, while prohibition of drug use does not appear to be a very effective deterrent of those problems, it certainly presents an enormous burden on the U.S. and Mexican criminal justice systems. In the end, any effort to evaluate the merits of current policy versus legalization must conduct a careful accounting of the likely costs and benefits of either approach.

Ultimately, without serious consideration of the legalization option—with careful anticipation of the potential impacts in the United States and drug source countries—it is not possible to evaluate its merits, or the merits of the current policy approach. Legalization is unlikely to be a magic bullet for improving public security since drug-trafficking organizations have shown remarkable adaptability to other forms of organized crime in response to changing market conditions. Yet, while further study and frank policy dialogue is needed on this topic, most U.S. and Mexican policy makers and experts are still reluctant to breach the drug legalization taboo. In this context, the problems of transnational organized crime and corruption will likely continue to complicate Mexico's challenging public security situation for the foreseeable future.

These, of course, are larger policy questions far beyond the scope of this particular monograph. In the end, regardless of whether the current efforts at prohibition are sustained, there must be more effort to regulate drug demand and address the public health problems associated with drug abuse, both in the United States and in Mexico (where traffickers have cultivated a substantial domestic market for drugs). Again, in terms of reducing demand, there appears to be a potential advantage to legalization, since drug use can be manipulated through market controls (such as vice taxation, dosage regulations, and so on). Still, with most drug control resources focused on law enforcement and security, there have been relatively few resources directed toward drug treatment programs. The National Institute on Drug Abuse (NIDA) estimates that in 2006 only 2.5 million U.S. citizens received treatment for drug and alcohol addiction, out of an estimated 23.6 million U.S. citizens in need. NIDA also estimates that illicit drug consumption costs the United States more than $181 billion annually, and that "for every dollar spent on addiction treatment programs, there is a $4 to $7 reduction in the cost of drug-related crimes. With some outpatient programs, total savings can exceed costs by a ratio of 12:1" (NIDA n.d.).

Hence moving toward a policy regime that emphasizes drug use as a public health problem could yield significant dividends, at significantly lower cost—particularly in terms of crime and violence—than both countries are currently paying in the war on drugs. Nonetheless, in terms of Mexico's police and judicial sector, eliminating drug corruption from the equation might be the single most important measure that could be taken in the coming years to produce a rapid and substantial increase in the integrity and security of the Mexican state. In the end, however, barring a substantial effort to evaluate, build political support for, and develop adequate preparations for the negative consequences of such a policy shift, we are left with rather few pleasing alternatives to the status quo.

CONCLUSION

Since the 1990s, Mexico's public security situation has deteriorated significantly. The Mexican government has an urgent need to strengthen and professionalize its law enforcement, juridical, and security institutions at the federal, state, and local levels. The end goal is not only to enforce law and order, but also to ensure that government officials are themselves accountable to the law and that the citizenry has prompt and equitable access to justice. As a central element of the judicial sector, domestic police forces are a critical component in the construction of rule of law. However, as the authors make quite plain in this volume, Mexico's police forces—both investigative and preventive police—have major limitations and inadequacies.

While attention is frequently given to the corruption of Mexico's police agencies, corruption is ultimately a symptom of deep-rooted institutional problems confronted by police. Likewise, resource deficiencies—poor compensation and the lack of adequate equipment—explain only part of the problems faced by Mexican police. To be sure, increases in police salaries will help to attract the best and brightest available candidates to the profession. However, in their daily lives, police lack access to basic protections and services that are now standard for professional law enforcement officers in other countries. These include non-salaried benefits, such as adequate health care (including optical and dental insurance), life insurance, burial insurance, and other similar provisions. Ultimately, increases in the levels of education, preparation, and training for Mexican police are certainly needed. However, without comprehensive measures to provide a professional work environment for police, competent professionals will not be attracted to the job.

Hence more careful examination of police and their circumstances is sorely needed. Excellent work is presently being developed by a number of U.S. and Mexican initiatives, such as the Mexico City–based Institute for Security and Democracy (Instituto para la Seguridad y la Democracia, INSYDE) and the U.S.-based Culture of Lawfulness Project. Still, considering the urgency of the issues at hand, there is an enormous gap in our understanding of the problems that plague Mexico's public security apparatus. To date, there have been few systematic social scientific surveys of police—or other justice sector officials, for that matter—in Mexico. An obvious next step in advancing knowledge and policy directions for Mexican law enforcement is to develop comprehensive, quantitative surveys of the "criminal justice system operators" (*operadores del sistema penal*). Such surveys should examine not only their professional profiles but also take into consideration their quality of life, technical knowledge, best practices and community relations, knowledge and understanding of professional ethics, and opinions about justice sector reform.

In general, more fiscal and intellectual resources should be directed toward developing and enhancing the field of Mexican criminological studies, with a view toward developing a new generation of dedicated experts and practitioners who can help guide Mexico toward more effective rule of law and overall public security. The next generation of police—as well as lawyers, judges, and other practitioners in the judicial system—will be the protectors of the Mexico that so many hope to see: a Mexico that is more secure, more just, and more prosperous. In the meantime, our hope is that this volume offers a small but useful contribution to the study of Mexican policing and public security in order to aid in the achievement of those ends.

REFERENCES

Althaus, Dudley, Ioan Grillo, James Pinkerton, and Patty Reinert. 2005. "Border Travelers Warned of Violence," *Houston Chronicle*, January 27.

Archibold, Randal C., and Andrew Becker. 2008. "Border Agents, Lured by the Other Side," *New York Times*, May 27.

Arrillaga, Pauline. 2006. "Feds Struggle with Border Patrol Corruption," *Associated Press*, September 22.

Bayley, David H. 1994. *Police for the Future*. New York: Oxford University Press.

BBC (British Broadcasting Corporation). 1999. "Colombia Murder Rate Soars," *BBC News*, December 30. http://news.bbc.co.uk/2/hi/americas/583197.stm. Accessed April 9, 2009.

Behnsen, Carlos. 2009. "Mexican Tourism Growth Defies Drug Violence," *Reuters*, April 2. http://www.reuters.com/article/worldNews/idUSTRE5306RF20090401. Accessed April 9, 2009.

Beltrán, Ulises. 2009. "Rechazan legalizar drogas," *Excélsior*, April 6.

Bustillo, Miguel. 2008. "Mexico Drug War's Costs, Risks Exported to U.S.," *Los Angeles Times*, August 17.

Calderón, President Felipe. 2008. *Segundo Informe de Gobierno*, September 1.

Cardoso, Fernando Henrique, César Gaviria, and Ernesto Zedillo. 2009. "The War on Drugs Is a Failure," *Wall Street Journal*, February 23. http://online.wsj.com/article/SB123535114271444981.html. Accessed April 9, 2009.

Castillo García, Gustavo. 2009. "Félix Gallardo acusa al extinto González Calderoni de repartir plazas a narcos," *La Jornada*, February 9.

Consulta Mitofsky. 2008. "Incremento de penas a delitos graves," December 4.

Corchado, Alfredo, and Tim Connolly. 2008. "Analyst: U.S. Anti-drug Aid Proposal Could Heighten Violence in Mexico," *Dallas Morning News*, January 3.

De la Luz González, María, and Francisco Gómez. 2009. "Histórico: PGR pega al gobierno en Michoacán," *El Universal*, May 27.

Díaz, Lizbeth. 2009. "Mexico 'Narco Junior' Teenagers Kill Drug Rivals," *Reuters*, January 14. http://www.reuters.com/article/latestCrisis/idUSN14467553. Accessed April 9, 2009.

El Economista. 2005. "AFI, entre la corrupción y la eficacia," December 6.

El Financiero. 2009. "Desaparece la AFI," May 29.

Grayson, George. 2007. "Drug War Allies," *San Diego Union-Tribune*, September 2.

Grillo, Ioan. 2007. "'Cop-killer' Guns from U.S. Seen Crossing into Mexico," *Associated Press*, August 18.

Hepburn, L., M. Miller, D. Azreal, and D. Hemenway. 2007. "The U.S. Gun Stock: Results from the 2004 National Firearms Survey," *Injury Prevention* 13: 15–19.

Krouse, William J. 2008. "The Bureau of Alcohol, Tobacco, Firearms and Explosives (ATF): Budget and Operations," *Congressional Research Report for Congress*, May 30. http://assets.opencrs.com/rpts/RL34514_20080530.pdf.

Lumpe, L. 1997. "The US Arms Both Sides of Mexico's Drug War," *Covert Action Quarterly* 61: 39–46.

Marks, Alexandra. 2006. "Why Gun Dealers Have Dwindled," *Christian Science Monitor*, March 14.

Méndez, Alfredo. 2009. "Nace este martes la Policía Federal; podrá investigar delitos e intervenir telefonemas," *La Jornada*, June 2.

Mexico Watch Weekly Briefing. 2008. "The 10,000-Dollar Question," August 29.

National Opinion Research Center. n.d. "General Social Survey." http://www.norc.org/GSS+Website. Accessed April 9, 2009.

NIDA (National Institute of Drug Abuse). n.d. "Treatment Approaches for Drug Addiction." Fact Sheet. http://www.nida.nih.gov/PDF/InfoFacts/Treatment08.pdf. Accessed April 9, 2009.

Office of Applied Studies, Substance Abuse and Mental Health Services Administration. 2008. *Results from the 2007 National Survey on Drug Use and Health: National Findings.* NSDUH Series H-34, DHHS Publication No. SMA 08-4343. Rockville, MD.

Ortiz, Francisco. 2009. "Difunden reglas del Subsemun 2009," *Reforma.* http://www.reforma.com/edomex/articulo/482/963299. Accessed March 17, 2009.

Parametría. 2006. "Confianza en instituciones: Disminuye credibilidad en el IFE," *Carta Paramétrica,* July.

Perez, Gloria. 2005. "Two Bombs Planted Outside Banks on Outskirts of Mexico City," *Associated Press,* November 18.

Presidencia. n.d. Programas del Gobierno Federal. http://www.presidencia.gob.mx/programas/?contenido=35024. Accessed March 17, 2009.

Ramos Pérezy, Jorge, and María de la Luz González. 2009. "Surge la Policía Federal Ministerial," *El Universal,* May 30.

Reforma. 2008. "Lidera Sedena quejas presentadas a CNDH," December 26.

Reuters News Service. 2005. "Mexico Scolds U.S. Ambassador for 'Punish' Boast," *Houston Chronicle,* January 27.

Serrano, Richard A. 2008. "U.S. Guns Arm Mexican Drug Cartels," *Los Angeles Times,* August 10.

SIGOB (Sistema de Gestión y Seguimiento a las Metas del Gobierno). n.d. "Tasa Nacional de Homicidios por año." http://www.sigob.gov.co/est/indicador.aspx?id=307&f=2019. Accessed April 9, 2009.

Trebach, Arnold S., and Kevin B. Zeese, eds. 1992. *Friedman and Szasz on Liberty and Drugs.* Washington, DC: The Drug Policy Foundation. http://www.druglibrary.org/special/friedman/socialist.htm. Accessed April 21, 2009.

United States Joint Forces Command. 2008. *2008 Joint Operating Environment: Challenges and Implications for the Future Joint Force.* November 25.

Vartabedian, Ralph, Richard A. Serrano, and Richard Marosi. 2006. "The Long Crooked Line; Rise in Bribery Tests Integrity of U.S. Border," *Los Angeles Times,* October 23.

Vernick, Jon S., Daniel W. Webster, Maria T. Bulzacchelli, and Julie Samia Mair. 2006. "Regulation of Firearm Dealers in the United States: An Analysis of State Law and Opportunities for Improvement," *Journal of Law, Medicine, and Ethics* 34, no. 4: 765–75.

About the Authors

Elena Azaola is a senior researcher and social anthropologist at the Center for Advanced Studies and Research in Social Anthropology (CIESAS) located in Mexico City. She received her Ph.D in Anthropology at the same institution, and her B.A. and M.A. degrees at the Ibero-American University. She also graduated as a Psychoanalyst. She was an advisor at the National Commission of Human Rights (1991-1993) and is a current Council Member at the Federal District Commission of Human Rights (since 2001). Dr. Azaola has received numerous awards and grants for the diverse research projects that she has conducted. Dr. Azaola has published more than 120 works in Mexico, as well as in other countries. Most of Dr. Azaola's research has been in the field of juvenile and women's justice institutions, human rights, violence, prisons and police institutions.

Carlos Antonio Flores Pérez is a researcher and political scientist at the Center for Advanced Studies and Research in Social Anthropology (CIESAS) in Mexico City. He received his B.A. in Political Science and Public Administration, and his M.A. and Ph.D. in Political and Social Studies at the National Autonomous University of Mexico (UNAM). His doctoral thesis, titled "The State in Crisis: Organized Crime and Politics," received the National Prize for Research on Corruption in Mexico from the UNAM and the Ministry of Public Administration in 2005. He has been an instructor for intelligence analysts at the Mexican Ministry of the Interior's Center for Research and National Security (CISEN) and has lectured on national security topics in Colombia, Ghana, Nicaragua, Norway, and Peru.

Robert A. Donnelly holds a Master's degree in Latin American Studies from the University of California, San Diego (UCSD), and bachelor's degrees in journalism and history from the University of Georgia. He is Program Associate at the Mexico Institute of the Woodrow Wilson International Center for Scholars in Washington, D.C. As Program Associate, Donnelly manages a MacArthur-funded research project on the patterns and practices of civic engagement and political participation by Latin American immigrants in eight U.S. cities. He also manages the Institute's borderlands research project, examining ways for enhanced collaboration on joint management by the United States and Mexico. Prior to coming to the Mexico Institute, Donnelly was Coordinator of the Justice in Mexico Project at the University of San Diego's

Trans-Border Institute over 2006-2008. From 1997 to 2002, Donnelly worked as a journalist in Mexico, writing for trade publications, wire services, newspapers, and magazines.

Marcos Pablo Moloeznik is a professor and researcher in the Political Science Department of the Universidad de Guadalajara. He received his B.A. in Political Science from the National University of Rosario in Argentina, his M.A. in Public Policy from the National Institute of Public Administration in Spain, and his jurisdoctorate from the University of Alcalá de Henares in Spain. Dr. Moloeznik has taught at universities in Germany, Argentina, and Poland. He has authored numerous publications on national security and human rights, including "The Debate Over the Participation of the Armed Forces in Peace Missions Under the Command of the United Nations Organization," (*Praesidium, Interdisciplinary Journal of Latin American and Cross Cultural Studies*, 2004–2005) and "The Nature of an Atypical Military Instrument: The Mexican Armed Forces," (*Revista Fuerzas Armadas y Sociedad*, 2005).

Jorge Rocha Quintero is a professor and researcher at the Center for Research and Social Formation at the Western Technological Institute for Higher Learning (ITESO) in Guadalajara. He received his M.A. at the International University of Andalucia in Spain, and specializes in human rights and local sustainable development. He is a member of the Directive Group of the Justice Center for Peace and Development, the first non-profit organization to defend human rights cases in Jalisco. He has also served as a citizen counselor for the Instituto Federal Electoral in the 2000, 2003, and 2006 federal elections, and as a commissioner in the 1997 and 2000 municipal elections in Tlaquepaque, Jalisco. He recently edited the book *Rural Sustainability and Local Development in Southern Jalisco*, and his commentary is regularly featured in *La Jornada Jalisco* and *El Puente*.

Daniel Sabet is a visiting professor and political scientist at Georgetown University's Edmund A. Walsh School of Foreign Service. Sabet's current research focuses on the obstacles to professionalizing Mexico's municipal police forces. This study explores the reform challenges of policy design, implementation, and institutionalization; the formal and informal rules of police and municipal governance; the negative impact of organized crime; the ambivalent relationship between the police and civil society; and new incentives being created by the federal government. Sabet's previous research, which has been published recently as a book entitled *Nonprofits and their Networks: Cleaning the Waters along Mexico's Northern Border*, examines how civil society organizations emerge to address local policy concerns in a political environment that has traditionally favored clientelism.

David A. Shirk is the Director of the Trans-Border Institute and Associate Professor in the Political Science Department at the University of San Diego. Dr. Shirk received his B.A. at Lock Haven University and his M.A. and Ph.D. in Political Science at the University of California, San Diego (UCSD). He conducts research on Mexican politics, U.S.-Mexican relations, and the U.S.-Mexican border. Dr. Shirk is the principal investigator for the Justice in Mexico Project (www.justiceinmexico.org), and has been a fellow at the UCSD Center for U.S.-Mexican Studies (1998-99 and 2001-2003) and at the Woodrow Wilson Center in Washington, D.C (2009-10). Publications by Dr. Shirk include *Contemporary Mexican Politics*, co-authored with Emily Edmonds-Poli (Rowman and Littlefield Publishers, 2008); *Reforming the Administration of Justice in Mexico,* co-edited with Wayne Cornelius (University of Notre Dame Press, 2007); *Evaluating Accountability and Transparency in Mexico*, co-edited with Alejandra Ríos Cásares (Trans-Border Institute, 2007).

María Eugenia Súarez de Garay is a Professor of Anthropology in the Gender Studies Center of the Universidad de Guadalajara. She is an expert on policing in Mexico and has conducted much ethnographic research on the lives of police officers in Guadalajara and throughout the country. Her most recent book is *Police: An Anthropological Approach* (2006), co-published by the Universidad de Guadalajara and Western Technological Institute for Higher Learning (ITESO) in Guadalajara; and the article "Notes for police diagnosis: the case of preventive police in the metropolitan area of Guadalajara," published by the Mexican Academy of Criminal Sciences. She earned her Doctorate in Social and Cultural Anthropology at the Autonomous University of Barcelona.

Guillermo Zepeda Lecuona is associate researcher at the Center for Research for Development, A.C. (CIDAC) in Mexico City and professor at the Western Technological Institute for Higher Learning (ITESO) in Guadalajara. He received his jurisdoctorate from the National Autonomous University of Mexico (UNAM). A practicing attorney, he specializes in institutional development, judicial reform, and criminal justice. In 1999, he was the recipient of Mexico's National Prize in Law and Economics. He has published several books and articles and is a regular commentator in Mexican newspapers. He is the author of *Crime Without Punishment: Criminal Justice Prosecutions and Public Prosecutors in Mexico.*

LaVergne, TN USA
07 January 2010
169129LV00003B/2/P

9 781935 551508